Speech/ Communication

Saundra Hybels
ITHACA COLLEGE

Richard L. Weaver, II
UNIVERSITY OF MASSACHUSETTS

D. VAN NOSTRAND COMPANY

NEW YORK CINCINNATI
TORONTO LONDON MELBOURNE

D. Van Nostrand Company Regional Offices:
New York   Cincinnati   Millbrae

D. Van Nostrand Company International Offices:
London   Toronto   Melbourne

Copyright © 1974 by Litton Educational Publishing, Inc.

Library of Congress Catalog Card Number: 74-2
ISBN 0-442-23623-9

All rights reserved. No part of this work covered by the copyright hereon may be reproduced or used in any form or by any means—graphic, electronic, or mechanical, including photocopying, recording, taping, or information storage and retrieval systems—without written permission of the publisher. Manufactured in the United States of America.

Published by D. Van Nostrand Company
450 West 33rd Street, New York, N. Y. 10001

Published simultaneously in Canada by
Van Nostrand Reinhold Ltd.

10   9   8   7   6   5

To Andrea A. Weaver and Robert Paul Dye

Preface

This book is designed for the introductory course in speech communication or interpersonal communication. For many students, the introductory course is the only exposure to communications study; these students need a practical approach that emphasizes the development of communication skills and an understanding of the communication process. *Speech/Communication* is grounded in contemporary communications theory, but our presentation relates communication in every instance to the student's everyday experience.

The basic course in speech/communication is changing. In many cases it is becoming more specialized, concentrating either on interpersonal communication, on the small group, or on the mass media. Understanding communication in our society, however, requires some knowledge of each of these kinds of communication as well as consideration of communication and the presentation of self, nonverbal and verbal communication, and public speaking. Our effort here is to provide a view of the breadth and diversity of communication in all of its various settings.

The conceptual framework of the book is given in the Introduction, where we present a basic communications model, which is then applied to all of the communications situations with which we deal in the text. The model provides a reference point and is used throughout the book to show that all forms of communication are interrelated and have certain similarities—that there are, for example, certain components of interpersonal communication that are also present in mass communication.

With the foundation gained from reading the Introduction, the student can read any other chapter of the book and in any order. Each chapter is a self-contained unit that can be read whenever appropriate to the particular student, instructor, or course. Thus, the book is adaptable to almost any fundamental communications course.

The sequence of chapters is based on our teaching experience and permits a comfortable integration of theory and practice in the classroom. Chapters such as Public Speaking and Small-Group Communication, which by their nature suggest activities to illustrate them, are placed between more theoretical chapters, such as Verbal Communication. This arrangement permits the student to read ahead into other chapters while class activities used to illustrate the "active" chapters are being completed.

The chapters are also integrated in that they move from a focus on the individual to an understanding of communication in one-to-one and one-to-few situations to communication in public speaking to, finally, that stimulus that touches all members of our society—the mass media.

At the end of each chapter we have provided an annotated list of suggested readings, selections of readily accessible contemporary books, most of them in paperback, which provide references for further exploration and growth.

We have written a book for the beginning student. We think that *Speech/Communication* will help the student to become more aware of those forms of communication that are designed to manipulate and to control; we also believe that the book will encourage the kinds of communication that foster a deeper understanding of the self and an increased awareness of and exchange with others.

Saundra Hybels
Richard L. Weaver, II

ACKNOWLEDGMENTS

My greatest acknowledgment is to the students I have taught over the past five years—both at Jackson State College and at Ithaca College. They have shared experiences with me that are so rich and varied that they could not help but be a major influence in my writing.

I would also like to thank Mary and Kenneth E. Anderson, who have greatly influenced my ideas about communication; Dawn Williams for her editorial assistance; and Marty Smith Petty for valuable criticism and moral support.

Saundra Hybels

I would like to thank our editor, Dawn Williams, for her patience, wisdom, and guidance. I would also like to express appreciation to my wife, Andrea, for her encouragement, observations, and insight. I wish to thank the other members of my family—R. Scott, Jacquelynn, Anthony, and Joanna—for their ever present, although unintentional, supply of experiences and situations which provide some of the content of this book and another perspective from which to view communication.

Richard L. Weaver, II

Contents

Introduction: The Need for Dialogue   1

    Communication: The Changing Emphasis   2
    The Process of Communication: A Basic Model   5

1 Self and Communication   9

    Who Are You?   10
    You Are What You Say (Maybe)   10
    Human Needs   11
    Roles   14
    Disclosure and Nondisclosure   19
    Disarming Communication   25
    Communicating the Self to Others: A Case Study   27

2 Interpersonal Communication   33

    Interpersonal Process: Three Essential Elements   35
    Speaker Roles and Listener Roles   38
    Perception of Self by Others and Others by Self   40
    Responding to Keep the Channel Open   50
    Emotional Messages and Rational Messages   54
    Improving Interpersonal Transactions   59

3 Nonverbal Communication   69

    Space   71
    Time   80

Body Movement 86
Voice 98
Objects 101
Mixed Messages 104
Culture and the Nonverbal 105

4 Verbal Communication 113

Style: Your Verbal Image 115
How Words Work 118
Meanings Are in People 123
Language Choices 128
Improving Your Verbal Style 133

5 Public Speaking 139

The Public-Speaking Situation 140
The Speaker's Image 142
Speaking and Anxiety 143
Analyzing the Audience 146
Choosing a Topic 152
Gathering Information 154
Organizing the Speech 156
Planning the Delivery 163
Choosing Visual Material 170
Delivering the Speech 171
Evaluation and Trying Again 176

6 The Power of Communication 181

Means of Persuasion 183
Suggestion: The Still, Small Voice 186
Protest: The Urge to Shout 191
Using Persuasion to Change Attitudes 200
Will the Change Last? 203
Resisting Persuasion 206
Ethical Considerations 208

7 Small-Group Communication 217

What Makes a Small Group Work? 219
Patterns for Communicating in Small Groups 230
Leadership 234
Evaluation in Small-Group Process 245
The Problem-Solving Group: A Case Study 247

8 The Mass Media 257

The Mass-Communication Process 257
The Economics of the Mass Media 263
The Power of the Mass Media 266
The Regulation of the Media 270
Planning a Political Campaign: A Case Study 271

Index 281

Speech/Communication

Introduction

The Need for Dialogue

The more you study communication, the more you are amazed that people communicate at all. Imagine, for example, a middle-aged insurance salesman who has always lived in Alabama trying to communicate his ideas and values to a young, "hip" woman student who comes from Chicago. Both speak the same language and come from the same country, but they probably differ in most of the following areas: ideas, experiences, attitudes, beliefs, knowledge, interests, group memberships, goals, needs, values, and communication abilities. Their only hope for communication is that they have a strong desire to communicate with each other and are willing to try to understand other points of view.

These two individuals will have difficulty communicating for the same reason that all of us have difficulty all the time. Each of us is an individual with a particular frame of reference, a way of looking at things that has developed since we were born and will continue to change and grow until we die. Every other person has a different point of view, his or her individual way of seeing the world. You can never get inside another person's frame of reference entirely, and he or she can never get all the way into yours. In this sense, we are all alone. But each of us also needs to communicate with other people, to share our lives and our thoughts with them. Understanding how communication works and becoming more aware of your own communication needs and skills can help you to share more of yourself and to understand more about yourself and about others. In fact, communication is the only way that anyone can come to know anyone else. As R. Buckminster Fuller has said, we are "only what each of us is communicating to one another in spoken words, gestures, postures, and flashes of the eye. We can't see one another; we can see only our respective communications devices."[1]

Communication, then, is of central importance. It is also a subject of increasing interest to Americans. There are numerous communication courses in colleges and universities, but its study is by no means limited to the academic world. A tough army sergeant is advised not to yell at the new recruits but to communicate with them. Magazines run countless articles full of advice about improving communication between husbands and wives, parents and children. Modern ministers, priests, and rabbis no longer spend all of their theological training learning to organize sermons and to explain the ideas of their faith—they are also taught to communicate with the congregation and to help members of the congregation communicate among themselves. Encounter groups form with the purpose of allowing strangers to communicate their feelings to each other. The list of people trying to communicate is endless; hardly a day goes by when we do not receive some sort of information or advice about communication.

COMMUNICATION: THE CHANGING EMPHASIS

So many Americans are engrossed and perhaps even obsessed with communication that one might ask why we are, as a nation, so interested in this subject. The question is so complex that it is impossible to give a complete and comprehensive answer. However, we can suggest some of the possible reasons.

The first is that contemporary American society has gone through great changes in its social structure. Look back at your grandparents. Chances are that they were born, lived, and died in the same community. Not only did they remain in the same place, they probably had the same job, went to the same church, and kept the same friends all of their lives. In the next generation—your parents—there was probably greater mobility and change. Their circle broadened; they changed jobs and

---

[1] R. Buckminster Fuller, "Thinking Out Loud: Physical Temporality and Eternal Principles," *Saturday Review/World*, September 11, 1973, p. 54.

living places more than your grandparents. In your generation, there has been even greater change. You will probably change your job, your house, and many of your close friends several times during different periods of your life. You also have a good statistical chance of changing your mate.

This increased mobility greatly affects our communication. We have been called a nation of strangers because we are often in the position of communicating more with strangers than with people we have known all, or even part, of our lives. When our communication is present-oriented, it is too exhausting and time-consuming to go through our entire life history with every new person we meet. Relationships must be established quickly—before we or our new friends move on to a new place. We have the choice, of course, of involving ourselves in superficial relationships in which we only exchange the information required by the day-to-day situation at hand. However, most people become increasingly lonely if they do not develop deeper, more personal relationships.

These relationships become even more important in the anonymity of a technological, industrial society. Many of us are best known to our school, our employer, and the government by our social-security number. The academic progress of many future students will be determined by how well they do on examinations graded by computers. Using the city and state on the address of a letter is becoming superfluous; the zip code is much more important. Although the assignment of numbers to individuals and to cities and states makes our society run more efficiently, it also creates a greater need for us to hold on to our individual identity. If our communication with humans increases and is satisfying, we feel less helpless about being numbered by the machines. Previous generations may have been able to take communication for granted; those of us who are impersonalized by institutions and organizations must seek out communication to retain our individuality and humanity.

The great social upheaval of the sixties has also been responsible for better communication. The greatest factor uniting sixties protesters was their need and desire to reject their roles, the behavior society expected of them. For example, women were expected to be happy cleaning house, cooking, and taking care of children. Blacks were expected to be content with being "good Negroes," accepting the few crumbs society offered them without complaining. Students were expected to be grateful for their chance to study; they were not supposed to challenge the structure of their educational institutions or of American society. When these groups, and several others, began to reject their expected roles, communication became an urgent priority. Protestors had to communicate to the institutions, the authorities, and the society why these roles were no longer satisfactory. Even more important, they had to communicate their new demands and expectations. Serious questions about communication were asked when society did not accept or even understand these needs.

Finally the increased interest of Americans in their psychological make-up has made an impact on communication. More and more people realize that it is psychologically healthy to communicate your feelings and to permit others to communicate theirs. Particularly during the sixties, people began to question the values and goals of the kind of communication that serves someone's own selfish interests. Critics complained that the intent of this type of communication is to command, force, manipulate, conquer, dazzle, deceive, or exploit. There is no mutual trust between the communicator and those to whom the communication is directed in such situations. The opposite of this self-centered communication is communication by dialogue. Although dialogue is not a new idea, it is a concept that came of age during the sixties. The "new" communication emphasized equal sharing in a process characterized by frankness, spontaneity, lack of pretense, intensity, and the responsibility of one person for another. Communication is no longer an ego trip; each person is recognized and listened to for his or her own uniqueness.[2]

All of these factors have led to a changing emphasis in communication study. Traditionally, communication has been studied almost exclusively from the point of view of public speaking, especially in an introductory course. Public speaking is a useful skill, but it is only a small part of the communication process. The new emphasis, and the emphasis of this book, is much wider. We will cover all of the following areas in the chapters that follow:

Self and Communication is concerned with the idea that the messages you send are intricately tied in with the images that you have of yourself and of others, that a message cannot exist apart from the self.

Interpersonal Communication involves how we communicate with one person or a small number of people on an informal, nonstructured level.

Nonverbal and *Verbal* deal with how we use nonverbal communication (a gesture, a frown, a touch) and verbal communication (language).

Public Speaking is concerned with how we communicate as speakers to an audience in a formal and structured setting.

2 Richard L. Johannesen, "The Emerging Concept of Communication as Dialogue," *Quarterly Journal of Speech* V. LVII, No. 4: 373–382.

The Power of Communication discusses how we can use persuasion and suggestion and how we are influenced by them. We will also examine protest communication—the communication that results when dialogue breaks down.

Small Group deals with how we work and communicate in small groups to solve problems, to run organizations, to make decisions, to heighten sensitivity, to facilitate social give-and-take, and so on.

Mass Media is concerned with how organizations and institutions try to communicate with us through the mass media.

Each of these types of communication is different, and we will be concerned with the various skills that each requires. The basic process of communication is the same, however, in that there are certain components that are always present in a communication situation. All communication works in the same way, and we will also be concerned with what all communication has in common.

THE PROCESS OF COMMUNICATION: A BASIC MODEL

Whether you are talking to a friend or a television network is sending a newscast to several million people, the process of communication is essentially the same. A model for the communication process is given in Figure 1.

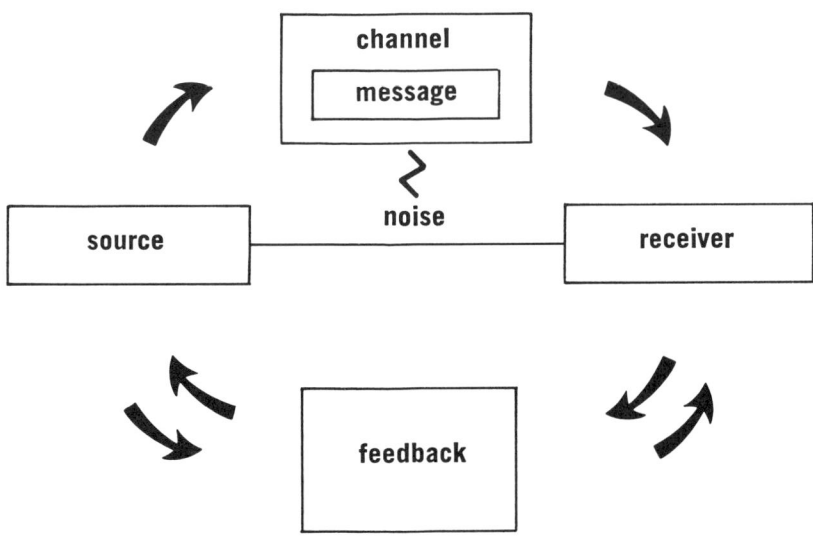

FIGURE 1

The *source* is the person or persons who originate the message. If a public speaker is delivering a speech, he or she is the source. In a television newscast, the network news organization is the source. Thus, a source can be a single person or an entire institution or organization.

The *message* is the actual communication the source is sending—the speech itself or the newscast, for example. The *channel* is the means through which the message is sent. Channels include spoken words, gestures and facial expressions, written words, airwaves, film, and so on.

The *receiver* is the person or persons for whom the message is intended. As with the source, the receiver can be a single person or many. In some cases, receivers meet together to hear the message, as does an audience for a public speech; in other cases, the receivers are separated from each other, as television viewers are.

Feedback is a two-way process—it is the response that the receiver gives to the source and the response that the source gives back to the receiver. If feedback is positive (the receiver shows interest and pleasure with the message), then the source will probably continue with the message in the same form. If feedback is negative, however, and the receivers lose interest or are not pleased, the source must revise the message to get back interest and attention.

Much of the success of communication depends on how well a source can adapt and respond to the feedback he or she receives. In some cases this is easily done; if you are talking to a friend who does not like what you are saying, it is fairly simple to change your message. If you are speaking to a large audience, changing the message is more difficult. In the mass media, change while the message is taking place is impossible because feedback is always delayed. A film producer does not know whether people like or dislike the film until the box office receipts are in. If many people attend the film, then the producer will probably continue to make similar films. If few people attend, then the producer must look for a new approach (or a new job).

Sometimes messages do not get through between the source and the receiver because of distracting and unwanted stimuli. This distraction is called *noise*. It can be either physical or psychological. Physical noise is obvious; someone is using a power mower outside the classroom window as you are trying to give a speech, or there is static on the car radio and so you cannot hear your favorite station. Psychological noise occurs in the mind of the sender or receiver and distracts him or her from the message. It is more complex and less easy to control than physical noise. If you go to a class right after you have had a quarrel with your roommate, you will probably be so distracted by thoughts of the previous communication that you will not receive much of the communication in the class. Psychological noise is a major cause of communication breakdown between the source and receiver.

A complete communication event, from the time that the source sends the message until it is received by the listener, is called a communication *transaction*. Most conversations between two people, for example, are made up of hundreds of sendings and receivings of messages, hundreds of small transactions. The most effective communication occurs when the message transmitted and the message received are identical. When there is no distortion of the message from the time it leaves the source until it is received, complete *fidelity* is said to exist in the transaction. Some communication theorists believe that complete fidelity can never be achieved, that no message is ever received exactly as it was intended by the source. This seems likely, since the source and receiver always have different frames of reference. It is clear, however, that the fidelity of any communication can be vastly improved if the sender and the receiver are aware of how communication works and are interested in achieving the greatest fidelity possible.

This book is written on the assumption that all of us can improve our communication, both as sources and as receivers. We hope to increase your understanding of the process of communication, of why people communicate the way they do, and of why some communications succeed and others fail. We will give emphasis to developing and improving communication skills. Finally, we are interested in making your own communication satisfying and rewarding to you and to those with whom you communicate.

1

Self and Communication

There is an exercise called Who Are You? that is commonly used in encounter groups and sensitivity training. The entire group is divided into pairs, and one person in a pair is instructed to ask the other person "Who Are You?" After the questioner listens to the response, he or she repeats the question again. The process may go on for ten or twenty minutes; although the question is always the same, the response becomes more varied and complex as the exercise continues. The person responding typically begins with basic information such as name, profession, relationships to others (mother, wife, brother), or perhaps the groups he or she belongs to (church, lodge, school). As the exercise continues, however, the respondent runs out of vital statistics and often begins responding with emotional information: "I am unhappy. I am hostile. I am a loving mother." Sometimes the respondent gets exasperated with the repetition of the question and begins to respond angrily or aggressively to the questioner. Other times respondents reveal more and more of themselves as the repeated question causes deeper and deeper probing.

WHO ARE YOU?

This exercise reveals how complex the self really is. Each of us is made up of a complicated web of experiences, knowledge, attitudes, and values, all of which help to define and explain who we are—both to ourselves and to others. *Self-identity* is the image we have of ourselves, or as R. D. Laing, a psychoanalyst and psychiatrist, puts it, "One's self-identity is the story one tells one's self of who one is."[1]

Some of us have considerable insight about ourselves. We know who we are, where we have been, and where we are going. Others of us may feel great doubt. Most of us combine certainty and uncertainty, depending on the circumstances. Our self-knowledge also changes over the years as we gain new information and experiences. The way we see ourselves at twenty is probably different from the way we see ourselves at forty or at seventy.

A self-concept is never created in isolation; it depends on the response and reaction of other people. The impressions people have of us and the way they react to us are very much determined by the way we communicate with them. This feedback process can also work in the other direction; when we see how people react to us and the impression they have of us, we may attempt to change our communication because their reaction is not compatible with the way we see ourselves. Thus, the image you have of your self and the image that others have are all intertwined in our communication.

YOU ARE WHAT YOU SAY (MAYBE)

Socrates once said, "Speak that I may see you." His words remind us that a person's identity and existence are closely tied to what he or she says. Yet we do not always say who we are; in many cases we make a deliberate attempt to conceal this information.

Our earliest identity and speech are not our own; they are conferred on us by someone else. Our mother, or the first person who takes care of us, tells us through her words and actions that we are good, bad, stupid, intelligent, lovable, or unlovable. She is also likely to teach us our first words and concepts and so, in many ways, we are her creation. From this early experience, Laing says, "We learn to be who we are told we are."[2]

---

1 R. D. Laing, *Self and Others* (New York: Pantheon Books, 1969), p. 77.
2 Laing, p. 78.

During early childhood we also learn to cover and hide unacceptable communication and behavior. Children learn not to throw their cereal on the kitchen floor. They learn four-letter words and then quickly unlearn them or avoid using them in the presence of their parents. By the time we are in our teens, most of us have a good idea of acceptable and unacceptable communication and behavior. On many occasions we may not communicate who we are at all. Sidney Jourard, a psychologist and author of *The Transparent Self,* says "Man perhaps alone of all living forms, is capable of *being* one thing and *seeming* from his actions and talk to be something else."[3] We hide our true selves in a variety of ways: we say things that we think people expect us to say; we play roles; we conceal our true feelings; our actions conflict with our words. Through these deceptions, deliberate or nondeliberate, we use words to disguise our selves; we no longer are what we say. If these deceptions go on long enough, we may lose a sense of who we are because our communication habits and our identity are closely related.

All of us can learn to communicate on a deep, personal, and rewarding level; it is possible to get who-you-are and what-say-you-are together. In the pages that follow we hope to show you why and where communication breaks occur. More importantly, we hope to show you how to overcome some of the communication problems we all face and to convince you that communication of your self to others, and of other people's selves to you, can become an enriching and rewarding experience.

HUMAN NEEDS

For many people, psychological *safety*—the approval and support that we get from people we love, admire, and respect—is an important need. Our safety needs cause us to seek out people who love and respect us and to avoid people we see as hostile and threatening. For example, many people face great anxiety when they are going to give a speech. Although they feel safe talking to friends and colleagues, the thought of facing an audience is very threatening because they are not assured of getting the kind of psychological support they need. A person's needs for safety may determine an entire life style. Do you go away to college or do you stay at home and go to a college in your own hometown? Do you make an attempt to meet new people with new ideas, or do you pre-

[3] Sidney M. Jourard, *The Transparent Self* (Rev. ed.: New York: D. Van Nostrand, 1971), p. 4.

fer to stay with old friends? The answer to these questions, and many others, may be determined by your safety needs.

Humans also have a need to grow. A child continues to try to walk even though she falls countless times. Her need to grow is far greater than her need to feel safe. If we were afraid of growth, we would never travel to new places or meet new people; in fact we would probably never leave our homes.

Abraham Maslow, the late psychologist who emphasized human self-fulfillment, put the human needs for safety and growth in the following diagram:[4] Maslow said that the more a person needs to feel safe, the

FIGURE 1.1

less likely it is that the person will be able to grow. Conversely, the individual is able to grow to the degree that he or she does not have a constant need for psychological safety. However, moving toward growth rather than toward safety can be very risky.

Margaret Mead, the anthropologist, describes such a risk in her autobiography, *Blackberry Winter*. She speaks about leaving the familiar safety of her home in the East to go to college at DePauw in rural Indiana:

> I arrived with books of poetry, portraits of great personalities to hang on the walls, and the snobberies of the East, such as the expectation that one dressed in the evening for members of one's own family. And I was confronted by the snobbery and cruelty of the sorority system at its worst. . . .
>
> When the invitations came out, I was invited to the Kappa rushing party. But when I arrived wearing my unusual and unfashionable dress that was designed to look like a wheat field with poppies blooming in it, my correspondent turned her back on me and never spoke to me again. I found the whole evening strangely confusing. I could not know,of course, that everyone had been given a signal that inviting me had been a mistake. Afterward, my roommates got the bids they expected, but I did not get a bid.[5]

4 Abraham H. Maslow, *Toward a Psychology of Being* (2d ed.; New York: D. Van Nostrand, 1968), p. 46.

5 Margaret Mead, *Blackberry Winter* (New York: William Morrow & Co., 1972), pp. 92, 94–95. Reprinted with omissions by permission of William Morrow & Company, Inc. Copyright © 1972 by Margaret Mead.

Mead describes a situation which you may have experienced in fantasy if not in reality. There are few things as uncomfortable as being in a room where you are not only ignored but are labeled as an unsuitable outsider. Thus, you may seek situations where you know this cannot happen—where you are assured of safety.

All of our communication behavior is closely tied to our need for psychological safety. We play roles that are expected of us by our peers and family; we communicate so people will like us; we often avoid communicating our most important feelings because we are afraid of rejection. However, when we communicate only what people want to hear, or what we think they want to hear, we can get into serious trouble. Our communication and our identity are so intertwined that it is impossible to separate them. If we get into a pattern of never communicating our self, the self no longer exists; we are only a reflection of how others see us. In the pages that follow, we will discuss how and why we communicate for safety and for growth and the implications these kinds of communication have for our lives.

ROLES

One of the most fascinating stories of childhood is "The Emperor's New Clothes." As you may remember, two unscrupulous tailors tell the emperor that they can make him a suit of clothes that can only be seen by those fit to hold office. The emperor agrees to have the clothes made. When they are "completed," they are admired by the emperor, his ministers, and all of his subjects. The hoax is not revealed until one small child, who does not know any better, says, "But—the King has no clothes on at all."

The tailors were shrewd psychologists. They knew that no person would admit that he or she was incompetent. They could count on the emperor to play the role of the qualified ruler and on the others to play admiring subjects, even if it meant admiring something that was not there. The child was so young that he did not know about the role that he was expected to play in the kingdom. The storyteller does not tell us what happened after the child uttered his fatal words, but we can assume that the social structure of the kingdom was badly shaken and that the role of the emperor and the relationship of his subjects to him was changed forever.

In its broadest sense, the term *role* refers to the factors that characterize your behavior at a particular point in time. When the emperor in the story was holding court, he was playing the role of the emperor by behaving the way an emperor is supposed to behave—wearing a crown, giving orders, and so on. After the hoax was revealed, the emperor may have gone into his private chambers to talk to his wife about the crisis; in that situation he would play the role of a husband in trouble—an entirely different set of behaviors. In each case, the role that the emperor was playing was partly determined by what he had learned from his culture about how emperors and husbands in trouble, respectively, are supposed to behave.

Distinctions are often made, especially in talking about the self, between the various behaviors that you exhibit in certain situations and the person you are beneath each of those sets of behaviors—between the role and the self. In this context, *role* might be defined as the behavior that society expects you to follow. Certain actions are expected of us; if we do not fulfill these expectations, we can cause considerable distress to ourselves and others. There are broad social roles that we are all expected to follow because we are Americans and share a common culture. There are also more specific roles that we are expected to follow as members of particular groups within the American culture.

We begin learning our sociocultural roles as small children. We are taught that it is impolite to spit in public; that children must behave in certain ways when adults are present; and that it is selfish not to share toys with a brother, sister, or visitor. By the time we are young adults, we know how to dress and behave at parties, at funerals, at work, and at school. We tell our host that we enjoyed the party when we were really bored to death. We do *not* tell our boss that he would do a better job of being janitor or our teacher that the assignment was useless busywork. These social behaviors are determined by our culture's definitions of roles such as child, guest, student, and so on; they may vary greatly from one culture to another.

Other roles are conferred on us as permanent members of certain groups. We are all members of broad, general groups such as men, women, blacks, and whites. As members of these groups, we are expected by our society and culture to play certain roles. For example, a male is expected to be strong, achieving, and unsentimental. If a male does not play this role, many people consider him inferior to other males.

The question raised by roles is what good and what damage can they do to the individuals and groups who play them? Roles, at their best, provide some psychological safety and a sense of identity. If you know the role you are playing, you can conform to the rules of society and be accepted. In a traditional role, for example, a teacher can go into a classroom and feel confident that, by virtue of his position, he will get a certain amount of attention and respect (or that students will play the role of giving attention and respect). He can ask for a term paper, give an examination, and fail those who do not play the role of the conscientious student. Although his traditional role may not stimulate motivation and intellectual excitement, it is safe.

Violating role expectations can be a threatening experience. Let's assume that the same teacher decides to abolish his traditional role. He enters the classroom and says, "Call me Bob. There will be no papers, and you will all grade yourselves." Now the students are in uncharted territory; they don't know what is expected of them or how to respond to this teacher who has changed both his role and the role of his students. The abandonment of these roles may prove to be very threatening to the teacher, the students, and even the school.

Role expectations can be damaging both to individuals and to society. Every role that you play defines you. If that definition is congruent with some essential part of you, then the role is comfortable and you can play it well. For example, there are some women who are happy with the role of housewife. They enjoy taking care of their home and children and have no desire to pursue a career or to find fulfillment outside the home. Other women, however, are angry when they are expected to play this role; they insist on more flexible roles for women. In the black movement, Stokely Carmichael's most revolutionary and far-reaching demand was to insist that blacks first reject all of the white definitions of black people and then define themselves. The new black definitions would, in turn, determine the role that blacks were to play in society.

One of the primary reasons for the turmoil of the sixties was that certain groups refused to play their roles. Blacks decided to no longer play the meek and submissive role, much to the distress of white society. The "happy Negro" could be (and had been) ignored, but the new black militant made demands on society that could not be ignored. More recently we have seen great protest against the roles that women, Indians, and Chicanos are expected to play.

Playing Somebody Else

What happens if the role or roles you play are not congruent with your self-image? Sidney Jourard writes:

> But what we forget is the fact that it is a *person* who is playing a role. The person has a self, or should I say he *is* a self. All too often the roles that a person plays do not do justice to all of his self. In fact, there may be nowhere that he may just *be* himself. Even more, the person may not *know* his self. He may be alienated. His real self becomes a feared and distrusted stranger.[6]

Carl Rogers, a psychologist with a special interest in communication, also writes of the role player:

> He discovers how much of his life is guided by what he *thinks* he should be, not by what he is. Often he discovers that he exists only in response

6 Jourard, p. 30.

to the demands of others, that he has no self of his own, that he is only trying to think, feel and behave in the way that others believe he *ought* to think, feel and behave.[7]

Ultimately, then, the question is to what extent our roles fit our own self-image. This question can only be answered in very individual terms for we all play roles according to our own needs. However, when roles become damaging to our sense of identity, they must be dropped or modified if we are to continue to grow. When the feminist movement gained momentum, for example, many women started to look at their housewife/mother roles and found them unsatisfying. Some dropped the role completely by getting a divorce and giving their husband custody of the children. Others changed their role: they split up the housework with their husband, put their children in child-care centers, and began to pursue their own professional interests. These role changes were not easy and were accomplished over long periods of time. Blacks have been redefining their roles for more than ten years, and there will probably still be many changes to come.

Most of us are not able to completely drop or change our roles. Our deepest and most vital roles are engrained in us from our earliest childhood; even though we might want to change them, they cling to us with great tenacity. If we are able to change, it is a slow, ongoing process. In many cases, our problem is to find a way to live with these roles which have been conferred on us by society. Jourard suggests that if we find a series of roles necessary, we must find at least one person with whom we play no roles. This is a person who knows and accepts us for who we really are. By permitting this person to know us, we are able to keep our sense of self-identity.

People who are struggling to change their roles may seek contexts in which extensive role-playing is not required. Sometimes these contexts can be misleading, however. For instance, in the beginning the hippie movement seemed to offer freedom from conventional, "establishment" roles until people began to realize that there was a hippie role that was just as restrictive as some of the more conventional roles. Some people find freedom from old role-playing patterns in groups which are specifically designed to encourage exploration of the self. These groups may be found in liberal churches, in the women's movement, and in encounter and T-groups run by trained sensitivity leaders. People who are forced to play many roles often find that participation in such a group gives them

[7] Carl Rogers, *On Becoming A Person* (Boston: Houghton Mifflin, 1961), p. 110.

at least one chance to play a role that is closest to their perception of themselves.

As well as becoming aware of what roles are doing to our lives, we should become aware of what they are doing to the lives of others. If we decide that we no longer want to play certain roles, it is only fair that we do not expect others to play them either. For example, some "liberated" women still expect men to open doors and pay for dates. If we work to abolish some of our roles, we should also work to the point where we can say, "I can be what I want to be, and you can be what you want to be."

Although many people talk of the good and damage that roles cause, they are seldom able to agree about where role-playing should begin and end. Most people agree that roles are important to the functioning of society but also have the potential to cause damage to the individual personality. Perhaps the only answer for the individual is to be aware of the extent to which he or she is playing a role and to know when that role is different from perceptions of the actual self. In other words, it may be necessary to admire the emperor's new clothes in order to hold on to your job—just do not delude yourself into thinking that the emperor really *has* new clothes! This seems to be the only way to keep the self intact.

DISCLOSURE AND NONDISCLOSURE

Disclosure is revealing your self to another person or persons. It also involves revealing information about yourself that the other person(s) would not ordinarily know, revealing your "private" self rather than only revealing your "public self." Before a person can disclose, he or she must have both self-knowledge and honesty. Disclosure, for example, could come after the end of a love affair. The man involved might disclose to his closest friends that the end of this affair has given him a feeling of great sorrow, loss, and inadequacy. He might use nondisclosure with people he doesn't know very well; he puts on a "front," says he is happy to be free again, declares that the woman was unworthy of his love, and begins to play the role of a playboy.

We all make choices about what to disclose and what to keep to ouselves. Our areas of choice can be seen in Figure 1.2.[8]

---

8 Joseph Luft, *Group Process: An Introduction to Group Dynamics* (2d ed.; Palo Alto, California: National Press, 1970), pp. 11–12.

	Known to Self	Not Known to Self
Known to Others	Free Area	Blind Area
Not Known to Others	Hidden Area	Unknown Area

FIGURE 1.2

The free area is the greatest disclosure area; it involves information about ourselves that we are willing to communicate as well as information we are unable to hide. A group of students, for instance, meet for the first time in a classroom and, following the instructor's suggestion, introduce themselves. Most of them will stick to vital statistics: their name, where they come from, and their major. Although a particular student does not give out much verbal information about his life style, many of his fellow students will judge whether he is "hip" or "straight" by such available information as his clothing and speech. At the beginning of the term, the students will limit their disclosure. As the term progresses, however, many of them will move more information into the free area. Some will do it with the entire class; others will do it with one or two individuals with whom they feel friendly. How much we communicate, of course, depends on who that other person is. To some people we may communicate almost everything we know; to others we may limit communication to information important to the moment.

The blind area is a kind of accidental disclosure area; there are certain things we do not know about ourselves that others know about us. This information often becomes known when others are able to penetrate our roles. For example, we may see that the man who must always have the latest model of an expensive car is really trying to hide his own sense of inadequacy and insecurity. Some people who see themselves as sympathetic and helpful are seen as bossy and manipulative by others. Advertisers like to play with our blind areas. They suggest, for instance, that you do not know that you have bad breath, but everyone else knows.

The hidden area is a deliberate nondisclosure area; there are certain things that you know about yourself that you do not want known so you deliberately conceal them from others. Most people hide those things that might evoke disapproval from those they love and admire.

Some of us have hidden areas that are not revealed to anyone. Others of us keep certain areas hidden to one person but open to another. For example, a woman is probably more likely to tell her best friend than her mother that she is no longer a virgin.

The unknown area is also a nondisclosure area; it provides no possibility of disclosure because it is not known to the self or to others. This is not to say, however, that unknown areas can never be known. Psychologists commonly help patients to discover these areas. Experience can also lead us into the unknown area. You might think that you would enjoy foreign travel or eating snails; you will never know until you try.

The disclosure and nondisclosure areas are not static and unchanging; disclosure varies with the person, the context, and with maturity. Masturbation may be a dark and hidden secret at twelve, but it may be easily discussed at twenty-five. You might have expressed your anger by screaming when you were three or four, but by the time you were in your teens you realized that anger should be toned down or hidden. If a friend keeps your secrets, you will probably reveal more. If you do not feel free and open with anyone, you may choose never to disclose or to disclose only to a stranger on a bus or train.

Many people do not believe that disclosure is a virtue. To them, revealing how one feels is an indulgence and somehow in bad taste. Our society has also developed the concept of being "hip" or "cool." To reach this state you must stand apart from others, never reveal your true feelings, and never get involved. "Being cool" allows no place for spontaneity or enthusiasm.

Other Americans have invented all sorts of devices to counter nondisclosure. In recent years, thousands (and perhaps even millions) of people have joined encounter or sensitivity groups. The main function of these groups is to permit the participants to say exactly what they want to say, to express their feelings just as they are feeling them, and to strip away the masks that they feel they must wear in everyday life. In academic life we have courses and entire majors devoted to the problem of reestablishing communication between people. There are also people who make a profession of advising companies and industry on improving communication.

Nondisclosure provides a person with great psychological safety. On the other hand, disclosure, writes Jourard:

> means taking the first step at dropping pretense, defenses and duplicity. It means an end to "playing it cool," and an end to using one's behavior as a gambit designed to disarm the other fellow, to get him to reveal

himself *before* you disclose yourself to him. The invitation is fraught with risk, indeed, it may inspire terror in some.[9]

There are many risks involved in self-disclosure. Some of us are afraid of the self-knowledge that disclosure might bring. We may suspect certain things about ourselves, but we would prefer that they would remain in our hidden area. Some of us are afraid of intimacy. Disclosure may cause us to feel responsible for the personal information we receive. For example, if a friend tells us that she is unhappy, we may feel a certain sense of responsibility for helping her to feel happier. Some of us fear that if we tell another person too much about us, he or she might try to control us. If we tell a lover of our great need for affection, he or she could withhold affection in order to manipulate us. Disclosure means that we must drop our roles. The role of a strong, brave male is no longer tenable to a wife who knows that her husband is terrified of spiders. Perhaps the greatest individual fear in disclosure is that of negative feedback; we are afraid that disclosure will mean that the other person will no longer love, accept, or want us.

If self-disclosure is so fraught with risk, why disclose at all? First of all, self-knowledge is obtained through disclosure. Jourard writes ". . .no man can come to know himself except as an outcome of disclosing himself to another person."[10] Through other's eyes, we see ourselves. Self-disclosure also creates a bond with other people. If we are willing to disclose, the person with whom we disclose may be able to reciprocate. This means that rather than only communicating roles, people learn to share the feelings, thoughts, and hopes that are vital to their lives. Unless we disclose our needs, we have no chance of their ever being met. Some people, for example, never show their anger. They appear calm and peaceful to their closest friends and associates even though they may be in inner turmoil. Because they cannot disclose their anger, they have no way of stopping the behavior that makes them angry. Other people are able to disclose anger at appropriate moments and in the right circumstances. They are able to distinguish between irritation and anger and to channel their anger in the right direction. Still others may overdisclose anger in inappropriate circumstances. We are all familiar with the man who kicks his dog and yells at his secretary when he is really angry with his wife or boss. There is a wide range of degrees in self-disclosure. All of us learn, through experience, which reactions are appropriate.

9 Jourard, p. 133.
10 Jourard, p. 6.

Some of us have seldom disclosed. Assuming you are willing to try, how do you go about it? One way to begin self-disclosure is to reveal something about yourself that is not too threatening to a person whom you trust. If this person accepts the revelation and reciprocates, you have the beginning of meaningful communication. We have also mentioned certain groups and institutions in which you can drop your roles. These same groups offer opportunities for self-disclosure since disclosure can only begin when defensive roles are dropped.

One of the great excitements of self-disclosure is that it gives us a chance to experience the fact that no human emotion is unique. Perhaps this can best be illustrated through an example of a group experience. An individual within a group was going through a very anxious period in her life. To cope with her feelings, she had developed a fantasy which she described to the group. It involved being committed to a rest home for six months. While she was there, all of her food would be prepared and brought to her, everyone would greet her with warm and friendly smiles and, most important, for the entire time she was there, she would not have to make a single decision or to think about the things that were making her anxious. At the end of the six-month period, she would be able to resume her previous life with calm and stability. After she told her fantasy to the group, every single member of the group admitted to having a similar fantasy at one time or another. This knowledge that others share your emotions is a great help to self-disclosure.

Self-disclosure can occur only in an atmosphere of trust and goodwill. There are people who can harm us or who would like to harm us; with these people we are better off playing roles. There are also people who will not understand our feelings even though they may feel favorably toward us. These people are generally not self-disclosers themselves, and they keep a great deal of their lives in the hidden area.

We should caution you about one other risk in self-disclosure. Although you may discover that honesty and openness are very good for you, too much openness may be harmful to other people—especially people who do not disclose themselves. Many people become threatened if they feel you are getting too close to them. Disclosure can also bring out hostile and aggressive feelings. These feelings can often be best expressed in groups with trained leaders who make certain that no individual is psychologically damaged.

Finally we would like to say that disclosure works best when it is an ongoing process. You can disclose occasionally and probably obtain some growth, but to continue to grow, you must continue to disclose.

DISARMING COMMUNICATION

At its simplest level, communication occurs when people get together to share information and feelings to the benefit of all those concerned. However, as we have already seen, communication effectiveness can be hampered and diminished by a variety of complex factors such as the communication of defensive roles and the inability to disclose true feelings. To these two factors, we would like to add a third which we will call *communication to disarm*. Disarming communication occurs when the sender wants (or needs) control; he or she sees the receiver as an opponent or an adversary, and the purpose of communication is conquest. In some cases this type of communication is legitimate because all participants understand and agree that "winning" is the purpose of the communication. A lawyer arguing a case in a courtroom and a speaker in a formal debate are examples. However, when "winning" or control is not the agreed-upon intent of the transaction, disarming communication can block effective communication.

Disarming communication is closely tied to one's self-concept. People who have a strong need for psychological safety often feel that it is important to win and to be in control. Thus, your intrapersonal communication (communication with yourself) affects your interpersonal communication (communication with others). On the other hand, if you can put aside your need for safety and aim toward growth, you no longer have a need to protect yourself; you can afford to listen and learn.

Disarming communication can take many forms. Four common types include defensive, aggressive or hostile, manipulative, and avoidance. These characteristics do not always occur separately; some or all might be present in a single communication act.

Defensive communication occurs when a person sees the communication situation as threatening. It may occur, for example, when it looks as though someone may be proven wrong. The topic under discussion becomes secondary; the individual concerned works to prove that he or she is right, to dominate, or to impress. One of the clearest characteristics of this type of communication is that the defensive individual does not listen; he or she spends all of the time when others are speaking thinking about how to improve his or her control and strategy. Defensive communication is filled with evaluative judgments; others' ideas are perceived as good, bad, moral, immoral, weak, or strong. The individual feels that his or her own ideas are unassaultable.

Hostile and aggressive communication involves direct attacks on other persons or their ideas rather than defense of one's own ideas. Again the disarming communicator may use evaluative tactics or engage in personal attack or sarcasm. Aggression is often used by those trying to maintain positions of power. An aggressive boss, for example, tells the employee, "Don't ask any questions—just do it!" As well as using hostile communications against others, the disarming communicator may use it against himself or herself. Politicians commonly use the "I'm just a country boy" approach. Not only is this a maneuver to downgrade their opponent; it is also an attempt to gain sympathy and, hence, power.

Manipulative communication is an attempt by the sender to control individuals or groups. This communication is characterized by self-interest on the part of the source. The source attempts to get the receivers to do what he or she wants them to do, not necessarily what is good or right for them. The manipulator often uses guilt as a strategy: "If you are my friend, you will stop studying and come shopping with me." "If you really love me, you will take me to the movies tonight." Manipulative communication is an integral part of American society. In addition to being used in individual communications, it is commonly used by advertisers and salespersons.

Avoidance is a tactic used by people who do not want to deal with communications that could be threatening. They stay away from the topic, change the subject, and avoid situations and contacts where threats occur. Avoidance of a subject may be the ultimate self-destructive control; if one refuses to ever deal with something, the problem can never be solved.

Defensive, hostile, and aggressive communication are often characterized by evaluative judgments. Carl Rogers suggests that the single greatest cause of communication breakdown is the individual's tendency to judge—to approve, disapprove, or otherwise evaluate the communication of other persons. For example, if a wife tells her husband, "I feel that you don't love me anymore. You haven't paid attention to me for weeks," and the husband replies, "You shouldn't feel that way. Of course I love you," there has been a communication breakdown. The husband has said the feeling is inaccurate without dealing with what is causing it. "That was dumb," "That was a stupid thing to say," "Don't be silly"—all of these are common phrases that contain evaluative, judgmental statements. Such statements usually cause the receiver to respond defensively or aggressively.

Rogers suggests that we stop making evaluative judgments and that we attempt to identify with the other person and to feel what the other person is feeling. However, as with dropping roles and disclosing, identification with other's feelings is very risky. He says:

> If you really understand another person in this way, if you are willing to enter his private world and see the way life appears to him, without any attempt to make evaluative judgments, you run the risk of being changed yourself. You might see it his way, you might find yourself influenced in your attitudes or your personality. The risk of being changed is one of the most frightening prospects most of us can face.[11]

We must become aware of manipulative and avoidance communication before we can change our behavior. Many of us try to manipulate people a great deal. ("If you clean your plate, you can watch television" or "I will go if you will go with me.") There may be circumstances in which manipulation is not bad—in fact there is a school of psychology devoted to manipulating behavior in a process called behavior modification. The emphasis in this school of thought is ignoring bad behavior and rewarding good behavior. The expectation for this manipulation is that the person rewarded will engage in more and more good behavior. Whether manipulative communication is justified really depends on the motives of the source. When the source works to further his or her self-interest, manipulation becomes distasteful. When the source interacts with the receiver with concern and care, manipulation may be justified if it genuinely aids the receiver.

Deciding whether to use avoidance communication also depends on the circumstances. You may change the subject in a conversation with a group of friends because it appears that if the talk continues, someone is going to be harmed or humiliated. If you constantly move away from things that are unpleasant or threatening, however, you will find yourself playing more roles. Manipulation and avoidance become less necessary when disclosure takes place and roles are dropped. When we are with people for whom disclosure is impossible, however, manipulation and avoidance can serve to keep some communication lines open.

COMMUNICATING THE SELF TO OTHERS: A CASE STUDY

We would now like to look at two groups that have used a combination of intrapersonal and interpersonal communication to solve the prob-

11 Rogers, p. 333.

lems of group members. These groups are Alcoholics Anonymous (A.A.) and Weight Watchers (W.W.).

Alcoholism and overweight are two problems that have caused distress to millions of Americans. Although there is a great deal of medical and scientific data on both subjects, doctors and scientists have come up with few practical solutions to help individuals with these problems. Most people who overdrink or overeat would probably agree that their behavior is dangerous to their health, but they still continue to do it. A.A. and W.W. have not eliminated alcoholism and obesity, but they (or similar groups) have made more progress than any other group in helping individuals with these problems.

Individuals in both groups must begin with intrapersonal self-disclosure. The member of A.A. says, "I am an alcoholic" and the member of W.W. says, "I am fat." No qualifications are permitted. For example, an A.A. member cannot say, "Sometimes my drinking gets a little out of control" and a W.W. member cannot say, "I have problems with my glands." Many people are not able to function in these groups because of this requirement for intrapersonal self-disclosure; they are not yet ready for this much honesty.

Once an individual has disclosed the problem to him- or herself, he or she is ready for interpersonal self-disclosure—to admit the problem to the group. Disclosing the problem in the group opens up the possibility that the individual can ask for, and get, the group's support. He or she is saying, "My problem is out of control, and I need your help [the group] to handle it." The meetings are filled with disclosures of personal experience. Alcoholics tell of experiences of losing jobs, beating wives, and waking up in gutters. Weight Watchers, similarly, tell of hiding food, of secret eating, and of airplane seat belts that do not fit. These experiences lead other members to disclose with the result that each individual learns that he or she is not the only one who has done these "terrible" things—there is always someone else who has done them too.

People play very few roles in these groups. Most members do not even know the professional roles that other members play unless the roles are directly related to their problem. Occasionally roles are attacked. W.W. tells members that the mother role does not involve eating all of the leftovers on the children's plates. A.A. may tell members that the role of an executive does not demand drinking at a company party. Generally, however, once self-disclosure has taken place, role-playing is no longer relevant.

Disclosure also eliminates the needs for disarming communication.

Although members may need it outside of the group to protect themselves, there is no need to be hostile, defensive, or to avoid the problem within the group. Members do not avoid the fact that they are fat or alcoholic; they do not defend the way they are nor do they criticize others with similar problems. Group members seldom make evaluative judgments of other members in the group because, in this setting, evaluative judgments of others would mean evaluative judgments of oneself.

Although these groups exist to solve a specific problem, they also serve as a model for other groups and other communications. The people in these groups are accepted; they are not made to feel inferior, weak, worthless, evil, or shameful. When people are given the opportunity to disclose and receive disclosure without receiving or making evaluative judgments, they are able to grow.

SUMMARY

Your self is a complex mixture of experience, knowledge, attitudes, and values. These factors, combined with the perceptions and reactions of others to you, all work to create the impression that you have of who you are.

We all use communication to present our self to others. Although we may attempt to communicate our true self, we may also use communication to hide the self. The greater our need for psychological safety, the more we will try to communicate in ways that are safe—ways that will obtain approval and respect from others. If we can get away from our safety needs and communicate our true feelings, however, we find that both our communication and our life can become more satisfying.

Carl Rogers has offered a personal communication model that might be useful to all of us. Several years ago he was asked to talk to a university audience about his life, his work, and what he had learned. In reply he said:

> 1) In my relationships with persons I have found that it does not help, in the long run, to act as if I were someone I am not.
> 2) I find I am more effective when I can listen acceptantly to myself, and can be myself.
> 3) I have found it of enormous value when I can permit myself to understand another person.
> 4) I have found it enriching to open channels whereby others can communicate their feelings, their private perceptual worlds, to me.

5) I have found it highly rewarding when I can accept another person.[12]

We believe that Rogers' discoveries about himself apply to all of us. His insights can lead us to fuller communication with ourselves and with others—to getting what-we-say and what-we-are together.

FURTHER READING

Maya Angelou, *I Know Why the Caged Bird Sings*. New York: Random House, 1969.
This autobiography tells an engaging story of growing up black and female in the rural South. Writing with great warmth and wit, the author describes her struggles with identity, love, and the oppression of self in such a realistic way that you cannot help but identify with her.

Sidney M. Jourard, *The Transparent Self*. Rev. ed.: New York: D. Van Nostrand, 1971.
The importance of self-disclosure to psychological well-being is stressed in this informal and readable discussion. The book is greatly enhanced by the author's willingness to disclose his own life and feelings.

Jess Lair, *I Ain't Much Baby—But I'm All I Got*. Garden City, New York: Doubleday, 1972.
This book contains practical advice about how to develop many of the personal insights we have discussed in this chapter. The author is particularly sympathetic to some of the problems and anxieties that are common to college students.

Abraham H. Maslow, *Toward A Psychology of Being*. 2d ed.: New York: D. Van Nostrand, 1968.
A complex but rewarding book on the subject of reaching one's full human potential, this is one of the classics of humanistic psychology. The author evolves a theory of the healthy personality by describing individuals who have found fulfillment in life.

Carl R. Rogers, *On Becoming A Person*. Boston: Houghton Mifflin, 1961.
This warm and easy-to-read book explores what it means to be a person. The author covers a variety of topics in a series of self-contained articles so you can choose the ones that interest you.

12 Rogers, p. 3.

Colin Turnbull, *The Mountain People.* New York: Simon and Schuster, 1972.
> This anthropologist's account describes a tribe in Uganda who lose the human values of love, respect, and compassion in order to survive. This depressing but fascinating book gives you a sense of what it would mean to completely lose your humanity.

2

Interpersonal Communication

The most crucial communication in our lives occurs in situations that are so common that often we do not think about them as involving communication skills at all. In a nation of strangers, being able to communicate with those around us every day can make the difference between developing nourishing personal relationships and being alone, alienated from others. In this chapter we will consider some of the skills which are involved in becoming more effective in communicating with others on a personal level.

When you seek an instructor's advice about a course or when you talk with an intimate friend about your future plans, you are involved in *one-to-one communication*—one source sending messages to one receiver. If three people, or even four or five, together discuss a movie that they have all seen together, those people are engaged in *one-to-few communication*—one source sending messages to a few receivers. In these face-to-face situations, all participants both initiate and respond to messages as they mutually influence each other; the roles of source and receiver alternate rapidly. Verbal messages—words—are sent and received in sequence while nonverbal messages are sent and received on a continuing, ongoing basis. Speaking together on a one-to-one or one-to few level is called *interpersonal communication.* It is the communication situation that most of us are involved in most of the time.

We take most interpersonal communication for granted. It seldom occurs to us to analyze it even though, at times, we might catch ourselves thinking something like, "Gosh, he acted strange when we talked today." Rarely do we, or could we, carry our examination to a point where we understood all the reasons why a person failed to communicate in an interpersonal situation. We spend nearly 75 percent of our waking time listening, speaking reading, and writing. Much of this communication occurs in face-to-face situations or is directly related to interpersonal relationships. Even if we wanted to analyze all of these communications, we would not be able to, simply because there are too many of them.

It is also impossible to set forth prescriptions which, if followed, would guarantee successful interpersonal communication because every interpersonal communication is unique. The Greek philosopher Anaxagoras said, in the fifth century B.C., that you can't step in the same river twice because the river is different and you are different every time. In the same way, you can't have the same interpersonal communication twice since neither you nor the other person will be the same. If a woman says "I love you" to a man on Monday night, he may react quite differently than he would to the statement, "I love you," on Saturday night. On Monday, it just happened that he had several exams coming up, a paper, and a speech, but on Saturday all that was behind him. He could breathe a sigh of relief and enjoy her company and attention. In this case, a different time made all the difference in the world. But not all Saturday nights are the same either.

Interpersonal communications are affected by all sorts of variables in the situation, the participants, and the message. Change any aspect of one of these and the nature of the communication is changed. The change could vary from a slight shift in attitude to a change in the weather. It might include the choice of a different word in the message or an alteration in emphasis on a word. Time itself—an aspect of the situation over which we have no control—also causes each situation to be different.

There are, however, certain skills that can be developed to improve interpersonal communication. Simply becoming aware of how this kind of communication operates can make you more effective in interpersonal relationships. To help you understand some of the factors involved, we will use three overlapping categories. In the first category, we will consider channels, feedback, and noise—three essential elements in the process of interpersonal communication. The second category includes the relationships between the speaker and the listener. In this area we will consider how you perceive the other participants and how they perceive you. The third and final category we will consider concerns the message. In this area, we will consider emotional and rational messages.

Interpersonal communication includes each of the components of communication given in the model in the introduction to this book, but the channel, the source and the receiver, and the message all have unique characteristics in this situation. Because interpersonal communication involves participants communicating in close proximity to one another, more channels are utilized than simply those of sight or sound. Lovers engage in a type of interpersonal communication just as a judge does when sentencing a criminal; the messages in these two situations vary greatly, and yet the physical closeness of the source and the receiver means that there are likely to be more channels available in these interpersonal situations than in public speaking or mass communication.

The relationship between the speaker and the listener also differs from the source-receiver relationship in the model. Rather than a speaker-to-listener orientation, interpersonal communication requires that the participants assume both speaker and listener roles. It is two-way communication, and to become effective communicators, participants need to develop their ability to receive as well as to send messages. The primary emphasis in interpersonal communication is on recognizing, and hence approaching or overcoming, barriers to understanding.

Interpersonal messages are unique in that the nonverbal level is often as important as the verbal level. The emotional content of interpersonal messages is likely to be significant to both source and receiver, and emotional content is often carried nonverbally. Interpersonal messages are also spontaneous—unlike the preplanned messages of public speaking, for example—and their effectiveness depends upon the flexibility and receptiveness of the source and the receiver.

One should remember that the major categories in the following discussion are arbitrary. They have been so designated for the purposes of explanation. They are overlapping—each not only affects the other, but often each becomes part of the other. They should not be viewed as exclusive—nor should they be viewed as definitive.

INTERPERSONAL PROCESS:
THREE ESSENTIAL ELEMENTS

The process of communicating with another person is ongoing, changing, continually developing. Effective interpersonal communication is organic rather than mechanical, and it generates new ways of behaving and new possibilities for growth in the participants. This growth is dependent upon the availability of channels, the amount of feedback, and the level of noise.

Channels

We tend to remember another person better if we can touch, smell, hear, and see that person than if we can only do one of these—hearing the person's voice on the telephone, for example. When you increase the number of channels you use to communicate with others, you not only heighten the interest that the others will have in your communication, but you also increase the support for your message, the level of possible understanding of your message, and your own image or credibility. If you are talking to another person about the damage done to your car in an accident, you are using one channel—sound, or hearing. If you show the person a picture, you double the channels—using both sight and sound. You can triple the channels by taking the other person to see the car so that he or she can touch it, see it, and hear you talk about it. If the other person were at the scene of the accident, he or she could also smell the burning rubber, the spilled gasoline, and the escaping radiator steam. The last image would likely be experienced, understood, and retained the best whereas the first description would soon fade from memory. When more channels are used, more of the receiver's senses come into play and, thus, the likelihood that the receiver will become more emotionally involved is increased. With emotional involvement—that is, when a person's feelings are affected—greater concern for the message, the ideas being conveyed, will occur. The more channels you use, then, the more effective your communication will be.

In interpersonal communication, because of the intimacy of the situation, it is easier for us to use all the channels. A handshake or an embrace, the strong scent of perfume or after-shave lotion, conversation that is reinforced by one person reaching into his wallet or her purse for pictures of the kids indicate some of the many characteristic ways in which channels are used in an interpersonal transaction taking place between two old friends who have not seen each other for awhile.

Feedback

When, instead of writing a person a letter, you decided that it would be better to see him or her in person, part of your decision may reflect a desire to see how the other person will respond to your message, what his or her feedback will be. Just as the source has more success in communicating through a number of channels, the receiver can increase feedback if it is communicated through a variety of channels. In interpersonal settings, we receive facial responses from our listener as well as vocal and verbal responses. Body movements, too, are sometimes used. You might question the truth of another person's generalization by raising an eyebrow. You might show that you are interested by looking the person directly in the eye and even squinting slightly. You acknowledge receipt of messages with vocal responses such as "yeah . . . yeah," "uh-huh," or "mmmm." You use verbal feedback such as "I know," "I see what you mean," and "Right!" A slouched posture may reveal apathy while turning away from the other person slightly may indicate disinterest. Because interpersonal communication is two-way, opportunity is available for extensive feedback through a variety of channels.

Feedback goes on all the time that people are engaged in an interpersonal communication situation. It is not confined to source or listener alone but flows from both throughout a transaction. Just as nobody can avoid communicating, nobody can avoid providing feedback. It is an important ingredient in increasing the accuracy of communication and removing barriers to understanding.

Noise

You have undoubtedly had the experience of talking to someone else about something you considered important and being abruptly interrupted. A husband and wife are discussing their plans when suddenly the baby cries; you and a friend are driving along the expressway discussing whether to pull off for lunch, and you are drowned out by a noisy trailer truck. Such interruptions cause frustration, especially if they are repeated. The term we have used in our communications model for such interference is *noise*.

Noise affects the message by causing a discrepancy between the message transmitted and the message received. *Physical noise* is technical interference. It may be caused by disturbance in the channel—a bad telephone connection, for example—or by a speech disorder in the source or deafness in the receiver. *Psychological noise* occurs within the communicator or within the receiver. When a speaker chooses incorrect words to express an idea and causes misunderstanding in the receiver, the speaker creates this kind of noise. Psychological noise could also be caused by distortion in feedback. Whenever the distortion occurs in the mind of the communicator or receiver, the interference can be labeled psychological.

The best way to reduce the influence of noise is to eliminate the cause. The couple in the first example can feed the baby and then go on with their planning; you can slow down so as not to miss the exit while the trailer truck passes. People dial a phone number again to get a better connection. Handling psychological noise can be harder; it may be more difficult to eliminate for it is often more difficult to perceive. Following the suggestions provided in Chapter 4, Verbal Communication, will help you to achieve an accurate transfer of meaning with a minimum of distortion. Often being aware of and willing to disclose your own state of mind during interpersonal communication will help to minimize psychological interference.

If noise cannot be eliminated, however, there are two other methods you can use to try to achieve accurate communication. The first is to use several channels of communication to say the same thing, thus providing a duplication of information. Multiplying the channels used will make your communication *redundant*. A smile, a nod of the head, a firm handshake or embrace, and the greeting "Hi! How are you?" often convey the same meaning—meaning that could be conveyed through a single channel or redundantly, through more than one.

The other method which will increase fidelity and reduce noise is to control the speed at which you are communicating. Information is processed by different individuals at different speeds. The rate varies for each situation and for each of the individuals in various situations. If you wanted to pass on some vital information to a fellow employee who was having a conference with a superior just after you, you might state succinctly as you passed him or her on the way out, "He's in a rotten mood" —but you would state it slowly and clearly so you would not have to repeat it. In talking casually to a few friends, you might speak very quickly whereas in talking to a large group of strangers, you might want to speak more slowly because of the increased possibility for misunderstanding, the intrusion of noise. Whether you should speed up, slow down, or become more succinct has to be a function of the feedback you gain. There is no specific rate that is ideal for all—except that rate at which a high degree of fidelity can be attained. It is the rate at which the amount of noise affecting the communication can be minimized.

SPEAKER ROLES AND LISTENER ROLES

Understanding and facilitating interpersonal communication depend upon each of the individuals who is involved in the transaction. Each

person plays the roles of speaker and listener in interpersonal situations, and each person can develop his or her ability to relate with others by understanding what these two roles require and evaluating his or her ability to play each role.

Sometimes we can predict how we will relate to other people and how other people are likely to relate to us. Attitudes can sometimes be predicted just as listener responses can. Your own communication skills and sociocultural experiences are fairly constant from one interpersonal situation to another and, thus, can also be predicted. Predictions should not cause you to become rigid in anticipating particular interpersonal communication situations, nor should you plan your interpersonal communication to the point that spontaneity is lost. Rather, predictions should allow you to consider alternative approaches, to anticipate circumstances, and to reflect on what you have learned about other individuals as a result of previous communications with them. You know that any person will not be exactly the same the next time you see him or her, but you also know that people do not change radically from one transaction to another. On the basis of previous transactions with a person, you can anticipate how a new interpersonal communication will go. Too, you know yourself, and you are the other vital element in the process.

Being aware of the variables in speaker and listener roles in the interpersonal communication process will also help you to send and receive messages with greater fidelity as you are communicating. This awareness of the process begins with an understanding that the speaker and the listener roles are intertwined in interpersonal communication; they influence each other to a greater degree than in any other communication situation. There is greater intimacy because it is a one-to-one or one-to-few situation. Roles are often exchanged rapidly—speaker becoming listener and vice versa with no definite pattern or regularity. When one knows that he or she must uphold, support, or provide one half of a one-to-one communication or a third of a three-way communication, he or she assumes the responsibility. Senses are sharpened, listening is keener, and responses are often better than they would be when more people are involved. Thus, speaker and listener roles are more directly and clearly intertwined—involved and interrelated with each other.

PERCEPTION OF SELF BY OTHERS AND OTHERS BY SELF

How you perceive yourself bears directly on your success in interpersonal relationships. If you perceive yourself as being liked, wanted, acceptable to others, capable, and worthy, it is likely that you will be successful in interpersonal relationships. It is likely, too, that communication in such relationships will be easy, open, honest, and satisfying for you. If you are anxious, insecure, cynical, and depressed, on the other hand, you are more likely to engage in defensive communication, that is, you will perceive a threat in communication situations. If you are unsure of yourself in a new job, and you receive some negative feedback from your boss on several tasks, you may begin to think that your boss "has it in for you"—that he or she does not like you or that he or she does not like your attitude. With such negative responses as a framework, you begin to interpret other things as negative that might not otherwise be considered negative at all. You begin to perceive that the boss is "picking on you" by walking by you or watching you while you work. If he or she asks for a report of progress—an otherwise normal procedure—you may respond with "Why me?" When you hold a negative attitude about yourself, often you think others hold a negative attitude about you as well.

Because you hold a negative attitude about yourself, it is more likely that others *will* hold a negative attitude toward you because the expectations you have about how others will react toward you often determine the reactions you receive. If you think your boss is against you, you will probably behave in a hostile or defensive manner with him or her; this may have the effect of turning your boss against you. In this manner, attitudes about yourself become *self-fulfilling prophecies* because the way others react to you is often determined by the way you expect and invite them to react to you. A person who is confident will appear capable and worthy and will, very likely, engage in less defensive behavior and communication than one who lacks confidence; thus, others are likely to see that person as confident.

How you perceive others will also bear directly on how you perceive yourself. We often use *projection* as we view others—projecting our faults and our weaknesses onto others. If you have trouble getting along with a neighbor, for example, you are likely to tell others that that neighbor has trouble getting along with people. Honest reactions to others result from security and confidence in ourselves. Communication is more likely to be open and honest when both parties are free from anxiety and sure of themselves.

The way you perceive yourself and others, and the way that others perceive you, are at the heart of interpersonal communication. If you feel anxious or as if the situation involves a great deal of risk, these feelings may become a barrier to effective communication. Sometimes the most helpful thing to do in a situation that feels risky to you is simply to acknowledge—to yourself and, if you can, to the other person—that you are feeling vulnerable. Disclosing your true feelings in this manner can help to build trust and to focus on the difficulty in the communication rather than avoiding it. Sometimes the anxiety is inevitable, and the best you can do is to be aware of what it is making you do in the situation. It is rare for communication barriers in interpersonal transactions to be created by only one person. If you can recognize your own contribution to the barrier, you are on your way to learning how to overcome such communication difficulties.

Role-Playing

The business of living from day to day requires that you play a wide variety of roles. Getting up in the morning with your family, you play one role. At work during the day, or at school, you may play a different role. Going for coffee in the afternoon with classmates may involve a third role. Socializing in the evening with intimate friends may call forth still another one. As a week progresses and you encounter a wide variety of situations, messages, and listeners, you portray still new and varied roles. With each person—the store owner, the neighbor, the filling-station attendant, the minister, the doctor, and the instructor—you are a slightly different you.

The source plays many roles in interpersonal communication. This is necessitated by different situations, by different topics of conversation, and, perhaps most importantly, by different listeners. Just as a speaker's role will change in response to different listeners, the listener's role will also change—a direct result of the interrelationship between speaker and listener. A person whose repertoire of roles is limited will have difficulty functioning effectively in interpersonal communication.

We all have a variety of roles, including some of which we may not be directly aware; we all role-play. As the number of experiences and encounters we have increases, the likelihood that we will play more roles also increases. The person who attempts to portray a single role throughout many different encounters will run into difficulty. One role simply will not suffice as situations, messages, and listeners change. The role that you portray at a "beer blast," for example, is not the role you would want your minister to see; the kind of self-disclosing behavior you exhibit when you are with close friends may not be the same behavior you wish to reveal to your casual acquaintances. Certain facets of your self are appropriate for some people, other facets for other people. All people do not see the same you, and people will react differently depending upon the you they encounter.

Effective communicators understand the importance of role-playing and have the ability to adjust quickly to different situations, messages, and listeners. They also are aware that others are playing roles and are reacting to the roles they create. They take into consideration their own expectations, their listeners' perceptions, and all of the other requirements of each communication situation. For example, a young man was at a party where he was being freer than usual; suddenly, in walked a possible future employer—a person whom he highly respected and with whom he desired to work. Not to adjust to the situation—altered now by the addition of an unexpected new listener—could jeopardize his plans. He reacted by pulling himself together a bit, showing more restraint and less verbosity. From the role of "life of the party" he changed to the role of "responsible and mature adult." Showing himself as responsibly mature was not phony; this man truly was responsible and mature—but this role had been left "at the office" and that of "party playboy" was being displayed. It is likely that if this man's parents had walked in, or if his minister had been a guest, other different characteristics would have been demonstrated. All these characteristics make up this person's self. They are appropriately varied according to the situation.

Becoming more aware of the use of roles and the fact that we all engage in role-playing is one way to increase your own flexibility and your ability to cope with interpersonal communication situations. This awareness will support your personal growth, helping you to become what Abraham Maslow calls "the healthy person" in his book, *Toward a Psychology of Being*.[1] If you accept yourself and others for what you are and they are, you are also more likely to be successful. You can be an individual—autonomous, resisting enculturation, and revealing uniqueness in your responses—even as you play a variety of roles. If you appreciate communication situations in all their complexity and allow yourself the richness of emotional reactions, your awareness will increase, and you are likely to enjoy a greater number of what Maslow calls "peak experiences," experiences that are rewarding and worthwhile. More flexibility and a better ability to cope with experiences—role adaptability—will increase your ability to identify with other human beings. You will experience improved interpersonal relations, increased creativity, and corresponding changes in your value system.

The most important characteristic of healthy role-playing is honesty. When you attend a play, you expect to see actors and actresses playing the roles of the characters in the play. A good actor or actress will play the part "without breaking"—that is, without deviating from the character being portrayed. Every action or reaction is what you would expect the character to really make. An actor or actress who "breaks" character casts a shadow of doubt on his or her own ability to act as well as on the honesty with which the character is portrayed. If you are playing a role

[1] Maslow, pp. 25–26.

that is not congruent with your self and another person penetrates your "cover"—the phony aspect of the role you are portraying—that person may doubt all your future behavior. The trust another has in you is jeopardized. To lose the trust of others may severely limit your future effectiveness in interpersonal relations.

Attitudes

Source and receiver attitudes also affect interpersonal communication. Your attitude toward the situation, the participants, or the message causes the interpersonal communication to be rewarding or unrewarding, successful or unsuccessful. Have you ever expressed an attitude of either extreme favor or extreme hostility to a topic under discussion and noticed that the person with whom you were talking stopped listening? The same would probably happen if the listener perceived an emotional message such as "I don't like you." A receiver will stop listening in these circumstances because he or she has determined your position or feelings, and further discussion is deemed fruitless. If the discussion continues, it is likely that distortions and misperceptions will occur because the receiver is no longer listening neutrally; his or her perception of the strong favor or hostility will color or alter all further conversation. Even if the speaker's attitude is not consciously expressed, the fact is that attitudes play an important role in interpersonal communication.

The speaker can avoid turning off the listener this way by either of the following closely related methods. The first method is *exploration.* If the speaker spends some time exploring the views and feelings of the listener first and detects an extreme position counter to the speaker's own—or a strong feeling of hostility toward the speaker as a person—then avoidance procedures can be used. The speaker can avoid further discussion on this issue, can dig deeper into the reasons why the listener holds these views, or can try to provide some reasons to counter the listener's position without ever expressing his or her own.

The second method involves *suspended judgment.* The speaker, in this case, withholds the expression of judgment so that his or her opinions will not close off the communication. There may be times when you will not wish to, or should not, counter the views or feelings of another. For the sake of peace and harmony you may avoid unnecessarily conflicting with the views of your parents or spouse; for the sake of security and your future plans you may avoid opposing the views of a boss or superior. It sometimes happens that a judgment is not crucial or that time will change the feelings of the other person anyway. Success in using exploration and suspended judgment has a great deal to do with *empathy,* mentally entering into the spirit or feeling of the other person, a concept that is treated in the forthcoming section on listening responses.

Selective Perception Attitudes can also affect your perception in the listener role. It may be that in listening to another person, you select only part of the other person's message to respond to. *Selective perception* means that you choose among incoming stimuli which to take note of—you hear what you want to hear and you see what you want to see. An instructor, for example, will often provide both positive and negative criticism regarding the performance of a student. The student may disregard all of the good comments made and concentrate only on the bad. This selective perception may be carried to such a point that if another student asked what the teacher thought, the student might reply by saying, "I was really shot apart!"

How you perceive messages is directly related to your perception of your self. People who have a stable and realistic perception of themselves are likely to have a positive outlook on life. They will, thus, be likely to perceive messages as they are intended whereas people who have an unstable and unrealistic perception of themselves will selectively perceive more of the negative aspects in almost every communication.

Selective perception also operates in a strictly utilitarian way. That is, you may perceive in any situation that which is or, perhaps, will be useful to you. Your attitude toward something, then, will be determined by possible use. Take three people looking at the same piece of land with an eye toward purchasing it. One person wants to use it as a rural retreat for camping. The second person wants to build a house on it. The third wants to make commercial use of it by building a store on it. All three people have different perceptions of the same piece of land—the first thinks about its limited accessibility, rough terrain, and scenic beauty; the second thinks about the way a house could be set on the property and how some convenient access could be gained; the third thinks about how accessible it is to main arteries of transportation and how access can be improved for large volumes of traffic. Each of these people is perceiving selectively. If instead of a store, the third person decided to build a house on the property, he or she might have to return to the land to see it again with that purpose in mind.

Selectivity in message reception works in still another way. If you feel strongly in favor of women's liberation and you think that others do too, it is likely that you will be highly receptive to any messages that seem to support it. In listening to someone else's conversation about women's liberation, you may hear that person as supportive of the movement even though the total thrust of the other's position may actually be contrary to your stand. In the same way, you may be against free love, and when you overhear someone on this subject, you may hear only that which is negative because this information seems to support your position, even though, if the message were examined in total, it might be found that it does not support your position at all. Often our attitudes can distort the message of another person by causing it to be more extreme than it actually is.

In speaking, listening, and responding to others, it is important to be aware of the problems that are likely to occur because we are more sensitive to perceiving messages that are consistent with our attitudes and because we may misperceive, or fail to perceive at all, messages that are opposed to our attitudes. Most of us are predisposed to associate with people whose attitudes agree with our own; thus, with those we choose to associate most, disagreement in attitudes will likely be minimal. We should, first, be aware that selective perception occurs. Simply recognizing the existence of this phenomenon is part of any attempt to solve the communication breakdowns that are likely to occur because of it. We should, secondly, be ready to change our perceptions when it becomes evident that we have misinterpreted a message, no matter who the source is. Fidelity in communicating interpersonally is something to be negotiated because communication in such situations is two-way.

To examine more closely this problem of selective perception and the manner in which fidelity is negotiated, find another person to be a participant with you and conduct a discussion on an agreed-upon controversial topic such as politics, religion, or sex. The controversial nature of the topic is important. This two-way interpersonal communication should be unstructured. After each participant speaks, however, a summary must be provided by the other person. The participant will, without notes and in his or her own words, summarize what has been said by the previous speaker. If the speaker thinks the summary is incorrect, he should be free to interrupt and clear up any misunderstanding. Following such a discussion, talk with your partner about the difficulty experienced in listening to each other. Did you find it difficult to formulate your thoughts and listen at the same time? When the other person paraphrased your remarks, was it shorter and more concise than when you said it? Did you find it easy to get across what you wanted to say?

Sociocultural Influences Speaker and listener attitudes can also be affected by the participants' sociocultural backgrounds. When you speak with a person in your class, for example, about your instructor's grading policy, both of you begin the communication with a common experiential base—the social experience of being exposed to your instructor's grades. When two people date each other for some time, they begin to think more and more alike (at least they come to more conclusions on which both agree) because the common base of experiences and opportunities for sharing information become greater. Individuals who have had similar experiences tend to have some advantage in obtaining greater fidelity in their communication. In some educational programs, for example, there is a demand for black instructors to teach black students because it is felt that blacks can understand blacks.

Our assumptions about what "shared experience" is are sometimes erroneous, however. For example, one black administrator from a local university went into a secondary school to determine the problems of black students by talking to them. He could not understand why the students would not open up to him. The black administrator had no direct experience with the problems that these black students faced because he was brought up in an upper-middle-class home, went to prestigious schools and universities, and became an administrator directly out of school. The black students detected this through his language, his dress, his mannerisms, and, in a sense, his whole style and were reluctant to communicate with him. "How could *he* understand *our* situation?" the students' reaction said. Just because you are black does not mean you understand blacks. A person's sociocultural background often requires time to emerge, and then emergence is likely to be partial, giving an incomplete view, and on a trial basis. Feeling the full force of another's base of operations requires patience and understanding.

In interpersonal communication, the accuracy of our message and the likelihood that it will be understood can be increased if we provide a sociocultural base from which the message can be viewed or interpreted. An outright condemnation of education, for example, might be effective if we told a listener that we come from a highly rated school system. If we had suffered from an inadequate, poorly supported, poorly supplied, inferior school system, our condemnation would be justified—but also expected, considering the circumstances. The black administrator might have been able to achieve some success if he had "leveled" with the students first by admitting his social and cultural advantages, which were shortcomings and limitations in the students' minds. Providing such a base alerts a listener to the environment that helped form our ideas.

The real problem in interpersonal communication as it relates to sociocultural experiences occurs, however, when we attempt to view and

judge other people by our own customs and standards, from an *ethnocentric* base. We become the center of the universe, a universe that is determined by our sociocultural background. The things we have done, the choices we have made, and the options we have taken become "right"—*the* course of action for others to follow. Thus, the greater the similarity of the action of others to our own, the more admirable and sensible it is; the more dissimilar, the more objectionable, strange, and bizarre. When we join an organization, we place it one cut above others. Our family becomes a model family; our nation is better or more moral than others. Such attitudes breed loyalty; such attitudes also breed problems in effective interpersonal communication.

Strong loyalty to a single club, cause, or country may generate hostility to members of other clubs, causes, or countries. Our hostility to another person's affiliations may be extended to everything that person does or everything that person represents: customs, mode of dress, food, art, tradition, and even race. How can two people interact successfully when one person views the other as a liberal lunatic, a rebellious radical, or a contemptible Communist? If we consider the social or cultural customs of others completely antagonistic, threatening, or even silly and ridiculous, we will experience communication problems. Moreover, extreme loyalty or faithfulness to one modus operandi may distort views of others and of the world. It can, when allowed to become excessive, even cause one to see the unjust as just, the immoral as moral, and the lawless as lawful.

Problems created by differing social or cultural contexts in interpersonal communication can be countered if we view customs or beliefs or actions that differ from our own in an objective manner. When the situation or the message involves a moral or religious context, it is likely that emotion may affect our rationality. Conscious awareness of the fact that bias in our own point of view and hostility from others is often intensified when we consider our own view the only "right" one may also help. In extreme cases, awareness may provide a stimulus to communicate when the willingness to do so may not otherwise be there. We too easily close our minds to others who do not share our point of view when we should be open to their ideas and perspectives—not only to increase understanding and to facilitate communication but to become better human beings.

These are, certainly, only a few of the ways that attitudes can affect interpersonal communication. If you are not aware of the ways in which attitudes operate, your interpersonal communication may be distorted, inaccurate, or misperceived. They are an important component in gauging the probable effects of a communication whether they relate to the situation, the participants, or the message.

Relationships: Complimentary and Symmetrical

Think about the last time you talked face-to-face with either or both of your parents. The way in which you spoke with each other and the information you conveyed revealed a definite relationship between you. You are probably aware, for instance, that the relationship between you and your parents is not based on equality. Your parents were brought up differently from you, in a different period, with emphasis on different values. They may think they know what is "right" or "best" for you and, thus, try to influence your life. In trying to influence your life, they maintain a somewhat "superior" position. All relationships are influenced by the degree of equality that exists between the participants.

Paul Watzlawick, Janet Beavin, and Don Jackson have published a study of interactional patterns entitled *Pragmatics of Human Communication,* in which they label relationships either complimentary or symmetrical.[2] A communication relationship based on equality is called a *symmetrical* relationship and involves participants who treat each other as equals and mirror each other's behavior. Such relationships sometimes occur between peers—people of the same rank with respect to mental and/or physical endowments, status, or other qualifications. In a *complimentary* relationship—based on differences—one communicator is superior to another. The instructor talking to the student, the doctor to the patient, or the boss to the employee represent the complimentary situation. Fewer relationships are based on equality than on differences; interpersonal situations are often based on a certain amount of both. Equality is likely to be a characteristic that easily slips away depending on the subject, the mood, or the situation. When you no longer have equality in a relationship, you either have no relationship at all or you have a difference. The difference might be as simple as one person knowing more about a topic than another person, one person expressing an "I'll take care of you" or "I'd like to help you" feeling, or a situation in which one person has been asked to take charge or be responsible. Whether a relationship is equal or different will affect the kind of communication that occurs. It may affect the amount of threat that permeates the situation, the courtesy and respect one person shows for another, or even the degree of openness and honesty that is permitted.

RESPONDING TO KEEP THE CHANNEL OPEN

A black woman was discussing a hypothetical case-study of a youth who had stolen a car from a parking lot. There were three other members in the discussion group, all white middle-class students. The task of the group was to decide the youth's fate—whether he should be placed in the state reformatory, on probation, or in the legal custody of relatives. The black woman believed the best solution was to provide close supervision of the delinquent youth's behavior by placing him on probation. The white members of the group felt her punishment was too severe for a

2 Paul Watzlawick, Janet Helmick Beavin, and Don D. Jackson, *Pragmatics of Human Communication: A Study of Interactional Patterns, Pathologies, and Paradoxes* (New York: W. W. Norton, 1967).

first offense. She responded by saying, "You say I'm wrong, but I think I'm right and you're wrong because I've been there and you don't know what you're talking about!" Such responses often occur in situations where feelings and emotions are deeply involved. In this case, what began as hypothetical became real for this young woman.

The problem with much interpersonal communication is that we carry with us a need or desire to judge, evaluate, approve, or disapprove of certain situations, certain participants, and certain messages. We move into communication settings with preset barriers to mutual understanding. *Evaluative responses*—indications that the listener has made a judgment of relative goodness, rightness, effectiveness, or appropriateness about the sender's message—are especially harmful in the early stages of a relationship or communication because once a value statement is conveyed, it is likely to generate another one. When a wife says to her husband, "You've been mean for the past three days," the husband's tendency is to respond with a comment like, "You've been mean since I married you!" We have a need to show our superiority to another person by using a technique commonly referred to as "one-upsmanship."

Evaluative responses are also harmful because once stated, they become public commitments to stands or positions and often force the one who makes the statement to defend it with further evaluative responses. Forced into a corner, a person becomes defensive and communication becomes emotional. Evaluative responses and judgments are appropriate, however, when you are specifically asked to make a value judgment or when you wish to convey your values and attitudes.

When we engage in face-to-face communication, we have certain needs as speakers and certain needs as listeners. These needs revolve around a basic desire for feedback which operates from both a speaker and a listener perspective. These needs are a shaping force in subsequent interpersonal behavior.

In communicating with other people, speakers need to know whether they are having an impact. They need to know, for example, if the listener is really listening—if he understands the message or if he feels the emotions being conveyed. Listeners, thus, serve as a necessary component in interpersonal communication because of the reassurance and support they can provide the speaker. Such support is readily noticeable when observing the listener's side of a telephone conversation. The "uhh-huh," "um-m-m," and "yuh's" that are heard are reassurances for the speaker that someone is listening. These responses do not necessarily mean that the message is getting through. Many people learn to provide reassurances for the speaker even though they are not fully attending. This will often pacify those who "bend your ear" at the slightest opportunity. When such reassurances are not received, the speaker stops and says, "Do you know what I mean?" "Do you understand?" "Do you see how I feel?" or "Are *you* listening to me?"

Effective listener responses often need to be more elaborate than simply a reassurance that someone is listening. More elaborate responses fulfill listener needs as well as speaker needs. For example, listeners may wish to indicate to a speaker how the speaker's behavior affects them— telling the sender what the problem means or how they really feel. Letting a fellow know that he has insulted you, for example, or telling a smoker that he or she is threatening your health by smoking in your presence would involve making such a response. If carried out with tact and skill, such responses can be a worthwhile and productive stimulus to further growth. They have the potential of providing insight.

Listeners might want to pacify a speaker or reduce the intensity of the speaker's feeling. When you sense that another person is depressed because he has been rejected by his girlfriend, you might engage in this type of response. Instructors often use a pacifying response when students come into their offices seeking justifications or explanations for failing grades or for doing poorly in the course. The student is reassured that the grade was justified by the work he produced, or he may be pacified by a comment like, "Don't get so upset, this isn't the end of the world; you will have other opportunities to bring up this grade." When a person needs to feel accepted or when he needs stimulation and motivation to solve a problem, a listener can give such a supportive response. In this way, reinforcement or the courage to continue is provided.

A listener may want further information. Oftentimes it is helpful in an interpersonal communication situation simply to gain a clear definition of a problem. Such a response may be appropriate when an instructor attempts to find a reason for a student's poor performance or when two people are discussing an issue and there is a misunderstanding between them about the definition of a concept or term that is being used. In such a case, one would need to probe the other person to determine a common base for further discussion.

Words like *heavy, morals, cool, hardhat, rock music, establishment, rights,* and even *love* often provoke immediate responses—conditioned responses—that differ among people. To these words, most of us have "gut" reactions. When someone tells you "That was a 'heavy' movie," it may be necessary for you to find out the meaning of *heavy* as it is being used in this context. Does it mean profound? Does it mean the movie was "a real drag"—another phrase that might require a probing response? How can you begin to intelligently discuss the movie until you know how the other person is using the word *heavy*? Anticipation of such responses would lead the source to define a term or terms being used at the outset of a discussion or communication, or immediately when they are used. Since terms are not often defined in this way, it is better to protect oneself as a listener from an impulsive response by reacting to words in a conditional way—realizing that meanings change from situation to situation, from person to person, or from message or context to message.

Understanding Responses

The strongest style of listener response, the one that provides the greatest amount of feedback, is an *understanding response*. This response leads to greater fidelity and clarity of communication between individuals because by using it the listener simply indicates a desire to find out whether he or she understood the sender correctly. The foundation of an understanding response is the ability to *paraphrase*—to restate an idea in a new way or in other words. The receiver paraphrases the sender's message in the receiver's own words, utilizing his or her own expressions. Repeating an idea in the sender's words does not really reveal understanding.

Understanding responses are appropriate in tone to the message received. The receiver should not respond humorously or lightly to a serious message just as the receiver should not respond with great seriousness to a shallow statement. An appropriate response to the speaker's tone would lead the sender to a slightly deeper feeling for the message. The receiver has communicated to the source that there is interest in the message, and, thus, the source is encouraged to continue, elaborate, and further explore the message.

An understanding response requires the receiver to see the source's message from the source's point of view. Further elaboration of a position clarifies it and avoids controversy so that a solid base or common framework can be established. Many conversations are best begun, then, by using the understanding response. We do this by completing a sentence or thought of the sender, by providing further illustrations to support those provided by the sender or to support the thesis presented, or by commenting upon the significance of the ideas. By doing this in simple, clear language we can better ensure accurate communication and, thus, fidelity.

An effective communicator will become aware of the various types of responses. Becoming proficient in using them when they are appropriate will enable you to help others with their problems and will aid you in building closer relationships. They are an aid to the speaker because they let him know whether meaning is being transferred. They are an aid to the listener because they are a means of gaining further information and insight as well as assuring fidelity. The different types of responses are not always separate categories; they overlap and, thus, can often be used in the same situation, with the same participants, and with respect to the same message. Using these responses increases the amount of feedback that occurs in a communication and helps insure that the speaker and listener will more accurately share each other's ideas and feelings.

EMOTIONAL MESSAGES AND RATIONAL MESSAGES

Interpersonal communication operates on two levels; the first is the emotional level, and the second is the rational level. Neither level operates exclusive of the other; however, most communications can be characterized as primarily one or the other. The emotional part of a message expresses the feelings of the speaker. The rational part expresses the speaker's thoughts. The guidelines for developing a rational message are fairly clear and easy to set forth. Those for developing an emotional message are not clear—especially when the situation is an interpersonal one. Concentrating on the other person, demonstrating warmth, expressing empathy, and maintaining genuineness in our dealings with others are, perhaps, the most important guidelines that can be suggested for developing better ability to send messages in emotional situations.

Improving Emotional Messages

To achieve the degree of openness in a transaction that allows you to communicate on the emotional level requires both courage and compassion. The interpersonal communicator must be willing to take a chance because entering such a transaction, or being involved in one, may result in misunderstanding, rejection, or being ignored, conned, exploited, or made to look ridiculous. You have probably been hurt by someone else whom you trusted. Once hurt, it is often difficult to exhibit the same openness soon again.

The compassionate communicator exhibits a feeling of sympathy for the other person in the transaction. He cares and keeps on caring—

despite the emotions exhibited and the disagreements encountered. Ralph R. Greenson, a psychiatrist, states that when one becomes emotionally involved, things matter, and when things matter there can be "difficulties, conflict, disappointment, misunderstandings, betrayals. . . ." He adds that "this can happen when you care."[3] Thus, the compassionate communicator must be willing to experience these emotions.

Interpersonal communication is often emotional because it is unplanned, unprepared, and unstructured. It is affected by the attitudes, needs, goals, past experiences, and assumptions of the participants as well as by their moods. There are also many other environmental and psychological factors that can affect the message. The effective communicator will attempt to take all of these factors into account without closing off the emotional level. Structuring a well-organized, verbally correct, factually supported discourse in interpersonal communication that is presented to the listener as if it were a public speech will only prevent meaningful interaction. Instead, the communicator can attempt to be-

---

3 Ralph R. Greenson, "Emotional Involvement," from *The Exacting Ear,* Eleanor McKinney (ed.) (New York: Pantheon Books, 1966), reprinted in *Bridges Not Walls: A Book About Interpersonal Communication,* John Stewart (ed.) (Reading, Massachusetts: Addison-Wesley, 1973), p. 61.

come personally involved with the listener, maintaining close perceptual contact, and creating and preserving conditions which will help the listener to receive the emotional meanings that are felt by the communicator.

Attaining such an interpersonal perspective involves several elements. It includes the development of interpersonal communication skills —to be outlined in a forthcoming section of this chapter—especially the technique of listening empathically. It involves knowing about your self and how your self relates to communication, as developed in the first chapter. It also involves knowledge of roles and role-playing. Only in the actual interpersonal-communication situation itself does one experience all the related components of communication coming into being, for it is the other person in the transaction who allows one to experience—to become fully human.

Improving Rational Messages

To improve the rational part of interpersonal messages, we should give more attention to the forms of support and to the structure of the communication. The support we offer and the structure into which that support is placed reinforce our message. Sound judgment and good sense are conveyed when our ideas are developed and when they appear to be arranged in some specific order.

Forms of Support Forms of support are the means whereby the communicator's main ideas are sustained or held up. They compose the "meat" of a message. Without forms of support, messages become assertions and generalizations—unsupported declarations and statements. Ideas can be developed with several different forms of support; they should, however, be supported appropriately—in a way that can be understood best by the listener.

One form of support is the *example.* An example is an instance or case in point. A woman talks to another woman about the problems of dating. She cites her own experience for support of the assertion that one of the problems is with the fellow who wants "to go too far" on the first date. She is using an example. In this case the example comes from the speaker's personal experience, an excellent support for interpersonal communication because the details of the example are well known to the communicator and because most people have a storehouse of examples on which to draw. Examples from one's personal experience are also revealing of the self and, thus, invite empathy from the listener.

One can also draw examples from the experience of others. Citing the experience of a roommate concerning the problems of dating might be useful. The well-read person will also have a storehouse of examples on a variety of topics derived from books, magazines, and newspapers. Another kind of example is hypothetical—the kind that is created by the communicator for a specific reason. Again, the person with a great deal of experience is often skillful at using such examples because they can be constructed by combining parts of many other examples. On the other hand, it can be totally ficticious. If you use hypothetical examples, it is important that the listener be aware that you are doing so.

Facts, another form of support, are those bits of truth which exist and which can be checked against reality for verification. If something is not disputable, it is a fact. We use facts all the time to lend greater emphasis to our ideas. When you talk to another person on any subject, you are likely to pull into your conversation a fact that you recently read; talking to another on marijuana, you might mention that a recent fourteen-year study linked continual smoking of pot to senility.

Group a number of examples or facts together and you get *statistics.* Statistics are numerical representations of groups of examples or facts that have been condensed to a single number. It is easiest to use statistics and it is easiest to remember them if you use round numbers. One student cited the fact that alcohol was the most abused and most dangerous drug available and supported the point with three statistics: 1) More than 50 percent of all crimes in America are alcohol-related; 2) more than 50 percent of all highway accidents are alcohol-related; 3) more than 100 million Americans drink. An example takes on more meaning with reinforcement from statistics. Knowing the facts makes what you say more meaningful and increases your credibility and reliability as a communicator.

Illustrations are extended examples. They are stories of facts or events, used by the communicator to shed light on an idea. They are especially powerful because they can kindle interest by revealing real persons in real situations. A good conversationalist will likely have a collection of stories that can be recalled on the spur of the moment to add interest to the message.

When we use the *opinions* of others to support our ideas, we are asking our listener to accept our idea because someone with whom they have some association, knowledge, or identification also has accepted the idea. When we use other's opinions, then, we must be certain that the listener knows who the person is. If the listener does not have this information we can do one of two things: eliminate the opinion from our communication or provide him with information that would enable him to judge the competence of the source on this topic. We must be sure that the person we use has a good reputation and can be considered reliable. Very often, *why* a person says something can be as important as *what* is said. This means that we not only have to know something about our listener but also about the personal interests, prejudices, training, and experience of the person we are going to quote or cite. In addition, in quoting or citing another person, we must strive to preserve the intent of the person being quoted or cited. Off-handed, inaccurate quotations bear on the credibility of the person being quoted as well as on our own. In using the opinions of others, make them specific and make sure they support and develop your idea accurately.

When you select forms of support to develop your message, seek a variety of types. Variety adds interest to your message. It provides a natural change of pace and, thus, holds attention. If you are going to use a personal experience, for example, cite a statistic and perhaps an opinion to reinforce your experience. Never feel confined to one type of support. You support an idea for the benefit of your listener so his or her interest and attention should be a paramount consideration.

Message Structure As communicators, we need to think about the listener as we structure our message. How should our communication be started? How much time should be devoted to the introduction? Which point should be stated first? How can the relationship between our main points be clarified? How should our communication be terminated? There is no way to predict precisely how a message should change in response to a changing situation or listener. There needs to be flexibility in structuring, and some interpersonal messages work best if they are not structured. To try to impose a predetermined order or structure on a listener will reduce feedback and undermine the whole interpersonal process. It is useful, however, especially with messages that are mostly rational, to think about the way you will structure a message for greatest effect.

A good salesperson is likely to change the order or structure of the communication—selling the same product—according to the way he or she perceives the receiver and the receiver's expectations. A good teacher will change the order of presentation of his or her material depending on the class or the time of day. If you had the same idea to communicate to an elementary-school student, to another student about your same age, and to an instructor, you, too, would probably change the order or structure of your communication with each receiver.

Being aware of possible alternatives in the structuring of messages should not lead you to using formal systems of arrangement such as the outlines used in writing or formal speeches. Such structures do not have a great deal of usefulness in interpersonal communication. There is one rule that can help the communicator to structure interpersonal messages. It is brief and easy to recall: first, tell your listener what you are going to say, then say it, and then tell your listener what you have said. Since most interpersonal communication is spontaneous and impromptu, this rule provides a basic structure or framework that can be remembered and put into practice.

It is unlikely that all the factors that affect fidelity in interpersonal communication could be listed. Those we have listed should be considered introductory. As you begin to analyze your successes and failures in interpersonal communication, you will begin to achieve greater understanding; you will also discover other factors that are important. It is impossible to establish any unvarying prescriptions for success in all interpersonal situations. Flexibility, adaptability, and variety should be considered in approaching each situation, each participant, and each message.

IMPROVING INTERPERSONAL TRANSACTIONS

Improving your interpersonal communication involves developing your role as a speaker, as a listener, and as a message (or meaning) analyzer. Knowledge and exercise of our responsibility in an interpersonal communication situation can help generate the exchange of accurate information and the establishment of greater fidelity in a communication relationship. We can also learn to gauge the probable effects of our communication—that is, we will be more likely to know, in advance, our chances of success.

Speaker Responsibilities

Becoming an effective communicator in interpersonal relationships involves a broad range of skills. Most of the skills require *adaptation*—altering our communications behavior to fit the circumstances. Most of them, too, are perfected over time because experience provides more information on which to operate. Through experience we learn what is appropriate and inappropriate for certain situations, people, and messages. We learn that certain contexts call for cooperation rather than conflict—or that certain relationships will be ongoing and long-range rather than temporary and short-lived. In an interview situation, for example, where you have a strong desire to gain employment, you will very likely assume a cooperative attitude or position. If you are involved in a debate with an instructor or an administrator over a procedure or policy that you dislike, the appropriate attitude would be one of conflict or opposition. You would use a different approach in talking with a visitor to your school or campus whom you knew you would never see again than in a conversation with a person with whom you shared a loving relationship. Adaptive behavior is normal and necessary, as we have seen in our previous discussions of role-playing. In addition to context, there are some other factors that the responsible communicator should consider as far as adaptive behavior is concerned.

The first factor is that interpersonal communication is a simultaneous process which involves sharing. All persons engaged in the process send messages and receive messages at the same time. Each is constantly sharing information, whether it be verbal or nonverbal, and is, thus, affecting the other persons in the communication. Perception of the process in this way involves or implies an important skill. The process is dynamic; since you are always a communicator as well as a receiver in face-to-face interpersonal communication, you must be more alert to the signals you are sending and receiving. Increased awareness is a skill which you can develop—a skill partially dependent upon recognition of the communication factors involved.

The second factor is your *credibility*—the extent to which you are worthy of another's belief or confidence. If your best friend tells you that your lover is seeing someone else on the sly, you will be much more willing to accept that information as true than if one of your "enemies" told you the same thing. In much the same manner, we would be more willing to accept as true the information that one of our local legislators cheated on his income tax if that information came from the governor, or another legislator than if it came from someone we distrusted or someone who did not seem to be in a position to know. Your credibility as a source for information depends upon how much trust another can put in you, how reliable you are, and, too, the dynamism with which you present your ideas. A person who does not know what he is talking about, or is in some doubt, can sometimes generate credibility, at least temporarily, by stating the ideas forcefully—with dynamism.

Credibility depends, in part, upon personal integrity. To be trusted by others, we must be seen by others as trustworthy. To be treated as loyal to the cause—any cause—we must be perceived by others as a loyal person. For our responses toward others to be taken as friendly, we must be perceived as a friendly, kind, and, perhaps, helpful person. A person who is seen as bitter or cynical could make friendly comments and be perceived as sarcastic rather than friendly.

Credibility is subject to reevaluation and change as the setting changes, the time changes, the receiver changes, or the subject changes. A professor of economics might be considered especially credible in speaking out on problems about the handling of the economy but no more credible than you or we in speaking out against problems in criminal justice. Credibility is also a characteristic that is determined or created over a period of time. A reputation for honesty is developed by a person who gives honest responses in a variety of situations.

A person's race, word choice, group affiliation, and social status affect the way we view that person's message because these factors also affect that person's credibility. For example, an American Indian who used revolutionary language might be considered a threat no matter what the situation. It would be great if we had moved beyond such evaluation in our society. A person's race (black, white, yellow, or red), group affiliation (Bircher, Ku Klux Klan member, or liberal), or social status (blue collar, businessman, or industrialist) can have much more influence on how that person's message is received than is appropriate. But since we *do* make evaluations on the basis of such factors, they should be considered when estimating probable effects. We almost always respond more to who a person is than to what he or she says.

The third factor which should be considered under speaker responsibilities is effective conversational delivery. An effective conversational presentation reflects directness and energy. Looking the other person in the eye and appearing interested and alert is likely to generate directness and enthusiasm in return and to add to the alertness and responsiveness that pervades the whole communication situation. Courtesy, tact, and fairness indicate that the communicators have respect for each other. A communicator who desires a specific response from a receiver can often obtain it by assuming the correct or appropriate mental attitude or set in delivering the message.

Listener Responsibilities

When you respond to another's joy with joy, to another's apathy with the same indifference, and to another's sadness with equal sorrow, you are showing *empathy*. You are entering into the feeling or spirit of the other person. The extent to which you are able to do this will often determine how well you can send a responding message. Total empathy is not possible for we cannot know exactly what the other person is feel-

ing nor the extent or degree of that feeling. Also, it is difficult to understand another's feelings if we have never experienced similar feelings ourselves. Can you know the emotion a person experiences when someone who is extremely close to him or her dies? Or the hate a person feels because his or her race has been put down and shoved around throughout history? Or the overwhelming exhilaration of a person who has just achieved the ultimate desire from life? One of the tips given to aspiring actors and actresses is to get out into the world and experience—feel! The more experience an actor or actress has, the more likely it will be that he or she can recreate a feeling or experience on the stage.

We can practice increasing our sense of empathy by role-taking—assuming the role of someone else. Imitation involves role-taking for you imitate the behavior, mannerisms, and responses of others. For example, take the role of a dean of students and have another person try to convince you that he or she deserves another chance at college after three failures. Take the role of an ex-convict trying to persuade an employer that he or she badly needs the cashier's job that is open. Take the role of your parents as they try to persuade you to cut your hair and beard or change your manner of dress. Your ability to respond to another person accurately may depend on being able to feel what that person is feeling. We all have feelings that may be part of the message. To empathize is to listen for and to respond to the feeling level of the message. It is like reading between the lines. Knowing that empathic listening is important often enables us to foresee, and thus resolve, potential conflict.

Listening, according to Charles M. Kelley, a writer on the subject, must be empathic because "a person understands what he has heard, only to the extent that he can share in the meaning, spirit, or feeling of what the communicator has said."[4] To overcome the obvious problems of not desiring to listen, or simply not having the ability to do so, Kelley suggests that you make a strong commitment to do so, that you prepare, that you focus on the sender as a communicator, and that you listen to him completely.[5]

Realistic Message Analysis

Good interpersonal communication involves more than the simple acceptance of everything that one hears. Acceptance, without analysis,

---

4 Charles M. Kelley, "Empathic Listening," in Robert S. Cathcart and Larry A. Samovar, *Small Group Communication: A Reader* (Dubuque, Iowa: Wm. C. Brown, 1970), p. 253.
5 *Ibid.*, pp. 257–258.

would breed a generation of people easily deceived or cheated. It would be a pleasure if all communication were in the best interests of all concerned with no deceit, trickery, or lies involved—but communication involves people. People rumor, people gossip, and people, too, enjoy receiving these messages in general circulation that cannot be confirmed in fact. Rumor and gossip are aften based upon guesses, hints, or inferences derived from incomplete, insufficient, or nonexistent evidence. There is, for example, a rumor out that the spouse of a prominent physician is an alcoholic or that the daughter of an esteemed congressman has an illegitimate baby. Rumor and gossip need not always be negative. Their negative connotations have been acquired over time because of the vicious level at which they often operate. Rumors are sometimes attractive because they let us in on "behind-the-scenes" information which most find interesting and exciting. You undoubtedly know at least one efficient carrier! Rumor is, though, poor evidence for what really goes on in the world. The best strategy for handling it in interpersonal communication is to suspend judgment. Rather than to judge based on rumor, one should wait until facts confirm the statement.

Because we are both communicators and receivers at the same time, we should always be aware of the importance of analysis. This is the only way we can counter those who threaten to manipulate us—those who persuade us to buy unnecessary products, those who encourage us to vote for unworthy political candidates, those who strive to have us see the foolhardy or despicable as wise and admirable. Analyzing another's verbal message is one of the most important roles that the proficient analyzer must assume; however, you can detect another person's lack of knowledge, lack of support, or poor reasoning through other cues. These cues might be communicated through the other person's bodily action, vocal action, attitude, language choice, or emotion. When you are talking to someone else, for example, and he or she makes an assertion that that person knows is weak, this assertion may be undermined by that person's lack of enthusiasm for the assertion, stiffness, lack of eye contact, fidgeting, or by inappropriate, unmotivated, or meaningless gestures. Reading another's nonverbal cues is an important part of analysis. The problem of nonverbal cues that contradict the verbal message is further discussed in Chapter 3, Nonverbal Communication. The person's attitude may be reflected through behavior such as making personal remarks, losing his or her temper, belittling others, lack of enthusiasm, apologies, antagonism, trying to be funny, or insincerity. Also, problems of thinking might be evident in unclear language, constant repetition, vagueness, indefiniteness, or constant misstatements. Finally, since our thinking is closely tied to our emotions, the proficient analyzer will be aware of inappropriateness of emotion, overdrawn emotion, or artificiality of emotion.

The person who attempts to analyze a message realistically should also be aware of appropriate emotional needs—his or her own as well as others'. Being aware of the potential for positive emotional exchange will increase the likelihood of engaging in rewarding emotional encounters. The expression of emotions can be inspiring, invigorating, and meaningful, and such experiences should be appreciated for the pleasure, satisfaction, and fulfillment they can provide.

The fully human person understands and accepts emotions. His or her emotions are balanced and integrated. According to John Powell, S.J., a writer on interpersonal communication, most human conduct is the result of emotional forces, most interpersonal conflicts result from emotional stresses, and most interpersonal encounters are achieved through emotional communion.[6] Because so much of your interpersonal life depends on how you handle your emotions, the way you deal with them and the way others "read" them is likely to determine your success in many areas of your life. Anybody who ignores emotional reactions or denies his emotions does not have his or her emotions under control. The proficient analyzer will dive below the surface of emotions for the sea of motivations underneath—even if this involves seeking the reasons why others lack emotional control.

None of the characteristics mentioned as possible focal points for realistic message analysis needs, of necessity, to be tied to problems of poor thinking alone. Unclear messages may reflect the lack of confidence of a communicator; hesitation in approaching a situation, another person, or a particular message; doubtfulness in the certainty of a course of action (or belief); and even, on a broad scale, a skeptical nature or insecurity regarding life itself. The guidelines for analysis given here are, however, cues about which an effective analyzer will be aware for they provide—especially as they combine with each other—evidence upon which we can base our evaluations. Not every communication must be judged; not every judgment must include all these guidelines. The most realistic approach is one of awareness and adaptability. If one is aware of the various characteristics and elements, it is more likely that he or she can appropriately adapt them to a situation, to participants, and to a message.

[6] John Powell, S.J., *Why Am I Afraid to Tell You Who I Am?* (Chicago: Argus Communications, 1969).

SUMMARY

We have placed consideration of interpersonal communication early in this book because it is the most common kind of communication. Within the interpersonal context, you form the most meaningful relationships of your life. Within this context, too, you can most easily communicate directly with another individual or individuals. You often use more channels when you communicate interpersonally—touching, smelling, and sometimes tasting as well as hearing and seeing. Feedback is immediate and, thus, people discover more information about one another than in any other form of communication.

To become more effective in interpersonal communication, you should search for the other person's meaning when he or she talks to you. This requires an understanding of how you are intimately intertwined with your listener. Perception, roles, attitudes, and other influences are operating on you as communicator, on the other person as listener, and on the whole situation or context. The meaning transferred will, likely, be emotional as well as rational because interpersonal communication is personal and involving.

A student who becomes skillful and successful in interpersonal situations will have less difficulty in approaching communication in the small group, in the public, or in the mass communication situation. These communication situations often depend on successful interpersonal communication as a prerequisite; the person who is effective in these situations has very likely engaged in rewarding interpersonal communication experiences first. Interpersonal experiences give people things to talk about publicly or in small groups. They are the means by which we decide how to approach a problem in the small group or in a mass-communication situation. They are basic to operating in a communication environment. Skill in interpersonal communication will increase one's self-confidence; it will also bring out those traits that make us most fully human—trust, honesty, openness, and love. Interpersonal communication is one means of developing fully functioning human beings.

FURTHER READING

Erich Fromm, *The Art of Loving: An Enquiry into the Nature of Love.* New York: Harper and Row, 1956.
  Care, responsibility, respect, and knowledge are essential elements to all forms of love according to the author, and "love is possible

only if two persons communicate with each other." To love, one must be willing to give; giving and receiving love are expressions of personal "aliveness." This is a learned work that will require some concentration, but the understanding to be gained is well worth the effort.

Reuel L. Howe, *The Miracle of Dialogue.* New York: Seabury, 1963.
Expanding on the ideas of Martin Buber, the author provides a highly readable discussion of authenticity, openness, discipline, and responsibility as the characteristics of effective communication. Borrowing examples from his pastoral experience, he develops the concept of dialogue as central to communication between persons as well as between individuals and God.

Nena O'Neill and George O'Neill, *Open Marriage: A New Life Style for Couples.* New York: Avon Books, 1972.
On the premise that free-flowing communication is crucial to the building of an open marriage, the authors relate nonverbal communication, self-disclosure, feedback, and roles to the development of a mutual bond between independent partners in which there is maximum individual freedom and growth. This paperback is relevant for anyone involved in an intimate relationship with another person, especially those who are married or contemplating marriage.

John Powell, S. J., *Why Am I Afraid to Tell You Who I Am?(Insights on Self-Awareness, Personal Growth and Interpersonal Communication).* Chicago: Peacock Books, 1969.
In this clear and succinct paperback filled with pop art and witty sayings, the author provides insights on self-awareness, growth, and communication. The material is presented in a warm and enjoyable manner that involves the reader in ideas that relate to his or her growth, emotions, and ego defenses.

Mary Caroline Richards, *Centering in Pottery, Poetry, and The Person.* Middletown, Connecticut: Wesleyan University, 1962.
With a tremendous sense of urgency and enthusiasm, the author of this paperback suggests that centering is the archetypal image used for the process of balance that is common to pottery, poetry, and people. In a person, it is the total capacity to respond using *all* the senses. This is a touching, personal, and stimulating work that creates a strong feeling for the integrity of the whole person.

3

Nonverbal Communication

The first day you walk into a class, before you say a single word, you are communicating. You are sending messages to everyone in sight. The way you present yourself, including how you dress and how you act, often says more about you and your feelings than anything you could say with words.

Albert Mehrabian, a writer on nonverbal communication, determined from his research that as much as 93 percent of the impact of a message depends upon the nonverbal.[1] *Nonverbal elements* include anything communicated that is not specifically verbal (expressed in words); thus, the way a person uses time, space, body movements (eye contact, facial expression, gesture, posture, and motion), voice, and objects is an essential part of every message that person sends. The cultural background of the sender greatly affects his or her use of nonverbal elements, and the list of elements could be expanded to include time of day, weather conditions, and any other variable that is not transmitted by the spoken or written word but might affect the communication. However, only those

    1 Albert Mehrabian, *Silent Messages*. Belmont, California: Wadsworth, 1971, pp. 42–47. Also see Albert Mehrabian, "Communication Without Words," *Psychology Today*, 2 (1968): 53.

elements over which we have some control or about which some awareness is important will be discussed here.

At the same time that you are sending nonverbal messages, you are also, of course, receiving them. You make observations about the instructor and the other students in the class on the first day just as they make observations about you. These observations are based on *cues*—specific indicators that are used to determine another's attitudes or feelings. (A mouth turned down at the sides, for example, might be a cue that a person is sad.) The cues you send provide the first impression your instructor and your classmates have of you. Later communications may change that impression, but many judgments are based on first communications. In male-female relationships, for example, the initial attraction between two people is generated by their mutual first impressions—and often the nonverbal messages are more importlant than the verbal ones.

The listener is greatly influenced by nonverbal cues. Some cues—like space, time, body movements, voice, and objects—can be controlled by the communicator to produce the desired effect in the listener. Over these elements the communicator can maintain conscious awareness. Over other cues—like sex, race, body size, age, region of origin, social status, and, to a certain degree, the communicator's emotional state while speaking—the communicator can exert little or no control. Whether control is exerted or not, all of these elements are part of any face-to-face communication situation, although, even as listeners, we are not always consciously aware of them. Much of nonverbal communication exists at a low level of awareness. It is significant, it is ongoing, but it is also widespread, diffuse, and difficult to define. We often send and receive nonverbal cues unconsciously.

The diffuseness of nonverbal communication results from the interrelatedness of the elements. It is unlikely that we would infer that a person is sad by a down-turned mouth alone. A number of elements would affect our judgment—eyes cast to the floor, no gestures, slumped posture, lack of energy in the voice. As we get to know people better, we also become more familiar with their mannerisms and their means of expression. Some of the cues we read for close friends are different from those we read for strangers. Cues become personalized—or person-specific. With more experience, we become aware of more cues, and nonverbal communication becomes even more diffuse. Think about how you indicate nonverbally to someone else that you are frustrated, angry, lonely or indifferent. Then ask someone else to demonstrate those same feelings without using words, and you will see how many different cues can be used to reveal the same emotion—an indication of the diffuseness of nonverbal communication. Some nonverbal cues will go unnoticed; others will become extremely important. A nonverbal cue, just like a verbal cue, takes on meaning when it is interpreted by another individual.

Concentrating on the specific elements of nonverbal communication means that the communicator or listener is examining the message part of the model presented in the introduction. You can divide the message into three parts: verbal stimuli (treated elsewhere), physical stimuli (space, time, body movement, and objects), and vocal stimuli (rate, inflection, loudness or intensity, and tone). In concentrating on the physical and vocal stimuli, we will try to answer questions such as these: What cues is your instructor reading as he first makes observations about you? What cues are you reacting to as you begin to "psyche out" your instructor? What cues make you decide to go out with a member of the opposite sex? Many of the cues have universal application even though the control and interpretation of cues varies from individual to individual and from society to society.

SPACE

The moment you enter a classroom you are faced with a decision that relates to how you use space. You have to decide where to sit. You may choose to sit in the back because you do not want to be noticed, because you feel that is a "safer" distance from the teacher, because you do not want people behind you staring at you, or because it will give you an opportunity to see other students' reactions and, thus, give you confidence. You may select a front-row seat because you have a great deal of confidence and security or because you want to be noticed. Why you choose to sit where you do is a function of how you use space.

An instructor might interpret where you choose to sit on the first day of class as an indication of your feeling about the course. Your choosing a seat in the back row might be seen as a sign of coldness or lack of concern; your choice of a front-row seat might be read as a sign of warmth or desire for intimacy. Of course, the instructor might not react to this particular decision at all. Your classmates may interpret the front-seat choice as "getting brownie points," "apple polishing," trying to get a good mark. They would probably not react to the choice of a back-row seat because that tends to be the norm—the place that is chosen most often and most consistently by students. A student who seeks to call little attention to himself or herself will probably find a seat in the middle or near the back the most comfortable and the least conspicuous.

Often we do not realize how we value space until we are restricted or our space is violated. A patient confined in a hospital loses space— the world shrinks from houses, fields, streets, and open spaces to an area sometimes less than ten feet by ten feet. The patient's space is violated by nurses, interns, doctors, and others who come right up and sometimes even touch. There is nothing the patient can do about it. Less dramatic examples can be found in everyday situations in which the violation of our space causes tension. Conflicts often develop between roommates over the control of their dormitory space. The head of a household sometimes has a special chair, and visiting friends can inadvertently cause discomfort by sitting in the "wrong" place.

Body space—a term used to describe the personal distance we use when we communicate with others or closely associate with others— operates in much the same way. We do not realize its importance until it is violated, and then we become nervous, uncomfortable, defensive and, sometimes, even unwilling to communicate. We make judgments about how others think and about how they feel toward us and toward the ideas they are communicating from the way they use their body space. Edward T. Hall, author of *The Silent Language* and *The Hidden Dimension*, two popular books on nonverbal communication, has labeled the study of space and distance *proxemics*.[2] In our approach to proxemics—a broad concept that includes body space as well as the other uses of space previously discussed—we will discuss the variables of warmth and coldness, formality and informality, and relationships and status. Following a consideration of these variables, we will discuss some of the important choices speakers can make regarding space.

Warmth and Coldness

How close you stand when you are talking to another person often reflects how you feel about that person or the strength of the attitude you have for that person at that time. Closeness generally reflects warmth. Think of yourself having a very intimate conversation with a close friend; the image of physical closeness comes to mind. Think of yourself taking a seat in a doctor's waiting room that is full of people; you picture yourself trying to find a seat that is separate or apart from

2 Edward T. Hall, *The Silent Language.* Greenwich, Connecticut: Fawcett, 1959, and *The Hidden Dimension.* Garden City, New York: Anchor, 1969.

the rest. It is more comfortable to sit on a couch with two close friends than it is to sit on a couch with two strangers. A gathering with friends is more relaxing than a party with strangers because it is more enjoyable to share space with people you know.

In intimate situations such as petting or making love, the nonverbal cues used to reflect warmth are intensified. Physical closeness multiplies the channels available for communicating. In expressing intimacy, you not only hear and see the other person; you also touch, smell, and taste. You become enveloped in the stimuli emanating from the other person. The lover's skin and hair, body heat and fragrance, breathing and movements intensify the intimacy—feelings of warmth seldom demonstrated in public. In accidental or forced situations like elevators and crowded subways, the same stimuli cause uneasiness.

To compensate for accidentally being placed in close physical proximity to a stranger, we often demonstrate characteristics associated with coldness. We frown, show disinterest, or assume a "poker-face." We often lean away from the other individual or become tense. We avoid looking in the other's eye, looking instead at the floor-indicator lights above the door of an elevator or down at the floor. If possible, we avoid touching the stranger. In all possible ways, we close ourselves to the other person—guarding and keeping him or her at some mental distance from us. Such nonverbal cues are often reinforced by the absence of any verbal communication.

To better understand the role of nonverbal cues in communicating warmth and coldness, try spending one hour responding to everything and everyone in the warmest possible way, and note the reactions you get. Do the same with coldness, and compare and contrast the results. Strive to use as many aspects of nonverbal communication as you can in your responses, and see which cues are most important in eliciting reactions from others.

Formality and Informality

The variables of warmth and coldness relate directly to the variables of formality and informality. A formal situation tends to be colder than an informal one. Most business discourse is conducted in a formal tone with participants standing at a distance of from seven to twelve feet apart. Eye contact at this distance becomes of utmost importance because if it is not sustained, communication stops. As the distance increases, so does the formality of the situation. Interpersonal communication and most social discourse are informal and conducted at fairly close range—up to about twelve feet—while public communication is more formal and conducted at quite a distance—from twelve to twenty-five feet. Speakers at public gatherings and classroom teachers are examples of those who often maintain the more formal distance.

As the distance between the source and the receiver is increased, the emphasis on nonverbal communication shifts to an emphasis on verbal communication. Words become more important because details of face and body are lost. The speaker becomes apart from, rather than one with, the audience and formality is, thus, emphasized. Communication from all channels is increased to compensate for the distance, but gestures and stance substitute for most facial expression and some of the eye contact that is lost.

To show how space affects the informality or formality of a situation, think about entering your instructor's office as it is arranged in Figure 3.1. The instructor has arranged the only other seat in the office

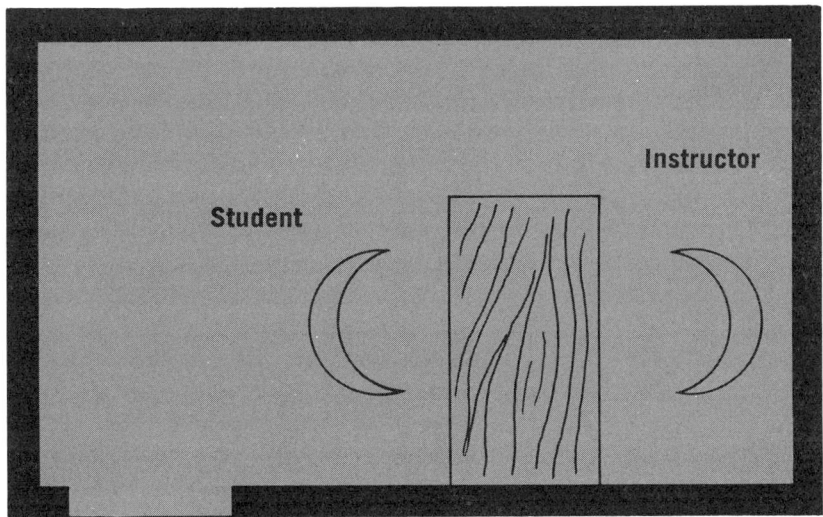

FIGURE 3.1

directly across the desk from where he sits. The desk provides authority and status for the instructor as well as a barrier to the communication. Conversation must occur across the desk. Formality, thus, is built into the situation.

Compare the above communication setting with that depicted in Figure 3.2. The instructor retains some of the formality by staying

76 CHAPTER 3/NONVERBAL COMMUNICATION

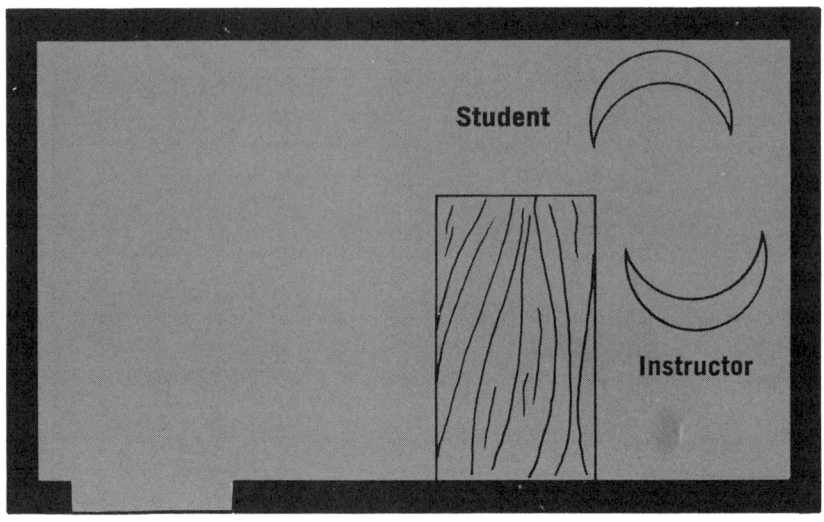

FIGURE 3.2

behind the desk but increases the informality by talking to the student directly—without having to speak over the desk. This spatial arrangement is probably still not conducive to full and free conversation because it is still the instructor's office and he or she is still in control of the space; however, the informality of this arrangement is likely to increase the student's willingness to respond.

Spatial distance will also be affected by the formality or informality of the message being transmitted. Chatting with a friend requires a comfortable but informal distance. Relating an experience to a stranger requires a different use of space. A serious message often is conveyed with some formality whereas a humorous message requires informality. Think of the distance you would assume in reprimanding your roommate for putting things on your desk—your space. Now think of the distance you would use in telling him or her a humorous anecdote that occurred on a recent date you had.

Spatial distance will also be affected by the informality or formality of the situation. Chatting with a friend in the campus hangout often involves the two of you sitting close together. Talking with him or her in the classroom or while being watched by another person may require more distance. The arrangement of many physical spaces is determined by what happens in that space. Churches, schools, and offices seem to exude formality and distance whereas bedrooms, some restaurants, and lounges often display the opposite.

Relationship and Status

The relationship and status of those communicating also affects their use of space. Equal relationships in which parties to the communication are both students, friends, relatives, doctors, teachers, employees, or whatever are likely to be warm and informal. The greater the discrepancy between the parties—such as in some student-teacher, doctor-patient, and employer-employee relationships—the greater the spatial distance when these people are engaged in communication.

To visualize the effect of the relationship and status on spatial distance, take a contemporary topic like pollution, no-fault divorce, or sex discrimination and think about discussing your views on one of these topics with several different people. What spatial distance would you use to present your views to the minister, priest, or rabbi of your church or synagogue? In talking about these same views with your parents, what space would be comfortable? What about your roommate? Your closest friend? Note that in thinking about the presentation and the spatial distance used, the relationships you have with the person affects the distance you would use with him or her.

One of the nonverbal factors affecting the communication in the settings illustrated in Figures 3.1 and Figure 3.2 involves the relationship between the teacher and the student. If, instead of a teacher and student, the participants were doctor and patient, one would expect the furniture arrangement to be more like Figure 3.1 than 3.2. If it were two friends, one would expect the arrangement to be more like Figure 3.2. If the student and the teacher "hit it off" well together, 3.2 would be preferred to 3.1.

In your mind, play with the spatial arrangements that you would expect to find in several settings and guess at the results. Imagine talking with the President of the United States standing within an arm's length of him with nothing between you. Imagine talking with an intimate friend about a personal topic standing twelve feet away. Next time you enter your instructor's office, think about taking the chair and moving it to a different spatial location—like changing it from that depicted in Figure 3.1 to that depicted in Figure 3.2. Relationships between people and a feeling of status are often sustained through spatial distances controlled by arrangements of furniture and other items within a spatial setting. To infringe on another's spatial distance could jeopardize a relationship or cause embarrassment to another's status; thus, to do more than simply conjecture about possible results could prove unwise.

Choices About Space For Speakers

How close a speaker stands to his audience can reflect anything from formality and coldness when the distance is great to informality and warmth when the distance between the speaker and the audience is small. The choices about space that a speaker makes are likely to be dependent upon the topic, the audience, the occasion, and the location. These factors will not always be clear-cut distinctions; they are directly related to each other in every communication setting.

The Topic If a speaker chooses to reminisce with an audience or to relate a series of anecdotes or stories, a close, informal, and warm distance would be appropriate. If, instead, the speaker chooses an issue which relates to the audience's physical well-being—trying to convince them to refrain from eating certain foods to aid in the maintenance of good health, for example—a more formal and cool distance would be appropriate. Convincing people to stop eating something to which they have become accustomed would involve the use of facts, opinions, and a certain rational objectivity that distance helps protect and maintain. Stories and glimpses into the personal life of the speaker require a different mood—a mood that distance might hinder or block.

A speaker who chooses to include both kinds of messages in the same speech might leave the lectern and move in close to the audience when delivering personal examples and return to the lectern to deliver the logical base for the speech, the facts and opinions. Personal insights or conclusions drawn from facts and statistics could also be delivered closer to the audience. The speaker's use of space reinforces the difference between a warm, personal message and "cold facts."

The Audience The audience should figure prominently in any decision the speaker makes about space, for their expectations may affect the success of the speech. Do they expect a formal address? Do they expect a warm, personal message? Would they be offended if the speaker left the platform and moved among them? Would they feel dismay if, instead, the speaker spoke formally from the lectern and never approached them personally at all?

The influence of audience expectations can sometimes be seen when a political candidate is going to speak. When the audience knows that the candidate is planning to deliver a major-policy address, there seems to be less of a desire to grab at and touch the candidate. If, on the other hand, the stop is just another of a whole list of stops, they demand that the candidate move among them, speak informally, and make specific references to the locale in a warm, personal manner. A major-policy speech requires the cool aloofness and distance of an important formal occasion whereas barnstorming demands immediacy and touch.

The size and the age of the audience might also be governing factors. A large audience demands distance so that all can see. Assuming the same distance for a small audience would be inappropriate. If the audience is composed of from three to fifteen people, sitting among them might be the most effective means of communication. An elementary-school audience might prefer this posture as long as everyone could see and hear. An elderly audience might prefer to have the speaker stand before them. Such generalizations, however, should be considered in the context of the total situation. The topic, occasion, and location should be reviewed along with the expectations, size, and age of the audience.

The Occasion Most Sunday sermons require some distance between the minister and the congregation. Most teachers lecture with some distance between themselves and the class. Formal occasions such as commencements, student-government meetings, and state-of-the-nation addresses require this same distance. In these cases, it is the occasion that governs the decision as to where the speaker will stand.

A folk concert might call for just the opposite, the audience gathering closely around the folksinger as young children would gather around their teacher to hear a story being read. In the rock-religious musical *Godspell,* which is based on the gospel according to St. Matthew, the traditional, formal space between the audience and the actors is broken. Actors not only mingle with the audience, but at the intermission, the audience is served wine on the stage by the actors. The message being conveyed to the audience seems to be that the people (represented by them) are an intimate and integral part of the play. The writers of *Godspell* attempted to create in the audience the feeling of the joyous celebration of life (the theme of *Godspell*) by making them part of the occasion.

The Location Choices about spatial distance may be governed by the physical setting in which the communication takes place. A campus assembly hall generally has a lectern located at the middle of the head table because speeches given there are often fairly formal. A campus organization having its first mass meeting in such a hall may wish to convey informality by having a table in front of the gathering on which the speaker can sit crosslegged. One may be given a great deal of flexibility in defining space in a public-speaking situation, or there may be no flexibility provided at all.

The effect of changes in the choice and use of space by the participants in a small group may be an important factor in stimulating active and enthusiastic participation. A small room is usually more suitable than a corner of a large hall for such communication. People find it easiest to communicate with those directly in front of them and hardest to communicate with those seated next to them. The person who sits at the head of the table is almost always looked upon as the leader of the discussion. Also, a strong feeling of cohesiveness or unity can sometimes be achieved if the chairs of the members are grouped closely together.

The topic, the audience, the occasion, and the location are always significant in how other people will respond to your message. Seeking the greatest amount of control possible over these elements help assure success; however, generalizations regarding one's use of space must be considered just that—generalizations. People function differently and generalizing about their behavior is not always successful. There are always exceptions. To become more effective as a communicator or as a receiver, one has to be aware of both the generalizations and the possibility of exceptions.

TIME

Another factor that very likely has some bearing on an instructor's first impressions about you concerns your use of time. When do you arrive for class? Are you the first one there or do you arrive after class has already begun? If you arrive late, you are probably noticed more than if you arrive early. Often, it is the extreme—the one who arrives very early or the one who arrives very late—that attracts attention, and of the two, the latecomer, in our society and with regard to certain occasions, arouses the most negative feelings. A student may arrive late due to oversleeping, not being able to find the room, or because he delays too long in talking to another student. On the other hand, he may decide to indicate to the instructor and students that he is in full control of the situation, to test the instructor's reaction to lateness, or to call attention to himself. The instructor and students may disregard the latecomer altogether, or they may interpret the lateness in any of the ways mentioned. They could also interpret it as an insult to the instructor or as evidence of selfishness or apathy on the late student's part.

As with space, we do not always appreciate the part time plays in our lives until control over it is taken from us. Just as patients in hospitals lose control over space, they also lose control over time and, like prisoners, are forced to do things when other people want them to. Tied to an institutional schedule, their lack of control over something considered second nature in other situations can cause anger, suspicion, and irritability. Students often feel similar frustration because so much of their time is spent doing other people's tasks. Teachers feel hindered and confined by the ritual of the fifty-minute class hour, which is often unrelated to the learning activity at hand. Workers, too, become frustrated by the five-day, eight-to-five, forty-hour weekly routine.

Chronemics, the word used by James C. McCroskey to refer to the use of time in communication, involves several overlapping and interrelated variables.[3] In our approach to chronemics, we will discuss selfishness and unselfishness, formality and informality, and the relationships between task and time. Following a consideration of these variables, we will discuss some of the important choices speakers can make regarding time.

Selfishness and Unselfishness

Patients who are comparing their doctors often discuss the amount of time the doctors give them. The more time, the better the doctor. We often speak highly of the instructor who will listen to us rather than brush us aside. We praise others who willingly hear us out. Friends are often treasured because they seem to care as much for listening to our ideas as they do for communicating their own. Unselfish use of time is universally admired.

Selfish use of time is reflected in behavior that does not respect the interests, wishes, and needs of others. A public speaker, for example, who feels no obligation to his listeners will show this by taking their

[3] James C. McCroskey, *An Introduction To Rhetorical Communication.* Englewood Cliffs, New Jersey: Prentice-Hall, 1972, p. 113.

time speaking to his own values rather than to theirs. The man or woman who is always late for a date might reveal, by this behavior, that he or she has little regard for the other person or for the occasion. On the other hand, such behavior might reflect the late individual's self-expectations or his or her desire to manipulate others. Again, generalizing about motivation for nonverbal behavior is somewhat difficult.

Satisfactory timing may depend upon the occasion or upon the synchronization of the expectations and habits of the people involved. You would likely be annoyed if your friend was late and you wanted to get to the theatre on time, but you might not be as unhappy if he or she were late to go shopping with you. Punctuality is much more important to some people than it is to others. Sometimes we develop a tolerance for a friend who is always late, even to the point of inviting that person to a party half an hour earlier than anyone else so that he or she will arrive when the others do!

Formality and Informality

Business appointments and arrangements to discuss ideas with superiors tend to be more formal than social get-togethers. You would worry about being on time for a job interview whereas you might not worry about being present for the beginning of a picnic or dance. The person who arrives early for a party scheduled for eight o'clock could find the host or hostess still preparing for the party—perhaps even in the shower. On the other hand, one who is late to a dentist's appointment may find that another person has already been taken and, too, may be billed despite the fact that he or she never saw the dentist. Considerations regarding time often change with the formality or informality of the occasion.

It is important for communicators to take note of the formality of the occasion when timing is being considered. A message designed for presentation on radio must be prepared with very careful consideration of the time element, whereas a message designed for most other occasions does not require the same exacting concern. Being prepared to make wise use of a fifteen-minute job interview requires preparation and forethought because of the formalized time restriction, as does making good use of the five minutes allowed for a class speech exercise. It becomes a question of when you can loosen up and relax a bit and when you need to be highly structured and fairly rigid. When in doubt, with good preparation and a tightly planned presentation, most people can decrease the formality if the situation calls for it.

Tasks and Time

If you are interviewing someone for a television newsclip, you will handle the time you have differently than if you are talking with a member of the opposite sex to find out if you want to date that person. A group of people with a time limit and a problem to solve operate quite differently from a group of people who want to explore a variety of feelings or ideas about a particular topic with no time restriction. The central issue—whether one is speaking of interpersonal or small-group communication—is the relationship between the time available and the task of those communicating.

The task may be evaluated by judging the quality and the quantity of the content one is able to cover in the amount of time provided. Some people have the ability of getting to the heart of an issue in a very efficient manner: the employer who finds out all he really needs to know in a matter of three to five minutes; the teacher who finds out with one or two questions whether a student has read the material she assigned the night before. Efficiency in communication is often what makes certain situations exciting or engaging. How many new, different, or relevant ideas are produced, how much is being said or done, or how many quality ideas are being generated is likely to be a result of how well time is used. Test the theory that efficiency creates interest by thinking about the last speech you enjoyed listening to and why you liked it. It is likely to be because the speaker used his time efficiently. This is as important in small groups as it is in speeches. Whether you come back to a small group or not may be determined by how efficiently the group utilized the time they had.

Efficiency in the completion of a task is important; however, it should not be sought to the exclusion of the thorough consideration of a variety of viewpoints, the thoughtful weighing of a number of different alternatives, or the sympathetic airing of emotions and feelings. Time should be allowed for exploration. Investigation and thorough inquiry provide a solid foundation for creativity since a creative effort usually evolves when your thoughts or your imagination are piqued by the ideas and opinions of others. Planning for the best use of your time includes some consideration of the facts that some tasks take longer than others to complete and the task can involve goals other than the solution of a problem or the completion of a decision. A task may include the gathering of information or the expression of personal feelings on a topic or issue. Thus, time must be related to the specific task at hand.

Choices About Time For Speakers

Public speakers operate under time restrictions; however, these restrictions should, in most cases, be more severe than they are. Speaking to a group of forty individuals for half an hour ties up twenty people-hours. The longer a public speaker is allowed to talk, the more likely it is that the audience will become bored and inattentive. The choices about time that a speaker makes are likely to be dependent upon the topic, the audience, the occasion, and the location. Just as in the case of space and its limitations, these factors will not always be clear-cut; they are directly related to each other in every communication setting. To say that one is more important than another is a judgment only the speaker can make in relation to a particular communication situation.

The Topic Select a topic that you can reasonably expect to cover with some depth and thoroughness within the time limits provided. You cannot expect to convince an audience to change the world in a ten-minute speech—nor the country, nor the city, nor even the college. You might have some chance in presenting arguments for a change in a particular class, but your best bet would likely be to approach a desirable change in just one class assignment in a ten-minute speech. The shorter the amount of time allowed for a speech, the narrower, or more specific, the topic should be.

In planning the delivery of the speech, the communicator should also be concerned about timing. The pacing of the information that supports the topic may make the difference between an exciting and a dull communication. Also, the location in the speech where the central idea, thesis, or proposition of the speaker is placed may determine whether it is received or not. The speaker may want to provide the audience some lead time—a warning that the message or topic is coming. Suspense can sometimes be created if examples and facts are stated first and the topic or essential message is delayed.

The Audience Martin Luther King faced a problem of timing with respect to his audience when he delivered his famous speech entitled "I Have A Dream" in Washington, D.C., in 1963. King was the last on the program; he was preceded by more than fifteen others. It was a hot August day, and the group of 200,000 had become edgy; many had begun returning to their buses. King had to open his speech dramatically and forcefully to turn their attention to the very reasons for this first march on Washington. He began speaking with these words:

Five score years ago, a great American, in whose symbolic shadow we stand today, signed the Emancipation Proclamation. This momentous decree came as a great beacon light of hope to millions of Negro slaves who had been seared in the flames of withering injustice. It came as a joyous daybreak to end the long night of their captivity.[4]

The power of Dr. King's rhetoric stopped his audience in their tracks. He began by alluding to Abraham Lincoln, using a paraphrase from the opening of the Gettysburg Address; this reminded his audience of the purpose of their protest. The rest of King's introduction builds emotional energy through a series of powerful similes and metaphors—"as a great beacon light of hope," "the flames of withering injustice," "as a joyous daybreak," and "long night of captivity." He lost no time in reaching out and grasping the attention of his audience.

An audience should feel that the speaker is eager and excited about talking with them. Often a sense of urgency can be generated by the timing used in the delivery of a speech. Obviously, a speaker who shows reluctance or appears late—just like a late term paper, business report, or press release—will indicate to the audience his or her low regard for them as well as for the message. Appearing on time with an impelling message will set the stage for the whole speech.

An effective public speaker says what he or she has to say and sits down. You show respect for your audience when you are terse, concise, succinct, and direct. Knowing when to stop talking is one of the most important—and one of the most abused—skills in public speaking. One way you can cure the habit of talking too much is by imagining that you are talking long-distance at day rates.

The Occasion Perhaps the greatest influence that an occasion has on the timing of a speech concerns the overall time restriction. An after-dinner speech calls for brief, usually humorous, comments. A commencement would require more lengthy, serious remarks. Think of a variety of different occasions—club, assembly, student government, class, church—and you can see certain imposed standards for how long a speaker at each occasion would speak. In most cases, time determinations and allowances are made for the speaker.

The Location If you were giving a rallying speech to a group of protest marchers located outside the administration building's main door,

---

4 Wil A. Linkugel, R. R. Allen, and Richard L. Johannesen, *Contemporary American Speeches: A Sourcebook of Speech Forms and Principles.* Belmont, California: Wadsworth, 1972, pp. 289–290.

you would likely give a shorter speech in midwinter or in the midst of a pouring rain than you would if it were a bright summer day. In the days of the American lyceum—a debate and lecture society formed in many communities during the nineteenth century—traveling lecturers often had to cut their speeches short because of poor heating or poor lighting in the buildings in which they were asked to speak. Ventilation, acoustics, lighting, and weather are some of the factors that might cause a speaker to speak for a shorter time, to increase his remarks, or to better adapt them to the situation.

BODY MOVEMENT

Jurgen Ruesch and Weldon Keys, pioneers in nonverbal communicaton research, divide the nonverbal world into three parts: sign language, action language, and object language.[5] We use *sign language* when we use a gesture or vocal tone to stand for a word, number, or punctuation mark. The clenched, upraised fist, for example, is a gesture used in the black-power movement to stand for strong support of the rights of black people. In the same way, a tone of voice may serve as an exclamation point, question mark, or period.

We use *action language* all the time; it includes all bodily movements that communicate but are not primarily meant to communicate; walking, running, and sitting are examples. A door-to-door salesman who is extremely pushy and who does not want to give you time to respond may unconsciously convey his aggressive intention by walking forcefully through the door and sitting on the edge of the chair. A woman who enjoys trying out natural-foods recipes can gauge how well a new dish is liked simply by observing the action language of her family—how they eat the food. Action language includes all the physical activities we perform every day to meet personal needs.

Object language communicates through the display of material things including the human body and its clothing. Both intentional and unintentional display are included. We wear an engagement ring or a wedding band with purpose. The way we wear our clothing, on the other hand, may be without conscious intent.

5 Jurgen Ruesch and Weldon Kees, *Nonverbal Communication: Notes on the Visual Perception of Human Relations*. Berkeley: University of California, 1956. Also see Jurgen Ruesch, "Nonverbal Language," in Robert S. Cathcart and Larry A. Samovar (eds.), *Small Group Communications: A Reader*. Dubuque, Iowa: Wm. C. Brown, 1970, p. 260.

Whether it is sign, action, or object language, we use the body for two nonverbal functions: to reinforce our verbal message—the words we use—and to reveal our attitudes and emotions. When you cannot believe what another person is saying, you might express your dismay verbally, "I can't believe you are saying that" and nonverbally by turning from the other person, shaking your head, and sighing. You have not only reinforced your verbal message of disbelief, but you have revealed your frustration—your feeling—as well.

Much of nonverbal communication relates, in some way, to body movement. Space and time refer, in part, to the movement of the body in a setting. The manner in which any part of the body is moved relates directly to both space and time, for it is moved within a specified space and in a specified period of time. Ray L. Birdwhistell, a founder of research in the study of communication through bodily movements, called this study *kinesics*.[6] Our treatment of kinesics will cover the nonverbal aspects of eye contact, facial expression, gesture, and posture and motion.

Eye Contact

The last time an instructor asked a question which you could not or did not want to answer, what did you do with your eyes? You probably avoided the instructor's eyes by looking down at the floor or at the notebook on your desk. By shifting your eyes away from the instructor, you were attempting to break contact—to show that you did not want to respond. The degree to which this cue was effective may have been a result of how many others wanted to respond or how aware the instructor was of your motives. Instructors who want to "catch" a student unprepared may be very alert to such a cue. If you have such an instructor, sometime when you do not know the answer you might try looking him or her straight in the eye.

To indicate the significance of eye contact, note the way that it can work in male-female communication on the street. As a man and a woman who are strangers approach each other, glances may be exchanged from a distance; however, when the two people reach a point about fifteen to twenty feet from each other, the woman's eyes will probably drop to the sidewalk directly in front of her. The man may

---

6 Ray L. Birdwhistell, *Introduction to Kinesics.* Louisville: University of Louisville, 1952. Also see his "Background to Kinesics" in *ETC: A Review of General Semantics,* 13 (Autumn, 1955): 10–18.

continue to look at the woman, but she will probably not raise her eyes to that particular man again. The rules that govern this nonverbal behavior are largely determined by the society in which these two people live. Eye contact between a man and a woman in our society often has sexual connotations; its rules permit a man to express sexual interest by eyeing a woman he does not know, but they prohibit this expression by a "decent" woman.

Eye contact between a man and a woman is likely to be interpreted by both parties according to these rules. Thus, looking into the eyes of a strange man closer than fifteen to twenty feet is a sign that the woman is "loose" or "available," and the man will probably interpret her behavior this way even if she is merely curious or from a small town and unfamiliar with the rules governing this behavior in the city. On the other hand, a prostitute may go out of her way to establish eye contact with a possible customer to reveal her desire and availability. Then the shoe is on the other foot. The man, in this case, who prolongs eye contact with the woman may encourage stronger or more direct solicitation. The double-standard implied by such sexist rules can make meeting strangers in big cities difficult for both men and women.

For the communicator, eye contact works in three basic ways. It aids in giving attention and indicating inclusion; it shows intensity of feeling; and it provides feedback. In treating attention, we will approach eye contact from both the source's and the receiver's viewpoints.

Attention and Inclusion The last time you spoke intimately with another person, you probably maintained very direct eye contact at the same time. When you look directly into someone else's eyes, you reveal that you are attending to him or her, and that you want that person's full attention. When communication is direct, eye contact is strong. By not looking at a person when you communicate, you effectively shut that person out of the communication. In small-group communication, stronger members can isolate weaker members by not communicating eye to eye with them. With full attention to everyone, by everyone, feelings of inclusion are intensified, and cohesiveness—the state of being united—becomes greater.

Effective communicators both send and receive messages. Many of the messages we could receive are missed because of poor eye contact. There is no surer way to lose a receiver than by avoiding direct eye contact—letting your eyes wander to the floor, to the walls, to the ceiling, or to notes. As a communicator, you need to be concerned about all your listeners. Too often, for example, in public-speaking classes, student have a tendency to direct their comments to the instructor instead of to the whole class.

Since we spend more time receiving messages than sending them, eye contact has to be viewed from the other side as well. A receiver who is interested in a communicator's message will listen attentively—revealing this attention through sustained eye contact. Receivers who do not look at the communicator often block the communication because the sender is cut off from the feedback he or she needs.

As the number of people with whom you are communicating increases, all must be included by your eye contact to feel that they have a part in the transaction. One neighbor can effectively give the "cold shoulder" to other neighbors by not looking at them as they approach. When you are engaged in a conversation with another person and a third person comes up to you, it is thoughtful and warm to shift your stance slightly to open toward the incoming person and to look the incoming person in the eye as he or she approaches. You are, in effect, receiving the other person and showing that he or she is welcome, even if you do not stop your conversation. In many cases, such eye contact can serve as effectively as if you had turned to the other person and clasped his or her hand in greeting.

Intensity Eye contact also reveals intensity of feeling. In intimate situations it often shows warmth; in other situations, coldness or anger. To say "I love you" or "I want to help you" or "I care about you" and to have the message received warmly, the one expressing concern must look the other in the eyes. One study found that happy newly married couples look at each other more frequently than unhappy newly married couples. Think of the courting behavior used in our society. Boy meets girl—girl looks away and down. As the relationship grows and more familiarity is established, eye contact becomes stronger, more intense, even more meaningful. The officer, on the other hand, who is "chewing out" a subordinate may look the subordinate directly in the eye with the intention of revealing the intensity of his anger. The father who is reprimanding his child may use intense eye contact to reveal his utter dissatisfaction with the child's behavior. He may demand of the child, "Look at me when I am speaking to you!"

Sometimes the absence of eye contact gives an impression of aloofness which is misleading. If you feel a sudden rush of warm feeling for another person, you may avert your eyes to hide the intensity of your feelings—fearing, perhaps, that the other person will be overwhelmed by them. Strong disapproval or anger may also be conveyed by refusing to meet the eyes of the offending person. Thus, either the presence or absence of eye contact may indicate strong feeling.

Feedback In addition to being an indicator of attention and feeling, eye contact also provides feedback. When you look into the eyes of another, you see all the facial expressions revealed by the other as they are communicated. You have probably tried to talk with a person who wore dark glasses and found the situation a bit difficult. You did not know if you had the other person's attention; you were not even sure he or she was looking at you. If you have experienced this problem—a barrier to effective communication—you know the value of eye contact.

An alert public speaker can also estimate the audience reaction if effective eye contact is maintained. Is the audience interested? Are they confused? Are they ready for you to end or are they content to listen more? Do you irritate them? Test the value of eye contact as a means of feedback by not looking at an audience as you communicate directly with them—just to see if the cue is perceived. Responsive, mutual communication requires both a stimulus and a response.

You begin to know how effective good eye contact is when you realize what it is like to be left out of someone's eye contact. If you have ever been an outsider, put yourself in the shoes of the listener. As the communicator, you can make receivers feel wanted; you can set them at ease; you can even excite them. Your eyes serve as the first electrical connection with your audience—they turn on the current. Often, how much enthusiasm and interest you generate once you have made the connection is dependent on how much current flows.

Facial Expression

The face is one of the most expressive parts of the body. The way you move your forehead, eyebrows, eyes, mouth, tongue, lips, and chin all communicate something about you. How others will react to these cues cannot precisely be determined, but they will react and they will react in different ways. Not all facial cues are subject to our direct and conscious control, however. Your age, sex, and race are also reflected in your face. A face-lift may alter the way one looks just as long hair may confuse some about one's sex. Such alterations and confusions notwithstanding, we do make generalizations about others' "mature judgment," "sexual bias," or "intolerance" based solely on the nonverbal facial cues of age, sex, and race. Our primary concern in this section will be with those cues over which we have some control while communicating.

What peoples' faces reveal when they communicate a message makes a great deal of difference in how that message is received. If you wish to convey a warm message, your face must support the message by revealing warmth—a smiling and interested face. If you wish to convey a very serious message, your face must support the message by revealing a grave, solemn, or, perhaps, thoughtful disposition. A single movement of the mouth or eyebrow could reveal acceptance, rejection, skepticism, even anger.

Birdwhistell discovered and catalogued twenty-three separate and distinct eyebrow positions. As you place the eyebrows into the context of the face, you begin to realize the tremendous variety of combinations possible. Our faces can make literally thousands of different expressions; thus, it is likely that people will respond differently to the "same" cue. What is one cue for one person can be a different cue for another person. Since we are continually being barraged with cues, and since most cues last for such a short amount of time—some for but a fraction of a second—it seems obvious that variations in interpretations will occur.

Facial cues are important in any communication setting, and the closer the receiver is to the sender, the more important the facial cues become. In intimate situations, the receiver is likely to be able to see more things in the sender's face than in settings where the distance between the receiver and sender is great. At a distance gestures often take the place of facial expression as far as the communication of attitudes and emotions is concerned.

The best facial cues are natural ones. One does not, generally, practice smiling to reveal warmth or practice frowning to reveal unfriendliness; however, if one is aware that the cue being received is not the one intended, then the sender is in a position to at least find out the reason for the discrepancy and attempt to clear it up. A public speaker can analyze the facial expressions revealed during a speech in a video-tape session. Seldom is criticism necessary for the video-tape speaks for itself. If the intention and the reception match, success has been achieved.

The importance of facial cues in communication is indicated by the number of colloquial expressions in the English language which describe the use of the face. The expressions, "poker faced," "straight faced" or "two faced" indicate use of the face to hide true feelings. A person may be condemned for telling a "bold-faced lie." When you are bold in another sense, one might say that you "have the face" to ask for or to do something; when you're in trouble, you may try to "save face." Facial expressions are important; thus, you should try to "put a good face on the matter."

Gesture

The various cues of the face must be placed into the larger context of cues that are made with other parts of the body. Some people "talk with their hands." A serious and thoughtful face is given further reinforcement with strong and determined *gestures*—movements of the hands or arms. Gestures provide numerous additional cues to which an aware listener can respond. Just as with facial cues, the varieties or kinds of gestures vary almost with the number of senders—especially when you begin to consider the gestures in combination with the facial cues.

Gestures are, generally, easier to practice than facial expressions. A person who practices a variety of facial cues to convey emotions may find that the cues—especially if they do not come naturally—reflect artificiality or insincerity instead. This is less likely to happen with gestures. Some gestures are better than no gestures; thus, if one's gestures are either weak or nonexistent, practice is encouraged. Having others critique your use of gestures can be of help. Self-critique, through the use of a mirror, is another way of gaining some feedback on your effectiveness.

In interpersonal communication when two people are standing very close to one another, gesture may be extended to include touch. Little children instinctively touch; however, they are regularly encouraged *not* to touch by adults: "Take your fingers out of your mouth," "Don't touch the furniture," "Don't touch yourself," "Don't touch strangers." Little boys are taught not to touch girls, and little girls are taught not to touch boys.

As children grow into adults, the desire to touch and to be touched remains, but the rules that have been stressed throughout childhood control that desire. Lovers are permitted the greatest degree of touch; between those of different status or class, no touching is permitted. You will also note that at social occasions men will shake hands with each other, but seldom do women or even a woman and a man shake hands or touch in any way unless the woman takes the initiative. Touching between adult men and women carries sexual overtones. Touching is so successfully forced out of us by society that many lovers, too, have to learn how to come alive again to their sense of touch. Some people just naturally touch others. Other people seldom or never do.

Have you ever found yourself showing concern for or serious interest in another person by reaching out and gently touching his or her upper arm? Have you ever known a person who showed appreciation for a joke or indicated kidding by hitting you lightly on the arm or the back? A handshake often reveals a great deal about another person: the person's strength or weakness, superiority or inferiority, enthusiasm or lack of enthusiasm. Through the touch of a hand you can feel security or warmth; you can also feel fear, coldness, or anxiety. A handshake is among the first nonverbal cues we get about the other person in interpersonal communication.

Gesture plays an important role in public-speaking situations. Often, because of the distance between the public speaker and the audience, gesture must take the place of facial expressions which are lost because the listener cannot see them. Gesture is closely associated with emotion for when the speaker becomes more involved in the material, or seeks to reveal greater intensity, the gestures, too, often become more expansive or more intense. If a speaker stands before you as an immobile body, how involved can you get with what that speaker is saying? The alert, animated, vigorous, and enthusiastic speaker often stimulates the audience to respond in kind.

Causing others to feel the emotion they perceive involves empathy, which can be aided by gesturing. The goal of the communicator is to achieve an empathic response; thus, the cues provided for the listener must be precise and accurate. Ambiguous cues—or no cues at all—provide the listener with a message that is open to various interpretations or to verbal stimuli alone with no reinforcement in the attitude or feeling channel of communication. Nonverbal communication of all kinds supplies the means for the responder to mentally enter into the spirit or feeling of the communicator or his ideas; gestures serve to support other nonverbal communication, thus adding seasoning to the entree to intensify its flavor.

Using gestures before an audience is sometimes difficult; many people become inhibited in front of others. Although we may "talk with our hands" in interpersonal communication situations, often we cannot successfully transfer that important skill to the public-speaking situation. If we try to overcompensate—overgesture—we will more than likely achieve the correct balance. Natural gestures that support and reinforce the verbal message being conveyed will seldom distract.

Gestures should never become a barrier to communication, however. When a listener pays more attention to what your hands are doing than to what you are saying with words—you are either gesturing too much or gesturing incorrectly. If the attention of a listener is distracted by a gesture—or anything else about the speaker's nonverbal behavior—that listener is not giving full attention to the speaker's verbal message. A story is told of a two-year-old who sat at the dinner table jabbering away at a furious rate while moving his hands in all directions. His parents finally discovered that he was mimicking the way they talked; they became more conscious of how much they gestured as a result. In their case, it took a two-year-old to create the awareness.

Posture and Motion

When you first come into a class, it is very likely that your posture reveals your feeling for the class. *Posture* is the arrangement and position of the body and the limbs, as a whole. It can reflect your inner motivation, your intentions in a communication situation, as well as your attitude. If you "drag" yourself into a class, reluctantly and with a great deal of skepticism and anxiety, it is likely that your posture will reveal this lack of enthusiasm. You may be bent over, slouching, and, perhaps, shuffling. Admittedly, this is an exaggeration; however, one of the best ways to reflect an I-could-care-less attitude is with your total body. Have you ever wondered why the armed services encourages the military posture? "Stomach in, chest out, shoulders back!" The military is convinced that posture reflects attitude. The serviceman who holds himself in an alert posture is likely to be alert. There is a certain amount of truth to this. The person who wants an alert and thoughtful response to a communication must appear alert and thoughtful in all aspects—including posture.

Pause sometime and note the way people walk, for it is often possible to speculate about the importance of their mission by the way they move. The carefree person who has time to spare reveals an entirely different posture than the person who is running slightly behind time in arriving at an important meeting. When you are relaxed, your whole body reflects an unconstrained looseness; when tense, a restrained hardness. The person who is a bundle of nerves, or who has an overactive thyroid, often manifests continual activity that one could interpret as the important pursuit of business, dedication to the task, or a "positive" use of time. The person who has time to spare is easy-going, often indifferent, and coolly unconcerned. It is the person's posture, in part, that provides the clue—even though we may not always be successful in reading the clue accurately.

Posture is important in communication because it can reveal the communicator's attitude toward the message and the receiver. The individual who is interested in conveying a message may lean slightly toward the person or persons for whom the message is intended. A positive attitude toward the other person with whom one is communicating may also cause one to lean toward him or her. A drooping, careless, awkward, or rigid stance could reflect disinterest and, perhaps, dislike. Albert Mehrabian, in a study of the transmission of attitudes by body posture, found that a communicator's body posture can reveal three different kinds of perceptions about the status of the person with whom he is communicating: a relaxed body posture is assumed if the other person is perceived to be of lower status than himself, a less relaxed body posture will be assumed if the other person is perceived to be of equal status, and a tense body posture will be assumed if the other person is perceived to be of higher status.[7]

---

[7] Albert Mehrabian, "Communication Length as an Index of Communicator Attitude," *Psychological Reports,* 17 (1965): 519–522; "Influence of Attitudes from the Posture, Orientation, and Distance of a Communicator," *Journal of Consulting and Clinical Psychology,* 32 (1968): 296–308; "Relationship of Attitude to Seated Posture, Orientation, and Distance," *Journal of Personality and Social Psychology,* 10 (1968): 26–30. Mehrabian's findings on posture are reported in Ronald L. Applbaum, Karl W. E. Anatol, Ellis R. Hays, Owen O. Jenson, Richard E. Porter, and Jerry E. Mandel's *Fundamental Concepts in Human Communication.* San Francisco: Canfield, 1973, pp. 114–116.

In the United States the word *slouch* has come to mean an inefficient or inferior person; thus, the way you carry yourself will probably reflect the image that you create when you are standing with another person, sitting in a group, standing before a group of people, or even reacting to another communicator. Just as the speaker's posture can reveal the speaker's attitude toward the topic, the purpose of the communication, or the listener; the listener's posture, according to Mehrabian, can reveal whether he feels threatened, whether he like the communicator, and whether he feels the communicator's status is higher or lower than his own. Whatever the observations reveal, posture is among the first cues both the communicator and the listener have an opportunity to "read," and both communicator and listener should realize that the way they carry themselves can set the mood for the communication as well as determine the results.

Body motion is often as important as posture in providing cues to which listeners can respond. Movement on the platform, movement while talking to another person, or movement before a camera can be important whether the audience is one or many. A skillful public speaker will, in general, try not to confine delivery to speaking from behind a lectern. Changes in thoughts and attitudes, as well as transitions from one idea to another, can be reflected by the body motion of a speaker in front of an audience. If you are changing a thought, moving in a new direction, or changing a mood, you may want to change your body position. A change in body position may involve coming out from behind a lectern, turning to face another part of the audience, or taking a few steps one way or the other. Changes in body position suggest that you are comfortable in front of the audience. They also reveal that you are in command of the situation; you appear to know what you are doing. We often use these same cues when we are talking to another person. In addition, we may turn our body slightly to include another person who is joining us or turn our body slightly to those we are addressing. Interest and involvement in a communication with another individual are revealed by facing that person squarely.

Body motions often reveal the intentions of a person to involve or exclude others—even if these are unintentional movements. Think of yourself getting onto a bus or train and sitting next to a person you do not know. It is likely that your body motions will reflect coldness; you may cross your legs away from the individual or lean away. You will try not to impose any more than you must on the other person's body space. If, however, you strike up a conversation with the person and you gain a

warm response, you may slowly change your overall position. You may uncross your legs for a moment and then cross them toward the other person. You may shift your position toward the other person and even lean toward him or her slightly. Infringement of the other person's body space no longer seems inappropriate for you have now shared each other's thoughts, and sharing each other's body space becomes a logical extension of that. As more participants contribute, in a small-group communication setting, for example, more thoughts are shared; the corresponding tendency is for members to lean in toward the center of the group. The person who slouches in the chair, maintains a lax body position, or fails to move his or her body toward the center of the group may be overlooked or slighted in the ongoing, active discussion. A person who looks and acts alert invites others to react by moving toward him or her.

VOICE

There is a clear distinction between a person's use of words (verbal communication) and a person's use of *voice*. *Vocal nonverbal communication,* or paralanguage, includes such characteristics as rate, inflection, loudness, and tone. These factors exist along with the words and serve to modify them in a variety of ways. In all speaking, vocal nonverbal communication has tremendous potential for influencing the meaning of the speaker's verbal message as interpreted by the receiver. Albert Mehrabian estimates that 38 percent of the social meaning in the communication process is stimulated by the vocal cues—not the words said but the way in which they are said.[8]

The rate, or speed, at which one speaks can have various effects on the way the message is received. A very rapid rate for five minutes or more can dull the senses just as a very slow pace can have the same effect. Variety is important. A message of high emotional intensity may require a slightly faster pace whereas a shift to a very important note or comment, one that the listener must get, might require a slow and very determined rate. Mehrabian suggested that a communicator's rate is increasingly affected by speech errors as his anxiety increases. Anger, stress, and fear can be associated with faster rates whereas grief or depression can be associated with slower rates. The speaker will hold the

---

[8] Mehrabian, *Silent Messages,* pp. 42–47. Also see "Communication Without Words," p. 53.

attention of the listener best if the rate of speaking changes with the nature of the ideas, the nature of the mood, and the nature of the feedback the speaker receives.

Inflection varies with the changes in pitch given in a vocal cue. The phrase "That is great" can convey a whole range of meanings, depending on the relative pitch one uses for the different words in the phrase. You might say, "That is *great!*" (it really is the most exciting and interesting thing you've heard all day). Or you might say, "*That* is great?" (you must be kidding; it's the dumbest thing I've ever seen in my whole life). Or "That *is* great" (it is surprising and delightful to discover the significance and interest of this thing). Note that the verbal message is the same in all three examples. The nonverbal use of voice inflection produces the intended meaning in each case.

Loudness is the strength with which the voice is used. No one likes to be yelled at just as no one likes to have to strain to listen. A speaker who always uses high intensity must learn to control the voice to gain variety. A loud voice is fine if used for a particular purpose and in moderation. Low intensity works the same way. Also, certain points, because of their importance, require more intensity or loudness than others. If all points are delivered with the same intensity, the delivery will, like a fast rate, tend to dull the senses.

A public speaker must make adjustments of intensity according to the distance from the listener or listeners. The size of the room, whether microphones are provided, and the acoustical features of the room all require adjustments for intensity. Warmth in interpersonal situations is often revealed by a relaxed and rather low intensity. The effective public speaker can often use much the same intensity as that used in interpersonal communication situations. Generally, one's personal conversation is full of a great deal of variety in intensity. One should attempt to capture this same variety in public speaking. Effective communication in these settings has been referred to by some writers as "extended conversation." The monotonous mumbler will create little enthusiasm for the idea being presented. Further discussion of the importance of verbal cues in public-speaking delivery is found in Chapter 5.

Tone is the quality or characteristic of a sound. It is a broad characteristic that varies, generally, according to the type of message being conveyed, the nature of the situation, and the kind of audience. A message of love being conveyed to a very intimate friend in the privacy of one's ·home requires a very different tone from a message of protest being conveyed to the administration in a meeting hall. A funeral requires an oration of a different tone than that required for a Fourth of July celebration. Finally, the kind of audience may influence one's choice of tone. For example, a speech about women's liberation before an all-male audience would be different in tone from the same speech before an all-female audience. We talk differently in the dorm before friends than we do in the classroom before other students or at home before members of our family. The whole tone changes.

A particular communication setting makes various kinds of demands in relation to tone. From the time that we are children and are told, in one situation, "Now, I want you to behave" as opposed to "BEHAVE!" in another situation, we begin to sense differences in tone. The way our parents talked to us in front of guests may have differed from the way they spoke to us at other times. A sense of tone is something that develops as we grow up and is very much a part of us. There are few guiding principles. The effective speaker will vary his tone according to the message, the situation, and the audience—depending on what tone is most appropriate to reinforce the communication and to best convey the attitudes and emotions of the communicator.

Receivers are likely to make judgments about the communicator's personality based on voice, especially if other nonverbal cues are absent. These judgments can be quite inaccurate. In telephone conversations with strangers, for example, our judgments about the other person often reflect sexist stereotypes. The smooth, breathy voice of a woman is often interpreted as sexy while the high-pitched voice of a man is considered effeminate. What a surprise when we find that she is unattractive in appearance and he is an immense muscular fellow! It is risky to react to another's personality on the basis of voice cues alone.

All the nonverbal cues often combine to tell the listener more about us than we want the other person to know. Although we have some degree of control over vocal cues, that is, we can often tell a person how to interpret the message we are sending by using the corresponding nonverbal cues, most of the time we do not give our use of voice a great deal of thought. We live with our voices all the time, and we often forget that others who hear us for the first time are making judgments based on them. No matter what the situation, the listener will receive important cues from your voice whether you intend to convey the cues or not. Because voice is an important nonverbal cue, we should all be more conscious of its effective use.

OBJECTS

Ruesch and Kees define *object language* as the nonverbal cues that are conveyed through the display and use of material things, including the human body and the way it is clothed.[9] In addition to objects of clothing, we will also treat objects worn with clothes, and objects used in communication settings. The mere presence of objects communicates nonverbally; thus, no one can avoid communicating through objects.

When you enter a classroom on the first day of class, your clothing may be one of the cues to which others, including the instructor, respond in making initial assessments about you. What you choose to wear is an area over which you exert a fair amount of control, although our culture, your particular society, your peers, and sometimes even the school exert pressure on you to dress in a certain way. Whatever the final choices you make regarding the way you dress, these choices provide cues to which others can and do respond. The judgments that we make of others on the basis of their dress tend to reflect the norms of our particular subculture or peer group; thus, what is perceived as a provocatively tight sweater in one region of the country might be perfectly acceptable in another. Choices of clothing tend to communicate a great deal about the personality of the wearer, and interpretations of this nonverbal cue reveal a great deal about the viewer.

The objects we choose to wear with our clothes also have communicative significance. Lapel pins, earrings, fraternity or sorority pins, college rings, eyeglasses, or cosmetics all say something about us.

Most of us like to feel that we are not greatly influenced by what another person wears; we would prefer to think that we judge a person by what he or she *is*. However, clothing is a powerful preoccupation in our society, and the advertising media encourage us to behave as if clothes *do* make the person. You can become more aware of the degree to which your own perceptions of other people are influenced by their clothing and also of the messages that you convey by the dress that you wear. Sit in some public place and observe the people around you, asking yourself what kind of people you think they are and how this perception is colored by their clothing. What, for example, do you assume about a

---

9 Jurgen Ruesch and Weldon Kees, *Nonverbal Communication: Notes on the Visual Perception of Human Relations* (Berkeley: University of California, 1956). Also see Jurgen Ruesch, "Nonverbal Language and Therapy," in Alfred G. Smith, ed., *Communication and Culture*. (New York: Holt, Rinehart and Winston, 1966), pp. 209–210.

conservatively dressed man who is carrying a leather briefcase? How do you react to a woman who is wearing disheveled, unironed clothing? Then, take a look at yourself in a full-length mirror as you prepare to go out for the day. What are you saying to other people?

The objects we choose to handle as we communicate also convey nonverbal messages. Teachers sometimes make unfortunate choices in this area. You may have had a teacher at some point who rolled chalk in her palms as she talked. It became especially distracting if she wore rings and the chalk clicked everytime it was rolled over one. Repetitive use of objects may reflect nervousness or boredom; some distracting mannerisms become unconscious habits that are automatic and difficult to interpret. The way cigarettes and cups of coffee are handled can give clues about people. Pencils, papers, and sometimes anything that is handy may become distracting diversions as well.

In communication situations like an interview, the objects in the room combine to form a total communication setting. The arrangement of furniture, as discussed in the section on space, may reflect warmth or coldness. A nameplate on the desk, what it says, and how it is made could convey formality or informality. Pictures on the wall and a carpet on the floor might reveal a cozy homelike atmosphere as opposed to a detached institutionalism. Magazines on the desk, depending on their titles, could disclose that the interviewer is informed of current happenings in his or her field or in the world. All of these are objects over which some control may be taken, but whether control is exerted or not, they do convey a message to those who see them.

When you are communicating in a public situation, you may have an opportunity to control the objects around you, or the objects may be controlled for you in such a way as to convey the impression that someone else desires. Whether you use a lectern may determine the degree of formality of the presentation. Whether a meeting is held in a classroom, a church, a large hall, a school, or in someone's home may determine the tone of that meeting. Whether you are seated in a chair in front of an audience or seated on a table certainly makes a difference. Flags, banners, and signs have a great deal of communicative significance. They add, for example, to the pomp and pageantry of a speech before a national-party convention just as picket signs help provide some of the mood for protest speeches whether they be antigovernment, anti-big business, or antimanagement.

The objects you select to wear, to handle, and to combine into communication settings convey a message. As with all other nonverbal cues, you should make sure that their message is the one you intend, for their message may, in part, determine the content of another person's message—even to the extent of determining whether another person might want to listen or respond to you at all.

MIXED MESSAGES

Many messages are sent simultaneously by verbal and nonverbal means. When the two channels confirm and complement each other, the total message is clearer because each channel reinforces the other. However, trying to make a correct judgment about the meaning of a message is often made difficult if the message being sent verbally and the message being sent nonverbally contradict each other. Such a contradiction between these channels will be referred to as *mixed communication*.

Perhaps on the first day of this class you heard your instructor say something like, "I feel that instructors should make themselves available to their students; thus, you can see me anytime." Then you tried to see him or her after class to find out a bit more about what this course included. As you watched the instructor pack away the lecture notes, snap shut the briefcase, and nervously look at the clock while talking to you and moving toward the door, you realized that he or she was saying one thing but meaning another thing. You were caught in the contradiction of a mixed communication.

What does a person really mean when he says, "I like you" in a cold tone of voice? What is a man to think of a woman who seems naïve but makes overt sexual advances toward him? What is a child to believe when the parent talks about getting to appointments on time and yet never seems able to get the child to the doctor's office on time? What is a student to believe when the professor encourages disagreement but gets very upset when she receives any? What is generally believed in these situations is the behavior that is hardest to fake.

Anyone can pay lip service to a belief, a creed, or a cause; it is what that person does that counts. Actions *do* speak louder than words. We tend to believe the nonverbal communication—not the words—because the nonverbal behavior is harder to counterfeit. It is more powerful in communicating feelings, and because it is more natural—that is, it is more a part of us—it is more difficult for us to control. To communicate our messages clearly and accurately to others, we need to be skillful in both the nonverbal and the verbal means of expression and also in making the nonverbal and verbal agree with each other.

Certain social situations may dictate that the nonverbal and verbal channels need not be in agreement. When you ask another person "How are you?", the inevitable reply, no matter what the other person's actual physical or mental condition really is, will be "Fine" unless, of course, the person is a very close associate and you have asked the question with deep concern or interest reflected in your vocal tone. We have many such verbal formulas that we use in a variety of situations: "It's a pleasure to meet you," "The pleasure is mine," "So glad you could come," "It's nice to be here," "You look nice," "That was a good speech," "Thank you so much, we had a wonderful time," "You will come again, won't you?" "See you later," "Take care." The list could be nearly endless. Such responses fill a need. They often serve as an acknowledgment of another person. They might provide a brief introduction for a more extended relationship. They often serve to terminate an encounter and let all people know "That is all there is; there isn't any more!" even though the literal content of the verbal message is often meaningless or actually false.

CULTURE AND THE NONVERBAL

Much of our nonverbal behavior is learned from childhood, passed on to us by our parents and others with whom we associate. Through the process of growing up in a particular society we adopt the traits, mannerisms, and activities of our societal group. The ways of living that are passed on to succeeding generations are known as a society's *culture*; they are a major factor in why people communicate as they do. A society, however, also contains subunits or *subcultures*. Although we may manifest the traits of the larger unit, smaller groups with which we associate become more specific frames of reference for certain ways of communicating.

An individual's membership in a youth subculture, the radical right, a black subculture, an ethnic subculture, the WASP middle class, the anarchistic left, or the "jet set" is communicated to others nonverbally by the cues that we have discussed in this chapter. Members of the gay liberation, for instance, which is a subculture that includes homosexuals who are committed to civil rights for gay people, have special ways of dressing, special vocabulary, and even special mannerisms which enable members of the subculture not only to identify each other but also to communicate with each other both verbally and nonverbally. Such systems of communication provide rewards for those within the subculture because using common terms and experiences to interact with each other is gratifying.

In most communication situations you have at least some control over your body movement, voice, and use of objects, but you do not ordinarily think of controlling cultural aspects. The various pressures to conformity that a culture imposes on you exert a great deal of influence on your behavior; those elements of your culture that are revealed to others are permanent and inseparable, for the most part. Changing or controlling communication behavior that is culturally determined is extremely difficult. It is useful, however, to become more aware of those behaviors which are a result of social training, especially when one is involved in intercultural communication. Nonverbal behavior is most noticeably affected by culture with respect to the way we control space, time, eye contact, touch, gesture, and voice.

Space

When you talk with another person, about how far away from that person do you stand? Notice that it is usually about an arm's length apart. The space is not consciously controlled every time you speak with someone because the appropriate distance is determined by your culture. In some cultures, the accepted distance between two people engaged in communication is smaller. In our country we tend to interpret distances between people that are smaller than an arm's length as reflecting a love bond between the people or at least a close relationship. Two people communicating close together may even be sharing a "big, dark secret."

Test the theory that an arm's length apart is the general, acceptable body space in which most Americans operate most comfortably by slowly reducing the distance between you and another person with whom you are talking. You will find that the other person will unconsciously withdraw to find the acceptable distance. Remember that in our culture, moving in on someone is likely to be interpreted as being pushy or overbearing. You are "coming on too strong!" If you move away slightly, your behavior may be interpreted in our culture as avoidance or concealment. You do not like the other person; you are avoiding or hiding something.

Time

The use of time varies between cultures as well. In our culture we tend to leave few pauses between our statements as we talk to others interpersonally. To leave a pause is a sign to another person that it is time for him or her to interject a comment. In other cultures, the length of pauses between statements is often greater; thus, a person from the United States is likely to interject more comments into a conversation with someone from another culture and to be perceived as overbearing as a result.

Time affects communication between cultures in other ways. A person from the United States does not like to be kept waiting. Often, five minutes is enough to make one edgy whereas ten minutes drives some Americans up the wall. Anyone who keeps us waiting, according to our cultural standard, shows no concern for us and treats us with contempt. But in some other countries, keeping a person waiting is one method by which influence or importance are indicated. The social codes of a culture often dictate how we are supposed to regulate our time. Although the use of time varies among various subcultures of American society, everyone has a pattern and that pattern is understood by most people with whom one associates. Violation of the pattern to which your group conforms may mean that other members will look upon you unfavorably.

Eye Contact

Eye contact is also governed by culture. In Pakistan it can be insulting to a woman if a man looks her directly in the eye. A woman who ascribes to the traditional customs still wears veils covering all or part of her face so that a man cannot cast his eyes upon her. An American who was to receive an award for outstanding performance in tennis in Thailand was instructed not to look the Queen directly in the eye as he received his award. Such an act would have been insulting. In the United States we communicate with others directly eye to eye, but in Nigeria prolonged eye contact is disrespectful. Not to look another directly in the eye in our culture may mean that you are not telling the truth. It may also mean that you are not interested in the other person or that you are shy. These are learned responses, just as when a man looks a woman directly in the eye for a long period of time, thus communicating to her, "I am interested in you. How about it?"

Touch

Touch, too, is heavily influenced by culture. In Southeast Asia, parts of Africa, and in some Arab states one often finds men holding hands.

This behavior has no sexual overtones at all in these cultures. You have probably seen leaders of the Soviet Union hugging and embracing each other when they meet and yet you would undoubtedly find it peculiar if you turned on your television set and saw the President of the United States hugging and embracing the Vice-President upon his return from a foreign country.

In some foreign countries, it is still not permissible for a man to have any physical contact with a woman before marriage. Holding hands in public in those countries might be taken as a contemptuous affront of one family to the other. Our culture also regulates touching behavior between unmarried couples to a certain degree. During the early stages of dating, there are definite and understood standards of behavior which vary according to the community and the age of the couple. A man who wishes to go beyond a mere kiss on an early date might be regarded as fast or as a wolf. Under certain circumstances, however, a woman may touch a man without generating the same kind of response. When standing next to him, for instance, she might touch the man lightly on the upper arm to indicate that she likes him or would like to date him.

Gesture

Many gestures are behaviors which are absorbed through cultural influences, and often we do not think much about them. In Pakistan, the gesture we use to wave "Good-bye"—the up and down motion of the palm—is used to beckon others to come. In Ethiopia, people put one finger to their lips to gesture for silence to a child but four fingers for an adult. To use one finger for an adult would be disrespectful, just as shaking an index finger from side to side to an adult in the United States would be disrespectful. Certain African groups point with an outstretched lower lip; they consider pointing with the index finger, as we do, rather crude. In Greece the gesture we use to signify "Stop!" is used nonverbally to curse another motorist. In Southern India, people shake their heads back and forth to mean *yes*. These are gestures we learn from childhood, and it is likely that most of us would not give their use a second thought no matter where we were.

Voice

Voice varies from country to country, perhaps, more than it does from one segment of a country to another. But it is important to realize that the area of the country you are brought up in could determine your chances for entering certain professions. A news reporter with a strong Boston or Brooklyn accent would probably not be acceptable as a network newscaster whose voice would be broadcast throughout the country. Southern accents, the midwestern twang, the western drawl, and other regional influences are cultural elements over which many of us have little control. We are likely never to realize the extent of our accent or peculiarity unless we travel to or are in a position to meet people from other regions. An Englishman would likely be ruled out as a network news announcer even more quickly than one with a regional accent; however, he would probably have more opportunities as an actor or a talk-show host in our country, depending upon the extent of his accent.

SUMMARY

Nonverbal communication is extremely important to the total communicative act no matter what the context is. More than 90 percent of the social meaning of a communication may be carried by nonverbal elements. These elements include space, time, body movements, voice, and the choice and use of objects. Social meaning is also carried by a cultural component, and cues regarding one's culture are reflected through most all the other elements. One's culture provides an umbrella under which all other nonverbal factors are found.

When we communicate with others we should attempt to integrate the nonverbal elements so that they provide us with support and reinforcement for the words we speak and for the attitudes and emotions we wish to convey. When we view the communication of others, we must be aware of the nonverbal as well as the verbal elements and attempt to analyze each as they relate to each other. They work together to create a total picture—we cannot overlook the forest because of the impressiveness of the individual trees, and yet, since so much nonverbal communication flows at such a low level of awareness for both the communicator and the receiver, we must not overlook the individual trees that make up the forest.

What we communicate nonverbally in a situation like the classroom is often a direct result of what we have communicated nonverbally all of our lives. Nonverbal elements are so much a part of us that it may be more important in communicating with others to be aware of the nonverbal elements than of the verbal ones. Often our nonverbal cues yield information about the depths of our personality; it is the means we and others use in a communication setting to "read between the lines." As we increase our understanding of the roles and functions of nonverbal communication, both as a sender of communications and as a listener of communications, we will increase our capacity to influence and to adjust to our surroundings. The old saying "What you are speaks so loud I cannot hear what you say" points to the importance of nonverbal communication in our lives.

FURTHER READING

Ralph Ellison, *Invisible Man*. New York: Vintage Books, 1972.
This is an extraordinary and exciting novel about what happens to a man when people look at him but do not see him. The hero is black, and as the story of his life unfolds, you experience how a person's race can make him invisible. The author dramatically demonstrates how one aspect of a person's nonverbal communication can distort both his concept of self and all of his relationships with others.

Bernard Gunther, *Sense Relaxation Below Your Mind*. New York: Collier Books, 1968.
This paperback concentrates on the expansion of consciousness by getting you in touch with a deep reality of your being. Beautifully illustrated with many photographs, this book gives explicit directions and suggestions for developing sensory awareness through the nonverbal communication medium of touch—one area that is seldom discussed or fully experienced by most people.

Edward T. Hall, *The Hidden Dimension*. Garden City, New York: Anchor Books, 1969.
In this paperback book, the author deals with spatial experience as it is molded by culture. The "hidden dimension" is man's use of space, and the book is very convincing in presenting the idea that virtually everything a person is and does is associated with the experience of space. This is an immensely interesting and exciting book full of examples and illustrations that develop the concepts of social and personal space and how they are perceived.

————, *The Silent Language*. New York: Fawcett, 1959.
This is a paperback book that examines the cultural component of nonverbal communication, especially how American behavior differs

from that of people in other cultures. The author is an anthropologist and uses numerous examples and interesting anecdotes to examine the human world of nonverbal communication that occurs around you. This book will stimulate you to make your own observations and analysis of the nonverbal behavior of others.

4
Verbal Communication

Think, for a moment, about the last time you communicated something in words to someone else. Was it just a minute ago when you told a friend that you had to study now? Was it at dinner when you asked someone to pass the salt? Was it when you asked someone in your last class what the reading assignment was? Whatever the situation, you did not merely utter words. The listener with whom you communicated received meaning through all of the various features of your communication, verbal and nonverbal, not only from the words you uttered. In this chapter, we will examine the use of words; it is essential, however, to remember that the significance of words as vehicles of meaning is always related to nonverbal elements in actual speech. Sarah Bernhardt, the French actress, is known to have moved audiences to tears or laughter, fear or anger, contentment or anxiety by speaking names drawn at random from a telephone book—an example of the insignificance of words when isolated from other elements of communication.

You do not speak meaning; you speak *to convey* meaning. Your verbal message is made up of words that you choose and arrange in a specific way in order to convey the part of your message that is transmitted in the verbal channel. You express your message, your meaning, in this combination of words with a particular intention in mind—having that message received and understood by the listener. The message that results, that is conveyed by the words, carries meaning to the listener. It is expressed in the language of the communicator, which is made up of units referred to as sentences, clauses, and phrases. Although these units and their subunits—words—will be the focus of this chapter, it should be kept in mind that meaning does not lie in the language but in the minds of the communicator and the listener.

Referring to the model described in the introduction, note that verbal communication is part of the message that crosses the channel. The intent of the message originates in the source, the communicator, and the meaning is perceived by the receiver, the listener. A portion of this chapter will treat the nature of the verbal units—words—that cross the channel. Most of this chapter, however, is concerned with the language behavior of communicators and listeners because to divorce words from how they are spoken and how they are heard is to look at them in isolation—and words are never so isolated in oral communication. It is impossible, for this reason, to discuss language behavior without discussing the people who are using the language. This applies equally to the communicator and to the listener. If you speak in perfect French to someone who does not understand the French language, you will not be understood, no matter how clear your words are. Successful communication depends upon the completion of the transaction, and much of our emphasis here will be on the two ends of the communication chain: the source and the receiver.

Part of the communicator's strength in conveying thoughts and emotions is derived from his or her language. In this chapter, we will first discuss language and style to provide a broad base for understanding the importance of language choices in determining your verbal style and the importance of style in how you are received or accepted by others. With this foundation, we will then examine how words work. Following this section, our focus will broaden to include the relationships between language and meaning and some of the issues involved in making language choices. Finally, we will briefly note several ways you can improve your style and language. An understanding of language will help you to express what you really want to say, honestly, clearly, and straightforwardly. When messages are misunderstood or when a communication has no effect on the listener, it is likely that the language of the communicator is, in part, at fault. The grandiloquent style of early orators has yielded to a modern communicative style that is direct, efficient, and vigorous. Communication that does not reveal these characteristics in the verbal channel is likely to be turned off no matter how skillful it is in other ways. Some understanding of language is therefore necessary to every other chapter in this book in which oral communication comes into play.

STYLE: YOUR VERBAL IMAGE

The words that you use are determined by all of your past experiences, by everything in your individual history. You learn words to express thoughts, and thought and language develop together. The way you think and the way you talk are unique; they form a distinctive pattern. In a sense, you *are* what you say because language is the chief means for most of us to convey our thought. Neither language nor thought can be viewed in isolation. They are related, constantly growing. Together, they determine your verbal style.

Style is the result of the way you select and arrange words and sentences. Everyone chooses different words to express his or her thoughts, and every individual has his or her own personal verbal style. Styles do not just differ among people; each person also uses different styles to suit the situation. The minister uses one style in the pulpit and another one in speaking to his family. The child uses one style on the playground and another one in school when talking to teachers. Actors have been known to use a different style among friends than among admirers; among admirers, they often try to manifest some of the stylistic qualities with which they have been identified on the stage or on film.

Inadequate style can destroy all the other good qualities a communicator possesses. A man who is skillful in remembering stories may be a very bad storyteller because he has difficulty in choosing words and in selecting and arranging sentences; thus, his poor style distracts so much from the stories that others do not enjoy listening. A woman who is very logical, or who has a keen sense for the arrangement of ideas as she speaks, may similarly lose this effectiveness in the expression of her ideas because her vocabulary is too complex to be understood. Even an individual whom we might be tempted to label glib—a person who is ready and fluent in conversation—may very well be unacceptable to others as a communicator because of a verbal style in which repetition is overused. Style, because of its power and influence over us, becomes as important to the acceptance of our ideas as do all the other aspects of communication. So what if we have experience; so what if we have information; so what if the occasion is perfect; so what, too, if we have a listener ripe for our message—if our style annoys, distracts, or confuses our listener, what we have to say is never received.

Impressions of personality often are related to verbal style. When you characterize a person as formal and aloof, part of that characterization probably results from the way that person talks. We sometimes "type" others as crude, colloquial, vulgar, or trite because of their verbal style. Since your style partially determines whether others will accept or reject you as a person, it will also determine how others receive your messages. Style, because of its importance, can cause you to influence one person's thinking about you, to win the friendship of another, to lose the respect of a neighbor, to win a sale, or to sway a teacher.

A young man in a pick-up truck stopped next to a group of college students at a prominent New England college and said to them, "Hey, ya'll, kin ya point out how a fella' kin geet to tha main bildin' 'round cheer?" Confused for a moment, the students decided he meant the administration building and pointed out the direction. "Thanks a heap, ya'll" they heard as the man departed. The looks and the comments of the students in the group following his departure revealed their amused contempt. The stranger's verbal style had made a very definite impression. We generally think less of a person who uses poor grammar. We show scorn for a legislator who cannot make a reasonably fluent explanation of a policy that he is advocating. We wince when we hear an actress we have admired in films show a very poor command of the English language on a late-night talk show. On the other hand, an adolescent boy who uses words far above his level of sophistication gains our surprise and admiration. It is certainly true that we are *not* only what we say; however, most people respond to what we say as if we were. Poor style in speaking is one of the biggest detriments to finding oneself accepted as a person in many circles, especially among the educated and those who consider themselves to be intellectually sophisticated.

Dialect

Our style of speaking is reflected in the dialect we use. A *dialect* is the one of various ways that people speak a language. There are a wide variety of dialects used in American English. Some dialects are spoken in particular regions such as Philadelphia, Boston, or the South. Other dialects are used by particular groups of people; blacks, Puerto Ricans, Indians, Hawaiians, and Japanese and Chinese Americans all have dialects within their cultural groups.

Most of our reactions to dialects reflect our feelings about the persons who use them. If we like the South, we may consider a Southern dialect charming; if we dislike the South, we consider it unpleasant. Few people considered John F. Kennedy's Boston dialect unacceptable but generations of teachers have tried to eliminate black dialect in schoolchildren.

A dialect, in itself, is not an inferior form of speech; it is merely a nonstandard form. Many dialects provide identity and unity within a cultural group, giving group members a way to express their ideas in a language and style that is unique to them. Because nonstandard speech is almost universally condemned in our educational system, however, there is a problem. Using a dialect which is essential to group identity may label the speaker as uneducated or uncultured if he or she uses it outside of the group.

Thus, every speaker who uses a dialect must make decisions about where and when to use it, and people who do not have a command of the standard dialect may find themselves quite handicapped in certain social situations and professions. If you want to make a career as an actor, actress, or television newscaster, you must obviously be able to speak standard American English when it becomes necessary.

Ideally, all people should stop stereotyping others because of their dialects. America has always been a melting-pot nation, and dialects give variety and color to American speech. If all dialects were eliminated and we all spoke standard American English, our language would be poorer and certainly more bland than it is today.

Language as Power

Because of its importance, effective verbal style acts as proof. When you speak to another person, your word choices reflect how familiar you are with what you are talking about and how much knowledge you have. When you select facts, examples, and opinions to support what you are saying, the power and the effect of that material will often be determined by your language. If you want what you say to make a vivid and lasting impression, your language choices will be important; otherwise what you say may be forgotten almost immediately. When a mother says to her child, "I don't *ever* want to see you do that again" after citing a number of examples of that particular behavior, she wants the child to remember that statement as a lesson for the future. When you tell your roommate, after several cases of torn, lost, and unwashed clothing,

"Never wear my clothes again!" you want your language to give support to your frustration. Your choice of language will help to give a lasting impression.

Effective style can also help your communication to hold attention and interest. Your style—the manner in which you express and relate ideas—can be interesting of and by itself. A distinctive and unique style is enjoyable to listen to; it is appreciated. Our fast-paced world has evolved an efficient, streamlined, get-things-done-fast style of communication. Some of the characteristics of the flamboyant, adorned, flowery language of our predecessors has been lost. Precision and vividness in verbal style are still prized, however, and success in many areas of life requires that a person be articulate and well-spoken.

HOW WORDS WORK

When you use a word orally, you are vocally representing a thing—whether that thing is a physical object like your biology textbook or an abstract concept like peace. The word is a *symbol*; it stands for the object or concept that it names. This is what distinguishes a word from a random sound. The sounds which are represented in our language by the letters *c-a-t* make up a word because we have agreed that these sounds will stand for a particular domestic animal. The sounds represented by the letters *z-a-t* do not make up a word in our language because these sounds do not stand for anything.

When you learn a language, whether it is your native tongue or a foreign one, one thing you have to learn is what the words stand for in that language; that is, you have to know the vocabulary. The other thing you need to know to use any language is how to put the words together to make clauses and sentences which express relationships among the words; this is the grammar of a language. Vocabulary and grammar are different in every language so that, for example, Spanish-speaking people use the sound *gato* to stand for what the English call *cat,* and in Spanish the verb is often at the end of the sentence while in English it usually comes near the beginning.

When you say that another person understands your language, what you mean is that he knows what your words stand for and how to put the words together to express ideas and relationships. You both have approximately the same thing in your heads for the verbal sound that is being made. Each of you has learned the connection between the sound and the thing, and each of you can use the sound to stand for it.

Notice, however, that what you have in your head for an object or a concept is never exactly what any other person has in his or her head, because each individual has different experiences. Your notion of what *cat* means comes from all of the cats you have ever known, read about, seen on television, heard others talk about, and so on. This *cat* is unique to you, but you can use the sound to communicate to someone else because cats have general qualities that are common and recognized by the other person from all of his or her experiences of cats. The fact that language works at all means, therefore, that those with whom you speak have a certain number of experiences that are similar to your own. If this were not true, the other person simply would not know what you were talking about!

Sometimes we assume that others know what we are talking about when, in fact, they have very little common experience with us. When you say that you *love* another person, for example, you use a word which stands for your experiences in being loved and in loving. Since these experiences, and their interpretation, vary a great deal from person to person, someone else may mean something very different when he or she says that word. The meanings of words change as our experiences broaden, as well. A twelve-year-old girl who says she is in love is expressing a very different range of experiences than a woman of twenty-five who says the same thing.

Words can be very easy to understand, or they may be very difficult. Distortions and misunderstandings often occur because people assume that everyone has the same thing in his head for a particular word. To you, *music* may be the latest folk-rock record released whereas *music*, to your parents, may mean a Strauss waltz or a popular song interpreted by Mantovani. To some, *vacation* means camping in a remote spot in some forest and roughing it; to others it means calling ahead and reserving rooms at Holiday Inns. Just as we have various reactions to things, we also have various reactions to words—the symbolic representations of those things.

Often, in our use of words, we simply do not say what we intend to say. You have undoubtedly caught yourself replying, "No, that's not what I meant" or "I know what I mean, but I just can't say it." The problem of not using words clearly and precisely is a common one. We do not select the "right" words; we omit words; we say too much; we are vague; we are ambiguous; we jumble our words. Difficulties in verbal communication occur for several reasons: it may be that you are not sure of what you want to say; perhaps you do not have the verbal skill to express your message in the best words. Often, however, the communicator has difficulty expressing his or her thought because he or she is not paying enough attention to the listener.

Who Are You Talking To?

When you seek a specific response from a listener, your words have to be within the other person's experience. This entails a fundamental principle that underlies many other parts of this book—the principle of audience analysis. The communicator must have *some* knowledge of the audience to know that there is a common core of meaning; without a common core, it is impossible for two people to communicate. The more the communicator knows about the listener, the better he or she can select clear and precise words.

Words are the conveyors of meaning—the means by which meaning is transferred from one person to another. The desire of the communicator is to have meaning occur in another person in response to a specific stimulus—the words which he or she uses. This requires flexibility in word use. The communicator cannot use the same words to communicate a similar idea to two very different people. As hearers change, so must words. You may have to sacrifice some of your choicest phrases, you may have to discard some of the trivial details, or you may have to give up your highly technical and professional vocabulary in order to communicate with a particular listener. *Discourse*—the words you choose to use—should be designed for the hearer. In conveying ideas to your parents, you generally avoid most of the slang and colloquial terms that you would likely use in talking to another student. You know your listeners well—through years of analysis—and you alter your words accordingly. Change the listeners and the words must also change.

Speaking Is Not Writing

Words also work differently when you speak than when you write. On most of the topics about which you normally talk, you use a vocabulary of 500-800 words. When you write, your vocabulary is considerably larger. When you read, it is larger still. The average high-school freshman has a general working vocabulary of 8,000 words whereas the average adult has a vocabulary ranging around 80,000 words. Obviously, the larger your working vocabulary, the more likely you will have the right word at the right time and for the right person.

Vocabulary size is not the only difference between spoken language and written language. Spoken language is usually more personal than written language because the communicator appears as a person before the listener. The communicator uses more personal pronouns such as *I, we, our,* and *you* in his communication. Because the communication exists between specific people—as opposed to a writer and his rather amorphous audience—the oral communicator is more direct, adapting his or her ideas to a specific listener. This directness often results in the speaker using more imperative, exclamatory, and interrogative sentences than the writer. Directness is increased by the possibility that the communicator can adapt to feedback—the reaction he or she gains in talking to another person. The writer does not have this advantage. Thus, if the oral communicator chooses imprecise words, they can be adjusted when feedback—misunderstanding in this case—occurs. In oral discourse the communicator and listener can make use of both visual and auditory stimuli in communicating, and in providing feedback, whereas the writer and the reader are limited to the visual stimuli printed on a page.

The writer has more time for choosing words, for phrasing sentences, and for checking construction. Because of this increased time, because of the receiver's greater reading vocabulary, and because of the possibility of the reader rereading the material, the writer can deal with more complex and difficult ideas. The speaker, in contrast, will use short sentences with greater variety of sentence length. In addition, and partly because of the pressures of time in creating messages spontaneously, the speaker will use contractions, sentence fragments, and slang.

Perhaps the greatest difference in how words work in speaking as opposed to how they work in writing is a result of the meaning that is transferred in speaking just because it involves living, breathing, reacting organisms. In writing, part of the meaning is lost because of the absence of the communicator's immediate presence. Even if the words used are exactly the same in writing and in speaking, the meaning will surely be different.

Words work best in the oral communication process if they are kept relatively simple. It is more important for communication to be instantly intelligible than for you to strive to use a large vocabulary. The listener has a limited amount of mental energy available; it is important that this energy be expended on apprehending the ideas rather than in trying to understand the words or the language construction. You should not insult the intelligence of a listener, but you should provide a stimulus—language—that is immediately understandable. This may involve building up a greater reserve of words from which to draw as well as doing a better job of drawing from an already existent pool of words.

MEANINGS ARE IN PEOPLE

For *meaning* to occur in the receiver, that is, for the receiver to understand what the source intends, the source should have something definite in mind. The more general the idea or impression the communicator wishes to convey, the more likely that catch-all words or words that are hazy, vague, or ambiguous will be used. *Understanding* is the core of meaning, and understanding is a two-way process; that is, the source is responsible for clearly presenting the idea and the receiver is responsible for trying to understand it accurately. Meanings are in people, not in words.

Even though an idea is clearly presented, it may still be misinterpreted. Meanings develop throughout our lives. From earliest childhood we build up a complex set of meanings from the associations and connections we make. Since each person grows up in his or her own personal world, it is easy to see why meanings differ; it is easy to see why a communicator who thought he or she was being clear might not have been able to effect an accurate transfer of meaning.

One example of how misinterpretation occurs is in communication across the "generation gap." The world of a parent or another adult is different from the world of a child or student. Communication often breaks down between parent and child because their development of the sets which establish meaning are so different. Their experiences are different and so are their values, opportunities, and vocabularies. As long as the person with whom we are communicating has values that approximate our values for the words we use, the message we transmit will stimulate a meaning in the other person that is similar to what we intend. The values of the parent often do not approximate the values of the child; thus, the message transmitted by either one does not stimulate a similar meaning for the other.

New meanings are continually created in all of us as we change our ideas, our feelings, and our activities. As we think, read, travel, contact others, and experience life, we alter the associations and the connections that make up our set of meanings. The word *ghetto* is likely to mean something quite different to a black person who has experienced ghetto life and a white person who has never been near a ghetto. The white person's understanding of the word would change some if he or she read Claude Brown's *Manchild in the Promised Land*.[1] If the white person

---

1 Claude Brown, *Manchild in the Promised Land* (New York: New American Library, 1965).

were to travel to a ghetto, further changes in his or her understanding of the word would probably occur. As he or she talked with others there, further changes might take place, and if he or she had the opportunity to live there for a while—experiencing ghetto life—even more changes might be effected. Talking to this person before, during, and after such a series of experiences would undobutedly reveal that his or her meaning for *ghetto* changed a great deal as a result of these experiences. As the white person's understanding of what ghetto life means increased, he or she would become more and more likely to be able to exchange meaningful messages with a black person who had experienced ghetto life.

There is still another reason why accurate meaning may not be transferred between two people. As we noted in Chapter 2, Interpersonal Communication, listeners often perceive messages selectively. A listener tends to filter the messages he hears according to his needs, expectations, attitudes, and prior knowledge. Two neighbors were discussing the grand opening of a local supermarket. Early in the conversation, the woman who had actually been to the store mentioned the number of "free" items available. Because of the other woman's concern over finances and the rise in prices, nothing her neighbor said after the mention of these "free" items was heard; anything that could be gotten free was a deal, even though the woman who had visited the store mentioned that she had had to wait thirty minutes to get into the store, had to push through crowds and crowds of people, had to wait while clerks restocked ravaged shelves, and had to stand in long check-out lines. In a way, the neighbor who heard about the free items created her own message. She filtered out the hardship part of the source's message and reconstructed what she heard in accordance with her personal predisposition—the desire to attain something for nothing. She did not hear about the tremendous expenditure of time, energy, and frustration that getting the "free" items would entail. In a similar manner we all hear parts of a communication that agree with our feelings and are likely to filter out other parts with which we do not agree.

Levels of Meaning

There are different kinds of meaning, as well, and misunderstanding can occur on any of the various levels. Hubert G. Alexander discusses four distinct meaning levels in *Meaning in Language*.[2] There is, first,

---

2 Hubert G. Alexander, *Meaning in Language* (Glenview, Illinois: Scott, Foresman, 1969), pp. 5–13.

meaning as the communicator intends it, or *intentional meaning*. Intentional meaning is what is in the communicator's head before he or she says anything. *Content meaning* comes from the content of the message itself, as it is expressed. The meaning that comes from our signs and symbols—including language—is called *significative meaning*. Finally, there is *interpreted meaning*, the meaning that happens in the receiver's head when he or she hears the message. Although each of the four kinds of meaning will be discussed briefly here, it should be clear to the reader that all are part of a simultaneous and continuous process.

Intentional Meaning The intention to express ourselves to others is one of the essential facts of living; there is a basic need to communicate. The intention to convey a message encompasses the desire to say something, the perception of someone else to whom you wish to send the message, and considerations about the language with which the message will be expressed. All three of these elements are included in the communicator's intention.

Misunderstanding can originate at the intentional stage if the communicator is unclear about any of the three elements: if you are confused or unclear about the idea you want to express, if you do not know the person with whom you are trying to speak, or if you can't find the right words to say what you mean, the message is liable to be misunderstood because it was not effectively prepared. The clearer you can be about your intention, the more likely it is that you will send a message that will be received with good fidelity.

Content Meaning The content meaning of your communication consists of the ideas and feelings you communicate as they are actually expressed in the message. When any verbal communication is attempted, more is conveyed than the things for which the words stand. Both you and your listener will also have feelings and sensations attached to the ideas. Sometimes the message is primarily about feeling; at other times, the intention of the communicator is to be quite objective, to express very few of his or her own feelings in the message. The emotional associations of both the speaker and the listener will, however, color the content of the message, no matter how objective it is intended to be.

The feelings associated with an idea may be the most interesting part of the message; however, feelings are a primary cause for misunderstanding. Individual emotions differ widely; feelings are subject to many different influences, and they are often beyond our immediate control. The feelings that a speaker associates with an idea may prevent him from expressing that idea clearly. They may also distract from the objective part of the message. In the listener, a particular emotional association may lead him or her to receive the message with his or her own extraneous feelings laid over the speaker's intention. Ideas about which the listener has strong negative feelings or associations may be completely blocked by those feelings.

Significative Meaning The chief function of the symbols of our language is to express meaning. We speak of significative, or verbal, meaning as that part of the communication that operates on the verbal channel; thus, significative meaning excludes nonverbal communication. The meaning of a verbal communication depends upon how the language is interpreted, and some words are usually interpreted with greater fidelity than others. A word that stands for a fairly concrete and emotionally neutral thing—like the word *mailbox*—carries the potential to be interpreted with good fidelity because most people respond primarily to its *denotative meaning,* the dictionary-definition meaning which designates the thing for which the word stands. Other words stand for concepts about which most people have strong feelings or extensive associations of a personal, individual nature; words like *freedom* or *moral* have the potential to be misunderstood because they carry a lot of *connotative meaning,* the feelings or associations that we have for a thing.

When there is a fairly direct relationship between the word and the object that it stands for, it is more likely that the significative meaning will be clear. Conversely, when the speaker uses words with strong connotative meanings, there is a good chance that misunderstandings will occur. This is simply to say that it is easier to be sure that you will be understood when you talk about mailboxes than when you talk about morals. We do not mean to suggest, however, that the best conversations are those which are limited to the mailbox level! Some of our most important messages have to do with ideas that have a great deal of connotation; they are important precisely because we feel strongly about them. It is well to remember, however, that when what you say has strong emotional feelings attached to it, you are more likely to be misunderstood.

Because significative meanings are dependent upon the way the words are interpreted, there is a strong likelihood that misunderstanding will occur at this stage. In addition to problems raised by the emotional charge on some words, interpreting what another person means by the words he uses is difficult for several other reasons. The meanings of verbal symbols are not fixed. Many words are subject to extremely short fads of meaning. Slang and jargon operate this way. Words like *hassle, rap, rip-off, trucking,* and *uptight,* to name but a few, have come into being within the last few years. Other words tend to change their meaning over time. Words like *bread, fuzz, pad, swinger,* the *pill,* and *trip* have taken on new meanings. The meanings of words also change quickly according to the context in which they are used. Words like *love, liberated, conservative, religion,* and *sensitivity* have different meanings in different contexts. Thus, one can see how fidelity of understanding can be affected at this stage.

Interpreted Meaning Interpretation becomes quick and automatic once you learn the fundamentals of a language. You are no longer even aware of the fact that you are interpreting—fitting meanings to words as quickly as they come to you. You make connections with previous experiences and prior knowledge in order to identify words, and you tend to assume that your meanings for those words are identical to those of the communicator who spoke them. As we have seen, this is never literally so, and misunderstanding can occur in the interpreted meaning as well as in any other.

In addition to the inevitable differences between the experiences of the listener and the experiences of the speaker, there are other factors which cause misunderstanding at this stage. A receiver, for example, who cannot identify the sounds he or she hears as symbols that have meaning will be unable to receive the message. Listening to Shakespearian lines delivered by a great actor would have little or no meaning for most of us if the actor were an Israeli speaking in Hebrew. Words may be garbled when they are received because the listener is inattentive or distracted by outside noise. Different backgrounds and differences in frames of reference between the source and the receiver can also cause errors in interpretation.

The responsibility for fidelity in communication rests with both the speaker and the listener since misunderstanding can be the result of failure at either end of the transaction. Whenever misunderstanding occurs in the process of spoken communication, both people can react to clear up the misunderstanding. Sometimes the speaker can correct misinterpretation by giving a secondary interpretation. He or she can repeat the point or elaborate upon it by giving further instances and examples. The speaker could restate his or her idea, phrasing the same idea in a different way by using different words. Restating an idea means approaching it from different avenues, showing it to your receiver in varying perspectives. The effective communicator will make use of these devices during every communication. In addition to using these methods, the communicator might also strive to make better language choices, following the suggestions in the next section.

The most important thing the listener can do is to respond to the message that he or she does not understand. A speaker can work to correct misunderstanding only if he or she realizes that the message has not been received. Sometimes the listener can also help the speaker to understand what is causing the lack of fidelity in their communication; you can say, "I can't hear you" or "I think that you and I have very different meanings for that word."

LANGUAGE CHOICES

It is impossible to lay down strict rules to govern choices of language for all occasions and for all circumstances. There are probably as many different standards and systems as there are communicators and situations. The ancients used a classification system in discussing language choices that included unity, coherence, and emphasis. In this book, we will use a system that involves four qualities: clarity, energy, appropriateness, and vividness. There are other requirements that are undoubtedly important for certain times and for certain effects; however, the following seem to be relatively important in all verbal communication.

Clarity

The language you choose should be *clear*. There should be as little doubt as possible about the meaning of the words you use. Clarity results from the choice of precise and accurate words, simple words and sentences, and fairly short sentences. Modern language is crisp, condensed, and concise.

Clear language underlies almost anything else the communicator chooses to do. A communicator may want to show power, authority, or a dynamic impressiveness; or he or she may want to be subtle, to evoke images, or to produce beautiful phrases. No matter what the communicator wants to do with words, that effort will fail if the words are not clear because the listener will not understand what he or she is talking about. For an audience to be informed, to be persuaded, or even to be entertained, they must first understand. A receiver will not listen to double-talk for very long. Frustration caused by unclear language may cause him or her to turn off any further attempts to understand.

Energy

The term *energy* implies the choice of words that reflect drive, excitement, urgency, and forcefulness. Energy does not necessarily imply a great deal of volume; it can be conveyed with a whisper or with a shout. A child, for example, will often respond immediately to a parent's demand that he or she "Get over here right now" because of the words used, whether they are shouted or whispered.

Perhaps the best way to describe the use of energy in language is that it is compelling. That is, it compels a listener to respond with attention. Because of the speaker's energy, the listener will try to understand and will be receptive to the persuasion or information—not that he or she *will be* persuaded or informed; he or she will simply be more open to the message. Gaining and holding the attention of a receiver is, after all, almost half the battle of successfully informing or persuading.

Energetic language is active. It creates images. It evokes emotions. It is direct. An idea is energized by the type of language used to support it. A brilliant or beautiful thought can be reduced to impotency by inadequate language. Note the powerful command of an instructor: "These term-papers must be in my hands by next Monday, or you will lose 25 percent of your grade." Your response to this statement would, very likely, be different from your response to a statement like "Papers are due Monday." Forceful language that manifests a great deal of energy will simply tell your listener, "Hey, look, this is important! Listen to me!" Often, that is all you want—an ear for your ideas and an open mind, ready to receive.

Appropriateness

Language that is *appropriate* is suitable for the communicator, the listener, and the occasion. It fits the material and the ideas. What is proper or timely for one situation may be improper or untimely for another. The alert communicator makes the adaptations that are necessary. You use different language when you are talking to your little brother or sister and when you are talking to the instructor of one of your courses, even if the topic of the communication is essentially the same. Can you imagine a doctor, a lawyer, or a business executive talking to his or her small son in the same way he or she speaks to a professional colleague?

When you consider the various elements that might affect your choice of words as you strive to make it appropriate, think about the sex

of your listener, where he or she is from, his or her occupation, social and educational level, and age. All of these factors may have a bearing on whether the listener understands your message. Each of them may affect the language you choose when you speak to this particular individual.

Using language that your listener can comprehend facilitates both understanding and acceptance. When a listener feels that you speak his or her language, the listener is more willing to open up to you and to like you. Adapting your language to your speaker is not being "fake"; it is being smart! If you have several alternatives as far as the language you can use, why not use that which suits the situation best—the words that will further the ends which you seek? Why not try to promote trust?

The communicator is cautioned of one danger in attempting to select appropriate words: the possibility that he or she will misuse words. This can prove fatal to attempts to create trust. A speaker who does not make the appropriate adaptations might evoke annoyance or irritation. A student, for example, will be successful in speaking to a faculty member if he or she remains a student and does not try to imitate the faculty member's use of language. The psychological distance between the source and the receiver becomes greater when the source uses unnatural language in an attempt to imitate the listener's style.

Making appropriate language choices does not mean that you must say what social ritual requires instead of expressing what you feel. Saying only what you think you should say often leads to the use of such formulas as the "How-are-you?-I'm-fine" routine discussed in the chapter on nonverbal communication. The meaning of these words—except as mere acknowledgment of another person—has been lost because of their frequency of use. Although most people find such words "appropriate" in certain social situations, they are not meaningful messages when they provide a cloak of banality for deeper feelings. It is easy, especially at certain formal occasions such as commemorations of birth, graduation, marriage, and death, to follow the script of conventional comments and responses. It may be more appropriate, however, to create original dialogue that expresses personal and unique feelings.

Vividness

When your senses are aroused by the words of another person, it is very likely the other person is using vivid language. You are able to see, hear, feel, taste, or smell the images that the communicator is trying to create. You can smell the perfumed fragrance of the rose described by the avid gardener. You can feel the agony of the motorcyclist writhing in a pool of blood on the highway after being hit by a car. You can hear the distant music, feel the vibrations of humanity, and smell the reek of garbage of an outdoor rock festival that attracted thousands. Vivid language serves to direct and hold the attention of a listener to an idea.

To call up sensory impressions, emotions, and experiences in others, you can do several things. You can select words and phrases that sound like what they are—this is a technique called onomatopoeia. For example, one of the things that makes outdoor barbequing enjoyable is the *sizzle* of steaks on an open grill. Children are often afraid of a *howling* wind. Snakes *slither* through tall grass. *Sizzle, howl,* and *slither* are naturally suggestive words and, like many similar words, may be used for rhetorical effect—that is, to arouse meanings through their sounds. These words need not be bizarre, foreign, or esoteric; simple, common, everyday words serve this purpose very well.

Another way to arouse vivid meanings is to avoid overused words and expressions. People who depend on words and phrases like *you know, right on, no way,* and *sorry about that*—to name but a few— often strike a listener as plain and ordinary. Their messages do not stand out from the crowd. The person who wants to add vividness to his or her speaking should strive to combine words and phrases in new and original ways. This requires some verbal skill, but it is essentially a matter of seeing things with a fresh perspective, much as the poet does. You can avoid stereotyped responses to things by coming at them with a new attitude, an individual excitement. Try seeing what you look at everyday with new eyes, attaching a new phrase or word to what has seemed ordinary and mundane. Doing this will help you to break out of the prison formed by your old word and meaning categories.

You can also achieve vividness if you choose specific words and phrases. Avoid generalizing and taking language shortcuts. When you are specific, the listener will know exactly what is on your mind because you provide a clear image in precise language. Next time you express appreciation for an evening spent at someone's house, try to be specific. You could say, for example, "I enjoyed the roast beef dinner and listening to all your old records was great. You know, I really hated to leave." Such details are more vivid than just saying you had a "good time." They are more effective in getting the message across.

There are so many elements, characteristics, and standards of good language that it would be impossible for us to cover them in a single chapter. Perhaps the best way for you to learn about language is to become aware of it as it is spoken and written by others. Good language usage in writing is not the same as good language usage in speaking—but, if you begin to perceive all language choices with sensitive ears and eyes, you will become aware, by teaching yourself, of how you can use words more effectively.

IMPROVING YOUR VERBAL STYLE

Improving language usage and verbal style is the business of a lifetime; skill and sensitivity in verbal expression are developed over a period of time. We tend to take language for granted, but a person who wishes to improve his or her style *can* do something about it through conscious effort and practice. Improved style does not result from the memorization of formulas and rules; because your use of language is such a clear reflection of your self, the project of improvement will be continued throughout your life.

The following three suggestions have proved useful for communicators in trying to improve their verbal style. You can become actively involved in one or all of these during the normal course of everyday human interaction.

1) *Increase your vocabulary.* Since words surround you every day, they are readily accessible and easily observed. When you become more conscious of the words of the television advertiser and how he skillfully and subtly tries to sell his product, or of the politician and how he presents his ideas, or of the teacher and how she teaches a lesson, you are simply taking advantage of a situation already present and available.

When you hear a new word, strive to understand it from the *context* in which it is used—from the parts that precede or follow and are directly connected with it. Although you may not always be able to stop another person to ask what he or she means by a certain word, sometimes it is helpful to do so if you can. People sometimes use words incorrectly, of course, and contexts can be deceiving or misleading. As you build your vocabulary, consult the dictionary regularly for denotative meanings. When you hear a word that is unknown to you or when you hear a word used in an unfamiliar context, check its meaning. You can also develop sensitivity to the connotative meanings of words by listening for people's feelings as they are revealed in verbal expression and in nonverbal cues. This will help you to become more aware of the emotional level in the expression of others and of your own responses to connotations. Sometimes you can get in touch with a feeling in yourself or in someone else by listening for the feeling level in discourse.

Another way to build your vocabulary is by reading, remembering new words as you read, and looking up their meanings. When you are reading, just as when you are listening to your friends talk, try to be aware of new words—then try to fit them into your own conversation. A word that is not actually used will not be remembered for long.

If you increase your vocabulary, you will increase the possibility that you will be able to get your intended meaning across to your listener. The more words you have at your command, the more likely you can be accurate and precise. This does not mean that you should search for big words—short, familiar words are often the best. In increasing your vocabulary, then, you will enrich your conversation. The beneficial by-product of reading and listening critically with an eye toward building your vocabulary is the broadening of your thinking. Words are the building blocks of communication and you can form a foundation which will help to assure that a meaningful, intelligible, and expressive edifice will grow.

As an adjunct to building your vocabulary, note how the words you read and hear are used in combination. It is the combinations that make style effective or ineffective. Thus, you should not just examine the individual trees—the words—but the way the trees combine to make the forest—the sentences, phrases, and the ideas themselves. Thoughts are expressed in groups of words—seldom as words alone.

2) *Adapt your oral language.* As you talk to people, become conscious of them as particular people for whom you need to adapt your message. Note the situation in which your conversation is taking place and make those adaptations that are necessary. Also, note the topic you are discussing since it, too, can influence your choice of words. Do not assume that any old word or phrase or sentence will suffice. Do not allow the first word that comes into your head to be the first word off your tongue. Be aware of what you are saying. This added consciousness will increase your sensitivity to other people as well as your awareness of language choice and use.

Sometimes people confuse personal authenticity with inflexible language usage. "Telling it like it is" becomes an excuse for pouring out the first words that come into your head, a stream-of-consciousness that could be labeled "verbal diarrhea." Our feeling is that such language choices can reflect a kind of self-centered indulgence which says to your listener, "Never mind who you are; listen to me!" Adapting your language to the individual with whom you are talking is more likely to result in authentic exchange between you.

Being aware of the entire communication situation and being able to adapt your oral language to suit the situation are marks of the mature speaker in any communication setting. The same words are simply not useful to express the same idea as the people or the situation changes. By consciously trying to be flexible, you will go a long way in freeing yourself from that prison referred to earlier—the prison in which your limited vocabulary and habit hold you. By trying to be flexible, you will reach out to make use of the other words that already exist in your vocabulary but which you seldom use because you really do not have to.

3) *Practice*. There is no substitute for practice. Communicate with others as often as you have the opportunity and as often as you have something worthwhile to say. Be your own critic; that is, be sensitive to your own performance. We all talk, but most of us do not stop to reflect on both what we have said and how we have said it. Practice using your language, and your verbal style will improve.

SUMMARY

Each person's verbal style is distinctive and unique. It is acquired through individual experience. To become a master of style, you should make a study of language itself, noting the relationship of language to things, but you must also remember that words are never isolated from the people who use them.

The verbal style of the communicator determines how his or her message will be received. Impressions of personality are also often related to verbal image, as are judgments about a person's level of education. Dialect is a function of one's cultural background; it is not inferior, but nonstandard. A strong verbal style adds support to all of the other intentions of any message.

Words work to communicate when the speaker and the listener both know what the words stand for. Distortions and misunderstandings occur when we assume that everyone else has the same experiences, and therefore the same meanings for words, as we do.

Speaking and writing differ in that oral communication is more spontaneous, personal, and immediate than written communication. Our speaking vocabularies are smaller than either our reading or writing vocabularies, and spoken discourse is most effective when it is simple and direct.

The responsibility for achieving fidelity in oral communication rests with both the speaker and the listener. Our ability to send and receive clear meanings depends upon our experience, our frame of reference, our perception, and our knowledge of the person with whom we are communicating. There are four different levels of meaning—intentional, content, significative, and interpreted—and misunderstanding can occur at any of these levels.

It is impossible to lay down strict rules for making good language choices. Language that is clear, energetic, appropriate, and vivid will be most effective, however, and you can improve your language choices by making a conscious effort to become more aware of these qualities. Your efforts to communicate more accurately will surely make life easier—for yourself as well as for those around you.

Language is a dynamic process. Personal experiences and the experiences related to us by others modify our meanings for words. Thus, verbal communication is really just a stirring-up process, changing meanings within, between, and among people. It is a human process for it is the variable that distinguishes us from all other forms of animal life. It is also a personal process for language usage is unique to each individual and, thus, varies with each individual.

Language gives your experiences and feelings a form that can be understood by someone else. It is the vehicle by which the substance of human relations is carried on. Language brings ideas to life.

FURTHER READING

J. L. Aranguren, *Human Communication.* New York: McGraw-Hill, 1967.
The author of this paperback book is thorough and perceptive in his examination of modern communication systems, which includes discussions of art, sculpture, music, secular and religious rites, traffic urbanization, computer tape, and the village gossip. Although the book is easy to read and is illustrated with numerous pictures, it is designed for the more serious student because of the thoroughness and breadth with which language is treated.

Robert L. Benjamin, *Semantics and Language Analysis.* Indianapolis, Indiana: Bobbs-Merrill, 1970.
This brief paperback textbook investigates the operation of language as a coherent system; it is a study of "how language means." The author looks at instances of the effective communication of meaning as well as instances of failure in communication.

Ivor Brown, *Mind Your Language!* New York: Capricorn Books, 1962.
In this brief paperback, Brown takes the reader on a witty and en-

joyable journey through the linguistic tangles created by overworked adjectives, slang and dialect words, scientific and technical words, as well as clichés and vogue words. His ideas are useful for those interested in avoiding the pitfalls of language, and for those who are interested in developing their own natural style.

Roger Brown, *Words and Things: An Introduction to Language.* New York: The Free Press, 1958.

This appears to be the *War and Peace* of psycholinguistics! In this nearly 400-page paperback, Brown takes a behavioral-science approach to language. A broad range of topics including meaning, symbols, pathologies, and propaganda, to name but a few, are treated in a clear and easy presentation which depends on numerous studies for support.

S. I. Hayakawa, *Language in Thought and Action,* 3rd ed. New York: Harcourt Brace Jovanovich, 1972.

Here is a comprehensive examination of the relationships among language, thought, and behavior. Language and people's linguistic habits are examined as they reveal themselves in thinking, speaking, listening, reading, and writing. This paperback book is "must" reading for the serious language scholar and includes Applications sections that are useful and interesting extensions of the concepts in each chapter.

William Strunk, Jr. and E. B. White, *The Elements of Style.* New York: The Macmillan Company, 1959.

Although designed for the writer, speakers take note: for the brevity, the clarity, and the truth that lies in it, this little book is worth considering. It treats the fundamentals—the rules of usage and the principles of composition most commonly violated. It will make you more conscious of the words you use.

Frederick Williams, *Language and Speech: Introductory Perspectives.* Englewood Cliffs, New Jersey: Prentice-Hall, 1972.

The assumption underlying this book is that speech is essentially language performance. The author examines speech from acoustic, phonological, linguistic, psychological, and sociological perspectives in a study intended for the serious beginning student who wishes to become acquainted with some of the technical terminology and writing in the language-behavior area.

5

Public Speaking

Public speaking has been practiced for thousands of years. People have always made speeches and generations of authors have written books about the art of speech-making. More than two-thousand years ago, Aristotle wrote *Rhetoric*, a philosophical and practical book about speech which scholars still read and use. In more modern times, authors have written anywhere from twenty-five to fifty new books about speech/communication every year.

Public speaking has been regarded in a variety of different ways throughout the ages. Some have seen it as a useful art in that it is a means of social control. Others have argued that it is a fine art because speeches often offer beauty, permanence, and insight into human experience. In the twentieth century many see it as a science, and they use behavioral science methods to measure its impact and to determine why some speakers are more effective than others. Regardless of the approach, most authors and speakers agree that public speaking is necessary to democratic decision-making. A public speech still provides a setting for people to meet and talk about their problems, and it encourages people to unite and act.

Throughout history the function of public speaking has gone

through little change. The Greeks saw it as a means of persuasion just as twentieth-century politicians do. In this century, however, there have been changes in form. Now public speakers must compete with the technology of the mass media. In a country of instant communication, the long, leisurely speech is dead. An old-time minister thought nothing of a two-hour sermon, but if a modern minister tries to speak more than twenty minutes, his church membership will probably decline. An African politician can give a two-hour campaign speech and hold attention, but most American politicians find they are more effective with television spot announcements. Influenced by a constant barrage of commercials, we now expect all of our persuasive messages to be short and to the point.

Historically the study of speech has revolved around the interaction of the speaker with the audience. Now the new technology has given us an entirely new phenomenon to study—many modern speeches are delivered to an audience whom the speaker never sees, and the interaction is delayed, if it occurs at all. When the President addresses the nation, he does it in his office to the television cameras, and public reaction will not be received until long after the speech is over.

Public speaking is in a transitional period. We still have the speaker at the Lion's Club luncheon as well as the nationwide television address. These two kinds of speeches have many similarities. In this chapter we will examine the more traditional public speech since that is what most of us will deliver throughout our lives. Still we must keep in mind that the new technology is influencing public speaking. For example, some advertising tactics for getting attention and creating concise messages may be useful to us as public speakers. Therefore our speech-making becomes a combination of the old and the new.

THE PUBLIC-SPEAKING SITUATION

Interpersonal, small-group, and public-speaking situations all share the same communication components: source, message, receiver, and feedback. Within the public-speaking situation these components are more strictly defined than they are in most other communication settings. In public speaking, a single source plans and sends a message for the specific purpose of evoking a precise response from his or her audience. Although one or more of these elements, the single source, for example, may be present in interpersonal or small-group communication, they are all found in public speaking.

The source is almost always the only person who plans the message, and the source determines the desired response *before* the message is sent. Since the source is the only person who is speaking, he or she has a heavy communication responsibility for the message. Whether the message is accepted or rejected will depend on the communication strategy that the source uses. Impressions of the source (and therefore of the message) are based on prior knowledge of the source, the content of the message, and how the message is delivered.

The message also has certain characteristics in a public-speaking situation. It has a specific purpose, is prepared and structured, and is generally static and unchanging. The message, however, does not stand alone; it is closely identified with the source. You have probably used the phrase "consider the source," which means that we can discount the message because we don't like or respect the source. The phrase illustrates the fact that source and message are practically inseparable.

The audience is also different in the public-speaking situation. Generally audience members are not known to the source as individuals, and therefore the source relates to them as a group. When the speaker plans a message to affect them, he or she makes broad assumptions about the group. For instance, if the audience is predominately Republican, the source may assume that they will probably be conservative and plan the speech accordingly.

The feedback in public speaking is limited and specialized. If the audience approves of the speech, they may laugh or applaud; if they disapprove, they may sit in silence or leave. There is little feedback that tells the source whether or not the message is being understood in the way the source intends. These feedback limitations put an additional burden on the source to prepare messages that are clear and can be understood within the context of this single speech.

One unique characteristic of public speaking is that it usually occurs for a specific occasion or a planned event—it seldom occurs spontaneously. The occasion may be informal such as a college class or a basic-training lecture in the army. Other occasions may be very formal—a President's inauguration, an after-dinner speech, or a graduation speech. The formality of the occasion helps to determine the nature of the speaker, the message, and the audience.

All communication is part of an ongoing process. No speech occurs in a vacuum. Audience response to a public speech is determined by the attitudes, values, and prior information they have brought with them. After they leave, they will get more information from other sources. There are few one-time communications that have the power to shake the foundation of an individual audience member, and a speaker who works to this end will probably not succeed. It is disappointing to discover we cannot be earthshakers, but as public speakers this perspective is the only realistic one from which to work.

THE SPEAKER'S IMAGE

The effectiveness of any public speaker depends on how he or she is seen by the audience. Audience perception of the speaker is determined by *ethos*—the speaker's personal characteristics which make him or her more or less believable and trustworthy in the minds of the audience.

For a speaker to be effective, he or she must have favorable ethos. Research has pinpointed three variables that go into the creation of this quality: expertness, trustworthiness, and dynamism. A speaker is seen as expert when he or she is competent in a subject; as trustworthy when he or she presents honest, acceptable arguments; and as dynamic when active, bold, and aggressive. For the greatest possible message acceptance, all of these variables should be present. For example, if a used-car salesman is seen as competent but not trustworthy, his effectiveness in selling cars is greatly hampered. A teacher may be perceived by students as both competent and trustworthy, but if her teaching is dull, passive, and tired, her effectiveness is reduced.

Speaker ethos is developed in an audience before the speech, throughout the speech, and after the speech is over. Prior ethos is based on the knowledge the audience has of the speaker before he or she begins to speak. This knowledge may be based on personal experience if members of the audience personally know the speaker, or it may be based on the vicarious experience of audience members who know the speaker through agencies such as the mass media. The audience may also have impressions of the speaker based on the groups to which he or she belongs. For example, if the audience knows that the speaker is a Black Panther or a member of the American Medical Association, they may have an impression of the speaker based on their impression of that group. Sponsorship may be another basis for prior knowledge. If the Ku Klux Klan sponsors a rally, we know that the speakers at that rally have certain attitudes—that is why they have been chosen to speak. Finally, prior knowledge may be based on mere physical appearance. The audience looks at the speaker seated on the platform and makes certain judgments: he is well-dressed; she looks kind-hearted.

All of this prior knowledge may either hurt or help a speaker. Because of negative prior information from the mass media, Stokely Carmichael often had to tell audiences that his purpose was *not* to spread hate and begin riots. Billy Graham's prior image as an emotional evangelist worked against him in an intellectual, university setting. Thus he would often begin a speech by asking if all of the members of the speech and psychology departments were present. This question let the audience know that Graham was aware that some people came to watch him "perform"—not to hear his message. One aid in establishing prior ethos is to have someone introduce the speaker. Introductions are especially useful in establishing the speaker's competence and trustworthiness.

Ethos is also created as the communication is going on. It can be created by the speaker's choice of topic, by his or her approach to the topic, by the extent to which the audience identifies with the speaker's ideas, and by the types of appeal the speaker uses. Dynamism is largely determined by the speaker's style of delivery. All of these factors help to develop ethos during the speech. We have only mentioned them briefly here—they will be developed more fully later in the chapter.

The ethos that occurs after the speech is mostly a continuation of the ethos that has been created before and during the speech. This ethos is no longer controlled by the speaker—it largely depends on whether the source has lived up to, has been less than, or has gone beyond the audience's expectations.

Ethos in public speaking is a function of the speech occasion, the speech itself, and, of course, the audience. All of these factors interact. A speaker may have great ethos with one audience and hardly any at all with another audience. Skillful preparation, including careful audience analysis, will help most speakers improve their own speaker ethos.

SPEAKING AND ANXIETY

Imagine a classroom sometime before the instructor comes in. The students are laughing and talking to each other; there are lively informal conversations going on all over the room. One young woman is telling a joke to a group of three or four other students; when she reaches the punch line, they all laugh. Then the instructor comes, and the class begins. The same person who told the joke gives a speech. She walks to the front of the room and begins talking. Although she had been at ease and comfortable when she told the joke, she now begins to resemble a Barbie doll—someone has pulled the string and out comes the recorded message.

What has happened to this student? Why did she change her communication behavior in such a short time-period? How does she feel when she is giving this speech, and what does her behavior tell us about her feelings? The answer to all of these questions is that she is feeling *anxiety*. This student is no longer in control; she has been assigned to give a speech by her instructor, and she knows that the entire class and instructor are watching and judging her. She responds to the situation mechanically—it is something to get through with as quickly as possible. Chances are that she really does not care about the effect of her speech. She only wants to get back to the safety of her seat.

The anxiety of performing in public causes all of us to respond in a similar fashion. Your heart beats faster, your palms perspire, your mouth gets dry, and your knees tremble. Although the audience is not aware of what is happening to your body, they are aware that you are nervous when you click your ball-point pen, play with your note cards, and speak in a decidedly shaky voice. This is called situational anxiety because it is present when we are in a certain situation—that of performing publicly—and it disappears when we are out of the situation.

Anxiety is a common feeling among performers. Brock Yates, who writes about car racing, says, "Men react to prerace jitters in many ways. Some great drivers, including Phil Hill, the first (and only) American world champion, tend to vomit. Others become testy and distant. Many yawn, a reaction that is often mistaken for devil-may-care bravado. It is, in fact, a common symptom of nervousness."[1] Bette Davis, who has had a long career as an actress, writes, "Opening nights! The nightmare of all actors. Lotte Lehmann once told me 'It will grow worse not better as you grow older.' She was right. It is always a kind of death before the curtain goes up." She also writes about the first time she ever played comedy. "I had nightmares every night during rehearsal that no one would laugh. I would wake up in a cold sweat. On opening night my first line got its laugh—and I relaxed."[2] Performers' biographies and autobiographies are filled with similar accounts of anxiety. There is probably not a single performer who has avoided anxious feelings.

Unfortunately there are no easy answers to the problem of anxiety.

---

1 Brock Yates, *Sunday Driver* (New York: Farrar, Straus and Giroux, 1972), p. 130.

2 Bette Davis, *The Lonely Life* (New York: G. P. Putnam's Sons, 1962), pp. 109, 111.

There are some things that you can do, however, to reduce it and put it into perspective. Our first and most important suggestion is that you recognize the feeling. Many people regard anxious feelings as somewhat shameful, something they should try to hide from themselves and others. If you can admit that you are feeling anxious, then try talking about it to others. You might raise it as a matter for class discussion, or you might talk about it with one of your fellow classmates. You will discover that other people feel just as anxious as you do, and while this discovery may not eliminate your own feelings, the anxiety will not seem so overwhelming.

A second strategy in overcoming anxiety is to prepare. Many students put off preparing speeches because they are anxious, and then they become more anxious because they have not prepared. If you find yourself in this trap, try to force yourself to prepare your speech. If you have discovered a good topic and good material and if you feel confident with your material, your anxiety will lessen. If your speech is scheduled for a certain day, plan to give it on that day. When you find a reason to delay it, ask yourself if that reason is really legitimate or if you are just putting it off because you are anxious. Putting off your speech will make you even more anxious.

Your choice of topics will also help you. If you speak on something that really interests you and is important to you, your desire to communicate the importance of the subject to the audience will help you to overcome your feelings of insecurity. You may remember a time when you were so excited by an idea or so angry about someone's reaction that you forgot how you would look to others and got passionately involved. You can have this same experience in speaking if you become interested in your topic and forget how you look and sound.

When the time finally comes to make your speech, remember the people who make up your audience. The more you can individualize them, the less threatening they are as an audience. Also remember that they want you to succeed. An audience, especially in a speech class, identifies with you strongly. They all know that they will be where you are in a matter of minutes or days. If you are successful, they feel that they have a better chance of succeeding. If you get into difficulty, their own feelings of anxiety grow.

There is one other helpful thing you can remember about an audience. Every audience has at least one person who gives particularly strong and reassuring feedback. This person looks at you sympathetically, nods when you have made a point, and smiles at your jokes. Look for this supporter when you speak. He or she will give you so much confidence and courage that you will begin to relate to all of the people in the room.

The first time is the hardest. Swimming, mountain climbing, foreign travel, riding motorcycles, making love, and giving a speech are all hard the first time you try. If you can get through it the first time, the second time may be easier. Although many speakers and performers have anxiety all of their lives, they manage to control it rather than letting it control them. Once a speaker manages to accept his or her anxiety and puts it into a realistic perspective, then the goal of speech becomes communication and anxiety becomes a minor hindrance to achieving this goal.

ANALYZING THE AUDIENCE

A good speech is audience-centered; it is planned, structured, and delivered with a particular audience in mind. In order to get the audience to respond to the message in the way the speaker intends, he or she must know as much as possible about the audience. Thus, much of speech-preparation time is spent in audience analysis.

A speaker will find many variables in any audience analysis, but the key to good analysis is *identification.* The more the speaker can identify and relate to the background, experience, interests, and attitudes of the audience, the greater the chance for speech effectiveness. Generally we can put audiences into three different categories: those who share common experiences and interests with the speaker, those who have different experiences and interests, and those audiences which are so large that it is impossible to discover common experiences and interests.

Identification is easiest when the speaker shares a common background with his or her audience. A Baptist minister has a good idea of the values of his congregation because the very fact that they are Baptists implies certain values and attitudes. A college student has little problem identifying with his or her classmates. They are basically in the same age group, probably examining various life styles, deciding on future careers, and sharing common interests in social activities.

In many speech situations, however, a speaker is unlike his or her audience and must spend time finding a common basis for understanding. A helicopter pilot must work to discover common ground with a bricklayer, and a college student must spend time to discover what experiences and interests she shares with the local Rotary Club.

The most difficult audience analysis comes when an audience is so large that no common interests can be found except for the desire to hear the speaker. Politicians face this kind of audience in large political rallies as do people who speak on television. Usually they solve their audience problems by making their message appeal to values that are held broadly.

Several approaches are useful whenever we analyze an audience. The first approach is to look at the audience variables of age, sex, socioeconomic class, racial-ethnic background, religion, occupation, and education. These variables can be important if one or more of them separate the speaker from the audience. For example, the white dean of a college for black students always mentioned in his speeches to the student body that he had grown up poor. His attempt to identify with his students was a failure because the students knew that growing up poor is considerably different from growing up black. The dean picked the wrong thing to identify with. Age is a critical factor if an adult is speaking to children, and the sex of the speaker may be important when a male is speaking to an all-female audience or vice-versa.

In other situations, these variables may not be important. If a Presbyterian is speaking in favor of better schools, his or her religion is probably not an important factor even though the audience is predominately Methodist. The speaker's sex should not be an issue when a member of the League of Women Voters is giving information about forthcoming municipal elections to the Lion's Club.

Every speaker must consider each of these variables as a possible factor in the success of the speech. If the speaker and the audience are significantly different, the speaker must find a way to bridge the gap within the speech. A speaker should not pretend that he or she has the same background and experiences as the audience, but the speaker can overcome differences by emphasizing common experiences. "I know that you are white and I am black and this has caused problems in the past, but our topic today is not race. Our topic is working together to get our street paved, and I hope that that will be our concern."

All of the variables we have been discussing—race, sex, age, class, religion, and so on—determine our beliefs and attitudes. These overall attitudes are more important than any single variable. How can a speaker determine the beliefs and attitudes of the audience? It is impossible to discover or deal with the thousands of individual attitudes which may be present in any one audience. Again we will say that if audience attitudes are basically the same as your own, you will not have any problem. But, what if they are different from yours and your speech purpose is to change some of these attitudes? How do you prepare your speech with this goal in mind?

First you must remember that your speech is one event in a continuing communication. It is not the only time that your audience will hear about your subject—they have probably heard it before and they will likely hear it again. Attitude change happens over a long period of time. Very few people will change their attitudes from hearing a single speech. They will consider what they already know, and they will consider what happens after your speech. When John F. Kennedy ran for President, many people thought he could not possibly win. Yet as election day grew closer, he gathered more and more supporters, and he managed to win by a narrow margin. Some political experts say that if he had had a couple more weeks of campaign time, his victory would have been even larger. Here we can see attitude change occurring over a period of time.

There has been considerable research in the area of audience analysis. Some general review of the findings may be useful to beginning speakers. The first area of research deals with *self-esteem,* the opinion that a person has of himself or herself. People who have a high self-esteem tend to be confident about their judgments and opinions and are therefore not easily persuaded. By the same token, people with low self-esteem are more easily persuaded.

On an interpersonal level it is often easy to discover whether a person has high or low self-esteem, but determining the collective self-esteem of a large audience is more difficult. If the audience is made up of professional people, you are probably meeting with a group that has fairly high self-esteem. An example of such an audience might be a group of lawyers. The best strategy for dealing with such an audience is to give them a pro-con examination of facts and let them make up their own minds. An audience with low self-esteem could be made up either of people who are not accustomed to making decisions or people who have had many failures in their lives. A group of people who have spent long periods of time in prison would probably fit this category. Low self-esteem audiences are more responsive to speeches which represent what they perceive to be the majority position. Therefore the best tactic is to show that what you are proposing is what most people want.

The second area of audience research deals with *dogmatism,* the extent to which individuals are committed to certain ideas. People are most dogmatic when their own lives are closely tied in with the issue under discussion. For example, someone in rural Indiana might be quite objective and liberal in a discussion about increasing low-income housing in urban centers. On the other hand, someone who is living in center-city Philadelphia might be quite closed-minded and strongly opposed to such housing since he or she could feel the housing as a personal threat. In planning message strategy, we know that open-minded individuals will listen to logical and rational approaches and closed-minded individuals may change if they perceive the change as proposed by a respected authority. George Wallace, for example, is a hero to many white Southerners. If he so desired, he could probably influence many people toward better race relations in the South.

The last area of audience research deals with *prior commitment,* the way the audience feels about an idea before they ever come to hear the speaker. If the audience is on the side of the speaker, then there is no problem, but if the speaker is on the "wrong" side of the issue, he or she must take care in planning the message. The speaker should work to convince the audience that although the message may seem to be unacceptable, it is really in keeping with the general philosophy of the audience. If a Roman Catholic speaks to a group of Baptists about the Catholic church, he would be wise to play down issues of doctrine—the virgin birth and papal infallibility, for example—and emphasize the ideas that all Christians have in common.

A Case Study in Audience Analysis

Let's see how these theories about audience analysis work in a practical speech situation.

A college-educated woman in her late twenties is interested in the subject of abortion. She had an illegal abortion while she was still in college, and the experience was so unpleasant that she has decided to work for greater public understanding and acceptance of abortion. Through her reading and experience she has become an expert on the subject, and she is willing to give public speeches about abortions throughout the community. Several groups have asked her to speak, and she has agreed to talk to four audiences: a group of radical feminists, a convention of the American Medical Association, a group of interested citizens at the city auditorium, and a group of Roman Catholic priests. How can she handle these diverse audiences? Each group must be analyzed separately.

1) The radical feminists are the easiest group for the speaker to relate to because they have taken a well-known public stand in favor of abortion. The speaker's main problem is not in identification but in her approach to the topic. She knows that her audience is on her side and agrees with her premise that abortion should be available to all women who desire it. Therefore her best strategy would probably be to get them to organize and to spread information about abortion, to join her in her own crusade of spreading public information and gaining wider acceptance of abortion.

2) The speaker has a moderate amount of identification with the AMA because they share a common interest in the medical problem of abortion. In this speech situation, the sex of the speaker is important; she is a woman speaking on a problem of women to a predominately male audience. Her education may also be a factor to this audience, and it would increase her credibility if she were to use correct medical terminology. The speaker realizes that doctors are crucial to the issue of abortions, and she decides to ask them to provide psychological support to patients undergoing the operation and to provide inexpensive abortions. In asking for psychological support she relates her own un-

pleasant experience of undergoing an abortion and points out that this would not have happened if she had had more sympathy and understanding on the part of the doctor performing it. The issue of inexpensive abortions is a delicate one since most people, including doctors, like to make money. Therefore she spends time describing well-run, efficient abortion clinics that are operating throughout the country and that are making profits for doctors as well as providing low-cost services. She has assumed that her audience will be generally in favor of abortion and she has given them information about ways to improve abortion services.

3) The speaker has less information about the citizens at the city auditorium than any of the other audiences. She can only assume that they have come to hear her because they are interested in the topic. In this speech, the speaker spends time in the introductory part telling why she is interested in and qualified to speak on abortion; she gives the audience a reason for listening and believing what she has to say. Since she does not know how the audience feels about the topic, she gives a general objective account of the status of abortion today. She discusses the present abortion law and the procedure a woman must follow to get an abortion. She concludes her speech with a discussion of the facilities that are available in the city and state of her audience.

4) The Roman Catholic priests are the toughest audience of all and therefore require the greatest advance preparation. The speaker knows that most of the audience has definite ideas about abortion and that these ideas are contrary to her own. She must deal with both dogmatism and prior commitment. Again she decides to be as objective as possible, and she covers many of the points that she covered with her audience in the city auditorium. The speaker is not able to find any high authorities in the Catholic church who have supported abortion, but she has found a group of liberal Catholic theologians who support the idea that individuals can and should make individual decisions regarding morality. After quoting one or two of these theologians, she cites examples of women who have chosen to have abortions, not for selfish reasons but for the welfare of their families. She knows that she has little chance of changing anyone's mind, but she hopes to leave the priests with the idea that in some circumstances, abortion may be the best solution.

As you can see by these examples, the speaker has made a number of choices. In every speaking situation she has adapted and changed her speech to meet the particular needs of the audience. This need for adaptation is present in most speaking situations. Giving a speech is somewhat similar to shopping for a gift. You don't go out and buy everyone the same thing—you take time to choose what is right for each person. If you take the time to make these choices for your audience, you have a greater chance of affecting your audience in the way you intend.

CHOOSING A TOPIC

Many people are asked to speak because they have expertise in a particular area. A civil engineer may be asked to speak to local businessmen on the need for a new city sewage system, and a member of the National Organization for Women might be asked to speak to a school assembly on the Equal Rights Amendment. Other people may choose to speak because they have a desire to accomplish a certain goal. Politicians speak to win elections, and Billy Graham speaks to save souls. Since these people are speaking for specific reasons, they do not have a problem of choosing topics because the speech occasion dictates the topic. Their main problem is their approach to the topic and, again, the key to their approach is audience analysis. As speakers they ask, "How can I best reach the audience with this topic?"

Classroom speeches, however, fall into another category. A student is not necessarily an expert, and the speech occasion is somewhat artificial because the student speaks to fulfill an assignment. Students are usually not given specific speech topics, but they may be asked to speak within a broad framework, for example, a speech to inform or a speech to persuade. Once you know your speech framework, how do you go about choosing a topic? It will probably help you to consider two questions: What will interest you and what will interest your audience?

Students sometimes deliver speeches on such broad and important social issues as poverty, tax reform, or inflation. Undoubtedly these are important topics, but they are not very good subjects for five-minute speeches. Chances are that you have very little knowledge or experience with such topics and that you would do well to stay away from them. You would probably be better off directing your attention to topics that you know something about and that can be reasonably discussed within your time limit.

Knowledge and *experience* are key words. What do you know about? How do you spend your time? What really turns you on? The best way to answer these questions is to look at how you spend those sixteen or so hours that you are awake each day. Do you spend your time working on your car? Buying new clothes? Playing cards in the student union? Working out a chemistry experiment in the lab? All of these activities could lead to very good speeches. In fact, with the right approach, almost any subject can be turned into a speech.

Your audience is another important consideration in choosing your topic. Speeches are more than exercises for speakers to hear themselves; thus, it is important for you to ask how you can present your knowledge and experience in a way that will interest the audience. There are several good ways of doing this.

Let's say you spend most of your free time working on your car, and so you have specialized knowledge about cars. You can assume that most of the members of your audience do not share that knowledge; if something is wrong with their car, they take it to a mechanic. Since you are limited to a five-minute speech, what approach can you take that will be effective? A good approach would be to apply your specialized knowledge to help the audience deal with problems about cars. You could speak on "How to Avoid Getting Ripped-Off in the Body Shop," "What to Look for in a Used Car," or "What You Should Do to Keep Your Car Running Well." All of these topics demand specialized knowledge on the part of the speaker, and each speech adapts this knowledge to the needs of the audience.

Maybe you are a chemistry major, and you spend all of your time in the lab. Many students barely manage to struggle through their chemistry classes, and they will probably never think about the subject again. How are you ever going to interest them? Think of it this way—every day of our lives we are touched by the impact of chemistry. Most of your audience is wearing clothes created by chemistry. Anyone who cooks is causing a chemical reaction. Chemical additives in foods and their effects on the human body are vital because they have life-and-death implications. Every kitchen and bathroom has a wide range of chemical products. All of these aspects of modern chemistry could well lead to an interesting speech.

If you are one who spends much of your time playing cards, then you have another possible topic at your fingertips. Have you ever wondered where all of those cards came from? Why do we use the terms *jack, queen, king*? Why do all decks have fifty-two cards? You can find the answers in a quick trip to the library. Interesting questions lead to interesting answers, and interesting answers lead to interesting speeches.

If you have several ideas for a topic, try placing yourself in the role of an audience member: Which topic would be the most interesting to you? Which would reach out and grasp your attention? When you think you have a workable topic, sit down and try to plan an approach. The majority of your preparation time can best be spent working on your speech rather than choosing your topic, but choosing a good topic will make preparation easier.

GATHERING INFORMATION

After you choose your topic, you should start gathering information. In the beginning it is not necessary to know just exactly how you are going to use it; you can arrange it later. You may find that some of the material will not fit into your speech and so you will want to eliminate it.

Your first source of information should be your own experience and the experiences of people you know. Personal experiences are effective because they get greater involvement from you and from your audience. It is easier to identify with personal experience than with any other kind of material. Using your own experience also enhances your credibility. In essence you are saying, "I have experienced this. I know what I am talking about."

One student used her own personal experience very effectively. She got up and said, "Today I am going to talk about contraceptives. I believe that this subject is important to all college students. If I had known about contraceptives, I probably wouldn't have had a baby in my sophomore year of college." From that point on, she had the full attention of her audience.

Information can also come out of your own community. If you are planning to talk about urban decay, be cautious about building your speech around New York City slums (unless you live there). Every city in the United States has slums. If your own community has lakes and rivers that can no longer be used, why discuss pollution in the Atlantic Ocean? Shoplifting occurs in all American cities and towns. Suicides happen in Big Ten universities, small private schools, and community colleges. Used-car salesmen use many of the same "come-on" gimmicks in every city. Your own community probably has all of the social good and evil of the entire country so consider it as a starting point.

Another source of information is local experts. Policemen, firemen, welfare officers, health department officials, doctors and lawyers—all of them are experts in certain areas, and they know a lot about your particular community and the problems in that community. Talk to them and quote them. A local authority will carry much more weight than some far-off remote figure in another city.

You don't always have to go to the top to get your information. If you decide to speak on the working conditions in the sanitation department, you will probably learn more from the man who picks up your garbage than from the Commissioner of Sanitation. If you want to find out about Sanitation Department policies, on the other hand, the commissioner will be the best person to help you. A prostitute will be able to say more about the life of a prostitute than all of the sociology instructors at your school. However, the story of one prostitute does not tell us very much about the state of prostitution in the United States, and to get this information, you will have to go to more traditional academic sources.

One of these academic sources is the faculty at your school. Instructors all have specialized knowledge within their given fields of study, and often they know how to get information in places that would not occur to someone who does not know about that field. If your topic is a fairly academic one—the history of prostitution, for example—you can probably get some information and leads to good sources from members of the faculty.

The library, of course, is the traditional source for information found in books. You have probably been using libraries since you learned to read, but most of us know about only a fraction of the sources and services that are available. Since you need to use these resources all the time, it would be worthwhile to spend an hour or two in the library just looking around and asking questions.

Several library resources are particularly useful to people who are gathering information for a speech. The reference section will give you the facts, or the bare bones, on any subject. Encyclopedias, although limited, are useful for general information and for short historical summaries. If you need information about people and their achievements, you can look in the *Dictionary of National Biography, Who's Who in America,* and *Current Biography. The World Almanac* and *Book of Facts* and the *Information Please Almanac* are good sources for current facts since new editions are published every year. If you want a quotation, look in *Bartlett's Familiar Quotations* or the *Oxford Dictionary of Quotations,* where quotations are listed by subject. The best source of statistical data for the United States is the *Statistical Abstract of the United States.* If you browse along the reference shelves, you will discover a wide variety of sources of information.

For a more detailed discussion of a topic, look in the card catalog under the subject. There you will find the titles and authors of all of the books in this library on the topic you are researching. Many of the cards may have similar call numbers because the books are shelved together in one or two sections of the library. If you go to that section, you will find several different books that handle the topic in different ways. Sometimes this kind of browsing will help you to find a unique slant on your particular topic.

The Reader's Guide to Periodical Literature is another useful source. This publication, which is found in the magazine or periodical section of the library, lists all of the articles in popular magazines that have appeared on your subject. Magazine articles are good sources for current information, and often you will find recent statistics and other material that you can quote in your speech.

After you have gathered all of your information, ask yourself again if this information is suitable for your particular audience. Will it help them to see, identify with, and understand the subject better? When you have gathered the best possible information, information that will work for you and your audience, then you are ready to begin building your speech.

ORGANIZING THE SPEECH

Earlier in this chapter we said that the purpose of a public speech is to elicit a specific response from the audience. One of the best tools available in helping you to get this response is good organization, which functions to direct all of your material toward the response you want.

Most speeches have the general purpose of informing or persuading the audience. An *informative speech* is one that presents the audience with information about a subject and lets them draw their own conclusions. A *persuasive speech* may also give information, but it tries to move the audience toward a specific commitment or action. There are some differences in organizing the two types of speeches, but their basic organizational pattern has greater similarities than differences. Both types of speeches require that material be organized into a statement of purpose, an introduction, a body, and a conclusion.

The *statement of purpose,* or the thesis statement, clearly states the reason for your speech in one sentence. "I am going to persuade the class to vote for Martha Smith." "I am going to explain why meat prices are so high." "I am going to convince the audience that excessive suntanning is dangerous." This thesis statement is particularly helpful in speech planning because you can test all of your speech material against it. If a particular piece of information supports your thesis statement, then you know that material is relevant. Although you may never actually state your thesis to the audience, it is implied and obvious throughout the speech.

The speech *introduction* has two purposes: it makes the audience feel comfortable with the speaker, and it creates interest in the topic. If an audience does not know you, you will want to make them receptive to you and hence to your speech. Many speakers use humor for this purpose. Sometimes a speaker needs to reassure an audience. For example, one speaker was scheduled to speak at a conference just before lunch time. She knew that the conference had gone on all morning, that the audience had heard many speakers, and that they were probably both tired and hungry. She began her speech by saying, "I know you are ready for lunch, and I have not prepared a long speech because I am hungry too. If any of you want to keep time, I am going to speak for exactly twelve minutes." Reassured that food was not a long time away, the audience sat back and listened with interest and attention.

You have already done an audience analysis and chosen a topic that is important to the lives of your audience. Point out this importance in your introduction—this is the best way of building interest in your speech. A college student began his speech to a group of classmates in this way: "You probably all know that the greatest epidemic in the United States is the common cold. Today, I am interested in the second greatest epidemic, one that involves a disease that is common among college students. This disease does not cause sneezing and minor discomfort—it causes insanity and blindness and finally death. I am speaking about venereal disease."

The organization of the *body* of your speech will depend on the type of speech you are giving. In an informative speech the best organization can be achieved by putting yourself in the position of an audience member. Assume that you know almost nothing about the subject, and ask yourself how it should be presented so that you can understand it. For instance, Julia Child, who appears on a television cooking program, always explains what she means by terms such as *baste* and *sauté* before she goes on to the more complicated aspects of cooking. The student who speaks about venereal disease realizes that his audience probably knows something about the subject, but he also might assume that some of the information they have is colored by fear and superstition. The best organization pattern for information is one that will present your material in a clear and comprehensible form to your audience. If you keep this in mind, you will discover a structure that will work for your speech.

Your speech might have a persuasive purpose; you are asking people to change in some way. One of the best ways of organizing a persua-

sive speech is to divide your subject into the problem and the solution. For example, some schools have dormitory curfew hours for women but none for men, and you want to change this. In explaining the problem you point out the present conditions, and you tell your audience that these rules discriminate against women. Your solution to the problem is to organize a five-person delegation from the class to approach the student government association and the dean of students to ask that these rules be changed.

Some speakers work to change an attitude rather than to ask for direct action. Again you can use the problem-solution order. In a speech called "What Do Women Want Anyway?" a student pointed out that there is wide-scale discrimination against women. In the problem part of the speech, she used statistics showing that women are earning less money for doing the same jobs as men, that they are slower to get promoted, and that employers often refuse to consider them because they are afraid that the woman might get pregnant. In her solution, she said that women want the same chances and opportunities in employment that are given to men. She knew that the men in her class were more likely to be students than employers now, but she also knew that some of these same men would be employers some day. She hoped to bring about an attitude change that would have long-term effects.

All speeches, whether they are informative or persuasive, will benefit from an outline. The purpose of your outline is to list the main points of the speech followed by the supporting material. Generally, a short speech should have from two to four main points. Let's say you are going to speak on "Common Sense About Pot." Your points might be 1) how pot is different from hard drugs, 2) the effects of pot when it is smoked, and 3) the laws in your state regarding pot. All of these main points should be supported by material that proves that your main points are true.

Supporting material includes examples, facts, statistics, illustrations, and opinions. It is based on your experience, the experience of others, and the information you find in your research. Each of these forms of supporting material is discussed in Chapter 2, Interpersonal Communication.

Your speech will also require *transitions* from one main point to another to tell your audience where you have been and where you are going. Transitions are a means of getting from one point to another smoothly. For example, if you are going from the point on the effects of pot to the point on your state laws about pot, you might say, "As you can see, smoking pot is a very pleasant experience for most people. But before you all run out to get some, I should warn you what could happen if you were caught." Now you are set up to speak about the state laws.

The *conclusion* of a speech says that the speech is over, the communication is complete. Have you ever talked on the telephone and had the other person hang up without saying good-bye? You know that this can be an unsettling experience. The same is true of a speech without a conclusion. You will find it useful to have a pretty exact idea of your conclusion before you begin speaking. There is no worse feeling than shuffling from one foot to the other, thinking to yourself "How am I going to get out of here?" A conclusion, prepared beforehand, will avoid this problem.

Many speakers conclude with "Thank-you" or "Are there any questions?" If the speech is a good one, the audience will thank the speaker. If there are questions, they are likely to be asked; usually this is determined by the format which is established beforehand. Thanking the audience or asking for questions does not take the place of a conclusion. As a beginning speaker, you should avoid this type of ending.

The minimal expectation for a conclusion is that it summarizes the major ideas in the body of the speech and gives a clear restatement of the major thesis. The conclusion will vary according to the type of speech. In an informative speech, it is often useful to summarize your main points. In a persuasive speech, you can also use a summary, but your main closing device will be to ask for commitment or action. No audience member who was listening should leave the speech wondering what the main idea was. Thus, a good conclusion lets both the speaker and the audience know that the speech is over as well as repeating the thrust or core idea of the speech.

For certain speeches, some instructors require a bibliography. A bibliography lists all of the sources of information that you have used in your speech. It is usually given at the end of the speech outline. In the pages that follow, there is an outline and bibliography that will guide you in preparing your own speeches. One side of the page gives an explanation of the outline process, and the other side demonstrates the process through a sample speech. You will notice that the speech we have used is a persuasive one and that it has a problem-solution order; the problem is explained and developed in the first three main points, and the solution is given and developed in the fourth main point. If you are preparing a speech based on experience or an informative speech, you will structure your material in the same way, including all of the parts of the outline as shown in the left-hand column.

Title	Danger In The Supermarket
Statement of Purpose	My purpose is to persuade my audience that many of the foods they are accustomed to eating are dangerous to their health.
Introduction	I plan to hold up a candy bar and to tell my audience that this candy bar is a useless and filthy food. Then I plan to hold up a bottle of red food coloring and to tell them that this popular food coloring contains a dangerous chemical. I will then tell them that many of the foods we find in the supermarket are dangerous to our lives and should be eliminated from our diet.
Body of Speech Main Points	I. Many foods have been stripped of their nutritional value to make them look and taste better to consumers.
Supporting Material	A. White flour and white sugar are stripped of nutrients in the milling and refining process. B. White bread is filled with air so it will feel soft and fresh when squeezed, and bleached to make it look white.
Transition from point I to point II	Food processors not only remove nutrients, they also add harmful ingredients.
	II. Many foods have dangerous chemical additives. A. Sodium nitrite, used to make hot dogs look fresh, is a dangerous chemical which can cause cancer and genetic damage. B. Red II, a food color used in hot dogs, processed cheese, cereal, soft drinks, and many other items, is dangerous to pregnant women and may cause fetal death.
Transition from point II to point III	Some ingredients, however, are not added intentionally.

III. The Federal Drug Administration tolerates high levels of filth in packaged and processed foods.

    A. They permit 50 insect fragments or rodent hairs in $3\frac{1}{2}$ ounces of peanut butter.

    B. In chocolate, they permit 150 insect fragments per eight-ounce sample.

    C. They tolerate 10 drosophila or other fly eggs in $8\frac{1}{2}$-ounce cans of fruit juice.

Transition from point III to point IV — Fortunately the consumer does not have to sit by and see food stripped of its nutritional value. We do not have to tolerate high chemical and filth levels.

IV. We can prevent nutritional deficiencies, dangerous chemicals, and filth in our food by a few simple procedures.

    A. We can read the labels of all packaged foods and refuse to buy any foods that contain dangerous chemicals.

    B. We can buy only fresh food at the supermarket.

    C. We can try to purchase as much food as possible from health-food stores that carry food which has not been sprayed with chemicals.

    D. Some of us with green thumbs might start gardens and grow as many fresh foods as possible.

    E. We should read consumer-oriented publications, such as *Consumer Reports,* which have information about the amount of filth and chemicals found in individual foods.

Transition from point IV to Conclusion — By following some of these suggestions, we no no longer have to be at the mercy of our local supermarket.

Conclusion	I will urge the audience to adopt my new eating program for better health and longer life. I will conclude my speech by throwing the candy bar and the food coloring into the trash container.
Bibliography	Hunter, Beatrice Trum, *The Natural Foods Primer*. New York: Simon and Schuster, 1972.
	"Frankfurters," *Consumer Reports,* February 1972, pp. 73–79.
	"The High Filth Diet, Compliments of the FDA," *Consumer Reports,* March 1973, pp. 152–154.
	"Red Food Coloring: How Safe Is It?" *Consumer Reports,* February 1973, pp. 130–133.

PLANNING THE DELIVERY

There are three methods of delivering a planned speech: speaking from notes, speaking from memory, and speaking from a fully written-out speech (called a manuscript). We strongly recommend that beginning speakers do not memorize the speech. When you memorize, you are so busy trying to remember what you are supposed to remember that you often sound very mechanical. This occurs because many people memorize in a word-for-word fashion rather than memorizing the outline of the speech. You limit your alternatives when you memorize words because one word depends on another; if you forget one word, you are likely to forget everything that follows. Also, concern about remembering your speech may make you tense, and we assume that you are anxious enough without adding this burden.

Many students prefer to write out their speeches and read them to the audience. This procedure is not recommended for a beginning speaker because it takes a great deal of practice and experience to write and read a speech so that it sounds like a speech. Most of us speak differently than we write. We use words in our written style that we would seldom, if ever, use in our oral style. Speeches that are written out tend to sound like compositions or term papers. Speech writers for the President of the United States write out his speeches because it is important that the President use his words exactly—Presidential speeches *can* be earthshaking! Most of us do not have to be so precise, however, and we will sound more spontaneous and natural if we choose some of the words as we go along.

Another major reason why a speaker should not read a manuscript is because audiences do not like to feel they are being read to. It is generally dull and boring; thus, to be effective, a speaker will consider the audience. Memorized or written speeches also allow no possibility for adaptation or change. If you are speaking from notes, you will have a better opportunity to notice the audience response. If they start getting bored, you can omit a section from your speech or insert an amusing story. If they look confused, you can add another fact or another example to clarify the idea. It is unlikely you will do this if your speech is memorized, and you will find it difficult to do if your speech is written out.

For a beginning speaker the best speech is usually the one that is made with note cards because these cards provide a good opportunity for natural and spontaneous delivery. They allow the speaker more opportunity to adapt to the audience. They encourage flexibility, too, because they are easier to use and easier to handle than a full sheet of paper. A speaker can move from behind a lectern easily with a note card in hand.

Note cards usually contain an outline of the speech as well as information you might not be able to remember such as statistics and quotations. Note cards should be an aid to your memory, not an audience distraction. Tapping, bending, and shuffling your note cards will draw your audience's attention to your cards rather than to your message. It will also distract your audience if you spend all of your time looking at your cards instead of at them. If your note cards are very complicated and include a great deal of information, they will become as binding to you as a manuscript. Number them, make them clear, keep them brief, and use only a few of them if you want to be effective.

After you have given a few speeches and have learned to use note cards, you may want to experiment with the other two methods of speech delivery. If you decide to speak without notes, we again caution you not to memorize all of your words. If you memorize just the outline of your speech, you will still have the opportunity to choose your words as you go along. If you use a manuscript, practice it several times *aloud* before you speak. When you come across words and phrases that sound unnatural, change them to a more oral and conversational style. Oral practice will also help to make the speech part of you; the better you know it, the more you can relate and react to your audience.

Most experienced speakers use a variety of methods in preparing their speeches—depending on the audience and the circumstances of the speech. Any method is effective when the speech sounds spontaneous and natural.

Planning to Keep Attention

Someone once said that the best speeches are those that have good beginnings and good endings—close together. Most Americans would probably agree. In a country of instant messages created by experts, a speaker has special problems in keeping the audience's interest directed to the topic. Other claims for their attention are always occurring simultaneously.

Most people are easily distracted, and few of us can concentrate on anything for long periods of time. Look back at the classes you attended today. How many times did your attention wander? If it was an 8:00 class, you were probably just waking up and you were not really alert. At about 11:00 you started getting hungry because you had skipped breakfast, and you wondered what you would get for lunch. In your 1:00 class you were feeling lazy because you had just finished a big lunch, and by the time you got to your 3:00 class, you were wondering what you would do when you got out of class. Maybe you were distracted by the thought of a date that you had the night before. Maybe the room was uncomfortable; maybe you wore cold weather clothes and the day turned warm. All of these factors kept you from concentrating on what was being told to you. Similar factors will keep your audience from listening to what you say.

Attention is the responsibility of the speaker. One wise speaker said, "If you find anyone asleep in my audience, come up and wake me up." This speaker assumed complete responsibility for holding the attention of his audience. Obviously we cannot command audiences to listen to us, but we can make them want to listen.

Most audiences will listen to things that are important and familiar to them. You might listen politely to a friend's problems, but when you get to your problems, you have your own complete attention. When you are talking about things that are close to your listeners, they will listen. Let's say that you want to talk about drugs to a group of college students. Drugs are a subject of potential interest to students if they are handled in the right way. Your audience might be interested in heroin traffic in the United States, but they are certain to be interested in drug traffic on your particular campus. By talking about your campus, you are talking about things of immediate concern to everyone. Are they pushing dope on the street corner? Did someone get expelled because she was smoking pot in the dorm? This is the kind of information that is important and, thus, interesting. You can keep attention by combining more remote material with information that is immediate and familiar. Seek variety in the way you organize your material.

The same is true of statistics. Statistics are real, but they are also remote and far away. For example, you can say that one million women had abortions in the United States last year. That is interesting information, but who can visualize a million people? It might be helpful to provide a comparison—"Do you realize how many women that is? If you filled the Rose Bowl stadium in Pasadena, California, with women—*ten times*—you would then have the number of women who had abortions in the United States last year alone." You might also follow up this statistic by telling about the experiences of one or two of these women who have had an abortion.

You can also keep attention by building suspense. A joke almost always holds an audience's attention because it builds to a climax, and they are kept in suspense until the punch line is revealed. Telling a suspenseful story can have the same effect. A speaker once kept an audience spellbound by telling an experience that had happened to her on Halloween. She and her brother always went to the local undertaker's on Halloween night to give themselves a good scare. On this particular Halloween, they entered the undertaker's parlor, and the door closed and locked behind them. At the same time, all of the lights went out. A single light came on over a coffin, and a body slowly began to rise up from the coffin. The two children stood rigid in absolute terror, unable to move. After what seemed like hours, the lights went back on, and the undertaker came out laughing. He had staged the whole thing to keep the kids away from his establishment on Halloween. This was a good story to hold attention because it was filled with suspense and built to a natural climax.

Also, look for the novel and the unusual—if you can relate it to the familiar. You could talk about the puberty rites among the Wasukuma, but since American society has no equivalent puberty rites, the information might be so remote that the audience would lose interest. But if you said that Wasukuma men hold hands with each other and that this has no homosexual connotation, your audience might find it very interesting.

Humor is another good attention factor. Many speakers use humor at the beginning of their speech and never use it again. If you can only find one funny story that is appropriate to your speech, you would be better off putting it in the middle when the audience's attention may be wandering. If you are a good storyteller, consider using some humor throughout your speech.

The ability to use humor is not a characteristic that everyone possesses. The best humor sounds natural and uncontrived. It is better to use no humor at all if it is either awkward or unnatural for you—or if it does not directly relate to your material. Some topics, some occasions, and even some audiences do not lend themselves to the speaker's use of humor. If you are unsure whether to use it or not—do not! When humor does not work, the failure can be embarrassing for both the speaker and the audience.

You can tell if you have attention by looking for feedback. A speaker must be free enough from notes and outlines to be able to look at the audience. You should be able to tell whether your audience is receiving your message. But what happens if you look at your audience and find that one half are passing notes and the other half are sleeping? They are telling you that they are bored, and it is up to you to do something about it. If you have prepared your speech carefully with attention factors scattered throughout, you will likely get their attention back. But you can also examine your delivery. Try moving. Change your voice. Are you falling into a monotone? Are *you* paying attention to what you are saying? If what you are saying is having meaning for you, it is more likely to have meaning for your audience. Try to realize the meaning of the words you are saying the moment you speak them. Think of the public-speaking situation as an extension of conversation. In conversation, your words come to you as you think of ideas. This will also be true in public speaking if the ideas are well-thought-out in advance.

Working on keeping attention is the most valuable thing you can do as a speaker. You like variety and change—so will your audience. Your attention wanders—that will happen to your audience too. A speech that interests you has a good chance of keeping your audience's interest.

Planning Language Choices

In the public-speaking situation, language choices can be made by answering the following questions: What language is best for the audience? What language is natural for you to use? What language is best for the speech situation, and what language will best express your ideas clearly and precisely?

During the late sixties, Stokely Carmichael gave many speeches on the subject of black power. He spoke to audiences ranging from predominately white college students to black people from a wide variety of backgrounds. These diverse audiences required that he use different materials and also that he make different language choices. One winter evening in Whitewater, Wisconsin, he began a speech to white students in this way:

> Thank you very much. It's a cold honor to be here tonight. I was just telling Mr. Hoover [the chairman of the meeting] that I am sure that the professors must have mandated you to come because if I came to this university, only Ben Bella would be able to get me out of the dormitory on a night like this, and he has to come from wherever he is at now.
> I have a problem in deciding which article to read. One I wrote in early September which appeared in the *New York Review of Books* which I condensed. The tighter and the next one is the one that appeared in the fall issue of the *Massachusetts Quarterly* and I still have not decided yet. I think I'll read the one in the *Massachusetts Quarterly* because it's much tighter.[3]

When Carmichael spoke to a black audience in Detroit, he began:

> I'm going to try to speak the truth. That's very hard to do in this country, you know. A country which was founded on racism and lies. It's very hard to speak the truth. But we're going to try to do that tonight.
> Now, these guys—those guys over there. They're called the press. I got up one morning and read a story. They were talking about a cat named Stokely Carmichael. I say he must be a ba-a-a-a-d nigger. For he's raising a whole lot of sand. I had to get up and look in the mirror and make sure it was me. Because all I said is that I'm just a poor old black boy, and I think it's time black people stop begging and take what belongs to them. And takes what belongs to them.[4]

Carmichael made certain assumptions about these audiences when he prepared his speeches. His main problem in the first speech was to move the audience away from the rabble-rousing image created by the mass media. He does this by identifying with his audience as a fellow intellectual. He refers to the *New York Review of Books* and the *Massachusetts Quarterly* because he knows that they are sources that are respected by his audience. Throughout his introduction and his speech, his language and style are standard English, the language of his white audience.

For his black audience he takes a completely different approach. He begins by stating that America is founded on racism and lies. This is

---

3 Robert L. Scott and Wayne Brockriede, *The Rhetoric of Black Power* (New York: Harper and Row, 1969), pp. 96–7.

4 *Ibid.,* p. 85.

something his audience already believes, and they identify with him because he has said it. He then goes on to tell about himself using a combination of dialect and slang. The black community often ridicules a black speaker who "speaks proper." If a speaker does this, the audience believes that the speaker thinks he or she is too good for them. Carmichael carefully avoids "speaking proper." He uses the idiom of his audience and by doing this says "I am one of you." Notice especially his shift to dialect in the last sentence of the introduction to the Detroit speech. Through his language choices he has achieved identification with his audience.

There are many times when this identification is important if the speaker wants to relate to the audience. Yet there are other times when an attempt at such identification can harm you as a speaker. If you are white and are going to speak to a black audience, it would probably be a serious mistake to begin with "Brothers and Sisters." The white cop in *Sanford and Son* looks pretty silly when he says "right out" instead of "right on." He is trying to use expressions that are unnatural to him, and they only have the effect of making him look foolish. Our language patterns are closely tied into our identity. If we use language that is awkward and uncomfortable to us, we appear unnatural and even phony to our audience.

Often our major language choices in public speaking involve whether we should be casual or formal. This decision is determined by the speech occasion. If the President speaks to the nation on television, his language will be formal and chosen with great care. However, if he speaks to a small group of party members in a meeting that is not covered by the press, he as apt to be much more informal. Audiences expect the speaker to be formal in speeches such as commencement addresses, television speeches, and church sermons. Formal speeches require that language choices be carefully planned and structured. With smaller groups such as club meetings, seminars, and conferences, the language is often more casual or conversational. If there is any doubt about the speech occasion, it is useful for the speaker to find out beforehand if the occasion will be formal or casual.

There are few opportunities for feedback in public speaking. If an individual receiver does not understand what the speaker is saying, there is little chance for him or her to request explanation. Therefore a speaker must make a conscious effort to make the message as clear as possible. One of the best techniques for clarifying information is restatement. Although restatement is necessary, it can become an insult to the audience if it is not done skillfully. When it is necessary for you to repeat your information, using different language will help keep your ideas fresh and interesting.

Clarity in speaking depends upon using language precisely. Some of the most imprecise language we use is slang and profanity. Think of the variety of meanings for such expressions as *wiped out, ripped off,* and *wow.* Using profanity involves additional difficulties. Some people are so offended by profane language that they react to its use by refusing to listen to the speaker at all.

A highly technological society such as ours has also created language problems. As groups become more specialized, so does their language. Truck drivers and bus drivers "deadhead;" film and television camera people "pan," "dolly," and "truck." Psychologists distinguish between "cognitive" and "affective" behavior. These terms are useful for communication within the group, but they can create great problems for outsiders.

In making language choices in public speaking, we must base our decisions on our analysis of the audience. Are we repeating difficult ideas? Are we being as clear and precise as possible? Have we made the best possible language choices for us and our particular audience? The right choices can make the speech come alive for both the speaker and the audience.

CHOOSING VISUAL MATERIAL

Visual materials serve three functions in a speech: they help to keep the attention of the audience, they give out information in the visual channel, and they aid audience retention. A study of visual materials showed that if an audience were merely told information, after three days they would only remember 10 percent of what they were told. If they were shown material without telling, they would remember 35 percent. However, if they were both told and shown the material, they would remember 65 percent after three days.[5] Just because you have an aid does not mean that you automatically have attention, however. You may remember sleeping through all of the films your teacher showed you in elementary school. An audience can sleep through visual materials as easily as they can sleep through a speech.

Your visual material should be chosen to help make your topic alive

---

5 Conwell Carson, "Best Memory by Eye and Ear," The Kansas City *Times,* April 19, 1967, p. 13A.

and interesting to your audience. There are several types to choose from. Architects and city planners often use models, a larger or smaller replica of an actual object. A first-aid instructor or a nurse might use another person to demonstrate mouth-to-mouth resuscitation or techniques in bandaging wounds. Some people are able to use the object itself. One student who was interested in car mechanics brought a carburetor to class as a visual aid. A wide variety of posters can be made or bought. Posters are often most useful when you are going to use graphs or talk about statistical material. Advertising agencies often use flip-boards, a series of posters held together by rings at the top, to give presentations to potential advertisers. For simple diagrams and drawings, the blackboard may be the best choice.

The first question you should ask about visual material is whether your speech is better because you are using this particular visual aid. Don't use it for the sake of using it. If it does not really enhance your speech, get rid of it and use something else. If the material is complicated, prepare it beforehand. Make sure that it can be seen by everyone in the room and that there is a way to display it.

When you present your visual material, take care to talk to your audience—not to your material. Many people have a tendency to turn their backs on the audience, especially when they are using a poster or a blackboard drawing. It is also important to display your material at the proper psychological moment. An aid can be distracting so take it out when you are ready to use it and put it away when you have finished with it.

Good visual material can make a speech lively and interesting, but it requires as much thought as the speech itself. Think about all of your speeches, not just the ones where visual aids are required. Is there material that you can bring in to help reinforce and highlight these other speeches? If there is material, then use it. Your visual material might just be that little extra touch that makes a good speech a great speech.

DELIVERING THE SPEECH

Many of us would like to think that what we say is more important than how we say it. Unfortunately, that is not true. Researchers in public speaking have discovered that *delivery,* or how we give our speech, is very important. Specifically they have made the following conclusions: 1) effective delivery raises speaker credibility and contributes to speech persuasiveness; 2) audience comprehension suffers when a message is delivered in a monotone; 3) speaker fluency and effectiveness are closely related; and 4) audiences retain more of the message when rate, pitch, volume, and voice quality are varied.[6]

In Chapter 3, Nonverbal Communication, we discussed how and what you communicate by your use of time, body movement, space, and objects. All of these factors are essential to good delivery. If you are ready to give your first speech, you might find it useful to reread that chapter. The remainder of this section on delivery concerns the voice. Specifically we will discuss pitch, loudness, rate, pausing, and articulation as they relate to public speaking.

Pitch is the range of tones we use in speaking. Most of us use a variety of tones when we are speaking—sometimes we speak in high tones and sometimes in low tones. If we do not vary our pitch and speak in a single tone, we are said to be using a *monotone*.

Movement from one pitch to another is called *inflection*. Inflection adds nonverbal cues to our words. For example, if we say "I am finished," our inflection drops at the end of the sentence to indicate that our thought is completed. Thus, we have said it verbally (using words) and nonverbally (using inflection). If we ask "Are you finished?", there is a rise at the end of the sentence. Rising inflections usually indicate questioning or uncertainty. In some cases we use a double inflection, and our pitch moves up and down within a single sentence.

Some people want to change their general pitch range because they believe it is either too high or too low. This is best done with the help of a speech therapist. Fortunately, most of use do not have a need for such drastic change. In public speaking we are more likely to face problems of a monotone because contrasts between high and low are not great enough. We can also fall into a pattern where we always go up (or down) at a certain point in our sentences. Children often use a fixed inflection pattern when they recite poems, causing a hypnotic effect on their audience. Once a person becomes aware of these problems, they can be corrected. One of the best ways to practice is to take some prose material, and mark it in the places where you think the meaning of the material requires a variation in your pitch. Then practice reading it aloud. The marking will help to increase your awareness of pitch. Once you have awareness and some practice, you will be able to apply this awareness to your speeches.

Loudness refers to the volume the speaker uses. Loudness serves

---

6 Ronald L. Applbaum *et al, Fundamental Concepts in Human Communication* (San Francisco: Canfield Press, 1973), pp. 144–5.

two functions: it helps the speaker to be heard and it adds variety and interest to the speech.

Often people have a problem of not being loud enough. Most of us think we are speaking more loudly than we really are. Generally, if you sound a little too loud to your own ears, you are probably just about right for a public-speaking audience. Anxiety causes some of us to speak too softly. We "hide" from the audience by not letting them hear us. In this case we must deal with our anxiety before we can conquer the problem of volume. A large hall or auditorium requires a special effort from the speaker if he or she is to be heard. Usually this problem can be solved by breathing from the diaphragm. This system of breathing can best be demonstrated by your speech instructor.

In large rooms or auditoriums, speakers often must use a microphone. Generally the microphone is mounted on a floor stand and can be moved up and down. The microphone should be about the same height as your mouth, and it should be adjusted before you begin to speak. It is not necessary to lean toward the microphone. This will produce an unnatural sound and will emphasize your *s* sounds. Most microphones will pick up a normal speaking voice when the speaker is anywhere from ten to eighteen inches away from it. If you have an opportunity, check the microphone before you start to speak to make certain it is operating properly. It is frustrating, both to the speaker and to the audience, to have to solve microphone problems after the speech begins.

Once you have solved the problem of being heard, you should work on using loudness and softness for emphasis. We usually use loud tones to show excitement, high emotion, or anger, and soft tones to show calm, peace, or boredom. Practice your speech beforehand and try varying your volume. Once you have discovered what spots should be louder or softer, you will probably find it useful to make notations about volume on your speech outline.

Rate refers to how fast or how slowly we speak. There are some occasions that demand a certain rate of speaking. A sportscaster giving a play-by-play account of a basketball game goes very fast—not only to keep up with the game but also to communicate the excitement of the event. On the other hand, a rabbi, a priest, or a minister will go slowly through wedding or funeral services for they are formal and serious occasions and call for a slow and more solemn rate.

The public speaker's problem is not to go so fast that everyone is lost or so slowly that everyone is bored. If the material is complex, the speaker will find it helpful to slow down. If the material is simple, the speaker may try to speed up. There are some individuals who speak too fast or too slowly in all of their speeches, but this is generally not a common problem.

More common is the problem of pausing. The pause can be an extremely useful communication tool if it is used properly. Used improperly, pausing will cause the audience to see the speaker as lost or confused. Jack Benny has always been a master of the pause. On one of his old radio programs, a thief approached the great tightwad and demanded, "Your money or your life." The long pause that followed was one of radio's funniest moments.

The pause can be used to get attention. Experienced speakers often approach the lectern, pause, look over the audience, and then begin to speak. This pause allows the audience to turn their attention to the speaker. A pause can also be used for emphasis. When the speaker comes out with an important idea, he or she might then pause, communicating "this idea is important—think about it." Sometimes the pause can give the idea that the *speaker* is thinking. His or her ideas are not all "down pat"—the thought process is still going on.

In a mass media world where our ears are constantly assaulted with sound, we are afraid of silence. Rather than tolerating a short pause in our own speech, we have a tendency to use "uh" or "you know." It takes practice to use the pause effectively; it is almost a matter of instinct to know how long or how short it should be. Try putting some pauses into your next speech. You will be surprised to find what a useful delivery tool they are.

Articulation is the speaker's skill in making the sounds of the language. The aim of articulation is to be understood. Although there can be physical causes for poor articulation such as a hearing loss or badly aligned teeth, most articulation problems go back to our language models. If our parents, teachers, or peers had poor articulation, then we probably do too unless we have made a conscious effort to recognize and change these patterns.

Three common causes of articulation problems are sound substitution, omission of sounds, and slurring. Sound substitution is very common. Many people say "der," "dem," and "dose" for "there," "them," and "those." In this case a *d* has been substituted for the more difficult *th* sound. Americans are often dismayed to find they cannot get water in a foreign country. They would be more successful if they asked for "water" rather than "wader." In fact, the substitution of a *d* for a *t* in the middle of a word is widespread in American English. If you need any proof, try pronouncing these words as you usually do: "thirty," "Betty," "bottle." Unless you have unusually good articulation, you probably said "thirdy," "Beddy," and "boddle."

We also commonly omit sounds. For example, we sometimes say "libary" for "library," dropping out the first *r* sound. We frequently omit sounds that occur at the ends of words such as "goin" for "going" and "doin" for "doing."

Slurring is caused by running words together. We frequently use phrases such as "yawanna go?" and "I'll meecha there." Slurring, as with other articulation problems, is usually a matter of bad habits, and it can be overcome with some effort and practice.

Many people believe that they have a speech defect, and they are therefore unable to make certain sounds. This can be easily checked. For example, if you always say "der" for "there," make a special effort to make the *th* sound. If you are able to make it, you have a bad habit, not a speech defect.

Once you are aware of a particular articulation habit, then you can try to change it. Changing a habit is not easy since it has probably been a part of you for a good fifteen or twenty years. Sometimes it helps to drill using lists of words that give you trouble. Other times it helps to have a friend who has a good ear for detection remind you when you fall back into an old habit. Once you have accustomed yourself to looking for the problem, you will catch yourself more and more. If you have several articulation problems, do not try to solve them all at one time. Work on one sound at a time and when you can handle that sound, then attempt another one.

EVALUATION AND TRYING AGAIN

Many speakers feel their work is completed after they utter the final words of their conclusion. However, some of the most valuable speech work begins after a speech is over. Now is the time to ask if you reached your goal and to discover what effect you had on your audience.

These questions can be answered by the feedback you receive during and after your speech. If you were looking at your audience as you were giving the speech, how did they respond? Did they look interested or did they look bored? Did you have their attention at the beginning of the speech and lose it later? If so, why? You may be able to answer some of these questions while the speech is going on, but you can probably best discover the answers after the speech is over.

Some of our most useful feedback comes in terms of questions and discussion following a speech. Questions often indicate whether the audience followed the speech and understood what we were saying. Lively discussion often tells us that we have stimulated thinking among audience members. Our most negative feedback may be no feedback at all. The audience is apathetic; they have no questions and no comments. If directly asked what they thought of the speech, they might reply, "It was a nice speech. I liked it"—a comment that is so general that it has little value.

Often it is necessary to interpret feedback. For instance, let's say that your object in speaking is to have an audience sign a petition. After the speech is over several audience members shake your hand and say "great speech" and go off without signing the petition. Now your problem is to evaluate their feedback. If it was such a great speech, why did they not sign the petition?

The classroom situation provides an unusual opportunity for speech analysis. During the first speeches, your instructor (and perhaps your classmates) will probably spend a lot of time discussing your speech—especially in terms of delivery. We would all like to think that we have delivered a perfect speech, but such a thing hardly ever happens on the first time or even the second. You will be receiving some criticism that will be useful to you. Sometimes this criticism may seem very threatening as most of us dislike being criticized in public. It may be useful for you to remember that this criticism refers only to the speech content and to the way you delivered it. If you accept it in this sense, you will be able to change bad habits and to become aware of and overcome some communication difficulties you may not know you have. Once you are aware of your problems, you are ready to try again. By the time you give your last speech, you may be very close to giving a perfect speech.

SUMMARY

Public speaking is an important means of communication in a democratic society. In public speaking, the source has most of the responsibility for the message. Whether or not the audience decides to accept the message depends on how well the source plans the message and how he or she is perceived by the audience.

In preparing a speech, the speaker first analyzes the audience. He or she attempts to find common ground with the audience in attitudes, values, beliefs, and goals. If the speaker's attitudes are different from the audience, he or she attempts to minimize the differences.

Speech preparation involves choosing a topic that is of interest both to the speaker and to the audience. After the topic is chosen, the speaker gathers information from personal experience, from the community, and from the library.

Most speeches are informative or persuasive. Informative speeches present the audience with information about a subject and let them draw their own conclusion. Persuasive speeches try to move the audience to commitment or action. Both types of speeches should be organized with a statement of purpose, an introduction, a body, and a conclusion.

As the speaker prepares the speech, he or she must build in information that will keep the attention of the audience. Attention devices typically include material familiar to the audience, suspense, novel material, and humor. A speaker can tell if the audience is interested by being attentive to feedback from the audience.

The speaker also makes language choices while preparing the speech. These decisions involve selecting language that is best for the speaker, the audience, the speech situation, and the clear and precise expression of the speaker's ideas.

After the speech is over, the speaker can learn by evaluating the past speech experience. The more the speaker is able to understand his or her successes and failures, the more likely he or she is to be successful in the next speech.

FURTHER READING

Royal L. Garff, *You Can Learn to Speak*. Salt Lake City, Utah: Wheelwright Press, 1966.
  A popular book that you can probably find in your downtown library, this guide covers many aspects of public speaking that are useful to beginning speakers.

I Have Spoken: American History Through the Voices of Indians, compiled by Virginia Irving Armstrong. Chicago: The Swallow Press, 1971.
  This anthology includes speeches and fragments of speeches made by Indians on problems of concern to them. Some of the speeches go back to the seventeenth century.

Arthur Smith, *Language, Communication, and Rhetoric in Black America*. New York: Harper and Row, 1972.
  This collection of articles by various writers about the communica-

tion experiences of black Americans ranges from discussion about dialect to rhetorical case studies.

Leonard A. Stevens, *The Ill-Spoken Word*. New York: McGraw-Hill, 1966. This interesting and readable book discusses the spoken word. The writer looks at the history of speaking and asks some provocative questions about the role of speech in contemporary life.

Harold P. Zelko and Marjorie E. Zelko, *How to Make Speeches for All Occasions*. Garden City, N.Y.: Doubleday, 1971.

A practical and easily read book on how to plan and organize a speech, this work will serve as a good reference.

6

The Power of Communication

Each of us is influenced throughout life by two opposing forces: the urge to change and the urge to remain the same. Part of us likes the old ways, the familiar, the friends we have now, the book that confirms what we already believe. Another part of us searches for the new, the better way, an experience we have never had before, a television program that gives us a whole new perspective. Trying something new, whether it is a new job or a new relationship or a new course, has an element of excitement—but change also carries the threat that we will not be able to handle the new experience or that we will end up worse off than we were in the old, familiar place. It is clear that change is not necessarily positive; it is equally clear that progress—in a person, in a nation, in the life of mankind as a whole—is possible only if some things change.

One of the chief powers of communication is the capacity to effect change. Talking to your father about your values may result in a change in your relationship, in greater understanding and trust between you. Reading about a new field may cause you to change your major. Working with others in a small group may produce a new stoplight on the corner of your block. Delegates from many nations may sit around a table and agree to stop a war. The power of communication to change people's lives is fundamental and all-pervasive.

This chapter is about that power; it deals with *persuasion,* communication that is designed to effect changes in attitudes or behavior. Persuasion involves the use of verbal symbols and nonverbal behavior by the source with the intention of producing a change in the receiver. Almost every time you say anything to anyone else, you are persuading. When you ask your parents for money, when you tell an Internal Revenue Service agent that your tax report was accurate, when you indicate to the instructor that the hour is over, when you tell the sales clerk you need time to think about the purchase—you are involved in the act of persuasion. Persuasion is common in all communication situations; it occurs in interpersonal relationships, in the more formal public-speaking situation, in small groups, and in mass communication. There is, thus, hardly a chapter of this book that does not concern itself with persuasion.

The persuasive speaker touches our lives from the moment we rise in the morning with "Its time to get up!" to the time we turn off the television after hearing an author promoting his or her latest book on the late-night talk show. It is as important in our society as it is necessary. Understanding some of the components of the persuasion process will enable you to better evaluate and analyze the persuasion of others, to improve your own ability to persuade, and to become a better contributor in decision-making processes involving change.

The communicator who intends to produce changes in others and fails is still involved in the persuasive process because of his or her intent. Persuasion may result because of the characteristics of a particular person who has the ability to produce changes in others. Persuasion may result from the message because certain elements in discourse are intended to alter behavior. But because the intention of a persuasive message is to change the receiver, the communicator is not really the persuader. The communicator simply provides stimuli that encourage the receiver to persuade himself or herself. Thus, the receiver is the persuader in the active sense. You may be persuaded to vote for a political candidate, for example, because you are satisfied that he or she is more honest or more concerned than the opponents. On the basis of the information you receive, you persuade yourself that your vote may provide you with "cleaner" government. The candidate only provides the stimuli to convince you.

Because persuasion really occurs within the listener, one primary function of the communicator should be getting and holding attention. If a listener's sensory receptors—eyes and ears especially—are not attracted to the stimulus—the idea or message—no persuasion can occur, even though symbols may be used by the communicator. The source's intent to persuade or the use of persuasive elements of discourse do not in themselves guarantee that change will take place. As in other forms of communication, success is measured by what happens at the receiving end, in the listener. The communicator who can use symbols and ideas that are familiar, have some variety, reveal more intensity than competing stimuli, are repeated, and show novelty or unusualness will grasp attention and hold it better than a communicator whose message does not manifest these characteristics. The next time you are trying to persuade someone else to do something, test this idea by changing your voice, your language, your meaning, your gestures, or your bodily action to see if such a change has higher attention-getting value. In persuading others, however, it is important that the technique should not become so obvious as to attract attention to itself. Also, persuasive techniques are usually used in conjunction with each other—seldom in isolation. The importance and value of the concept of attention should be kept in mind as the other components of the persuasive process are discussed.

Because major portions of the material that could be treated in a chapter on persuasion have been treated elsewhere in this book, we will focus here on six major areas that concern persuasion directly: 1) the means of persuasion, 2) suggestion and protest as forms of persuasion, 3) attitude change, 4) the effects of persuasion, 5) resisting persuasion, and 6) ethical considerations in persuasion. The nuts and bolts of putting a persuasive speech together have been discussed in Chapter 5, Public Speaking. The persuasive proposition is treated in Chapter 7, Small-Group Communication. Ethos—the image of the communicator in the eyes of the receiver—is of major importance in persuasion; it may indeed wield a stronger influence than other devices for persuasion such as argument, evidence, appeals to motives, or appeals to emotion. You may want to review the discussion of ethos in the chapter on public speaking.

MEANS OF PERSUASION

If you have ever been asked to make a case for abolishing a requirement at your school to the faculty or administration or if you have ever planned an argument against pollution to present to a group of industrialists or if you have ever been motivated to convince someone else to join a cause or organization to which you belong, you have probably been faced with decisions that concern *means*—how to most effectively influence a receiver or group of receivers.

There are, basically, three means of persuasion: 1) *logos*—using sound reasoning and dependable evidence, 2) *pathos*—relating the desired change to the attitudes and emotions of the listeners, and 3) *ethos*—demonstrating the good will, wisdom, and character of the communicator.

The three elements are not mutually exclusive, nor should a persuasive communication be designed to contain only one of them; different situations require varying degrees of logos, pathos, and ethos. A balance is the ideal in most situations. Making a case before the faculty or administration would very likely require more evidence—cold facts—than the other two situations. Faculty members or administrators tend to value logos and to make judgments only after serious consideration and study of the matter. An emotional plea would probably detract from the credibility of the communicator since a student would, very likely, be seen as immature if he or she pleaded the case with passion. The more evidence the student could amass, the more probable he or she could make the desired change in the receivers.

Arguing against pollution is a different situation. It is unlikely that the facts and other data that you could gather would have significance to an industrialist. In many cases, they already know the facts, or think they do. Although your credibility may be low, you might have a chance to persuade them by making an impassioned plea for the salvation of our earth and the preservation of something inhabitable for future generations. Another use of pathos might be even more effective: presenting the possibility of a boycott of the products produced by this particular industry. This would have an emotional impact since industry's primary goal is making money.

Finally, to convince someone to join a cause or an organization might require some logic, some emotion, and a good deal of ethos. Your ability to persuade the other person in this case would probably depend, to a great extent, on what he or she thought of your own wisdom regarding this choice and your other choices as well—those to which the other person may have been exposed in the past. How important your character is to the other person, whether he or she wants to be associated with you, even your good will in approaching the other person may affect your success in convincing him or her to join. People sometimes forget that the establishment of high credibility—effective ethos—is not a function of a specific situation. It begins when your association with another person begins and develops throughout your relationship.

There is no formula for choosing the best means of persuasion. Sometimes you need to use more logic—a clear purpose, strong evidence, a unified structure, and cogent reasoning—as opposed to appeals to the audience's feelings or to the straightforward establishment of your credibility in the other person's eyes. Choosing the best means requires audience analysis; you need to know who the audience is, how old they are, what sex they are, how they feel about your ideas or topic, and what they know of you as a communicator. Such analysis may be made of one other person, of a group of people, or of the public at large.

If your analysis of your receiver(s) indicates that the audience's attitude seems to favor your idea, you could heighten this feeling by giving an emotional plea. The addresses given before conventions of political parties are examples of this kind of persuasion. In personal conversation, you can give a personal example or anecdote to indicate that your feelings about this idea are the same as your listener's. In a small group, facts and additional evidence are often provided to heighten the unanimity of feeling.

When receivers are neutral or apathetic, which is the common state of most receivers, some evidence along with some emotion and a strong case for the source's credibility may cause them to change their behavior. Listeners are so consistent in their neutral reaction to most ideas that we have coined another definition: "Persuasion is the art of moving apathy in your direction." Richard Nixon once used another phrase to characterize the general public—he called them "The Silent Majority."

With a hostile audience, the evidence should be powerful. To provide support for strong evidence, one's credibility should also be strong. The person bent on the persuasion of a hostile receiver should be warned that this is a difficult situation; there is little hope for success in changing the behavior of someone who is truly hostile. An informative approach—establishing the idea as an important one through the presentation of facts and opinions with no emotional pleas whatsoever—may be an effective tactic. With sufficient information, and given time to think over the ideas and to contact others regarding them, the receiver may at least become more open to your message.

It is likely that anything you do before, during, or after a persuasive communication will bear in some way on your logos, pathos, or ethos. The more concerned you are with influencing, the more care you should take in controlling the means you use to persuade. Think about these factors next time you are in the receiver's position. What does the communicator have to do to make you say "I'm sold—you convinced me!" to a salesperson, "Wow—that was an impressive speech" to a public speaker, or "That was a compelling advertisement" to your television set? Logos, pathos, and ethos should blend together to form the means of persuasion in such a way that they are neither distracting nor obvious. It is not the technique, after all, to which the listener is to respond— it is the idea or the message. Generally speaking, and with regard to the use of these means in an honorable fashion, it is not as important to note *how* one is convinced (whether it was logos, pathos, or ethos) as to note *that* one is convinced—that someone's behavior has actually changed as a result of a stimulus you produced through means of persuasion.

Occasionally you will see a persuasive message that has been designed without careful audience analysis or a message that is clearly designed for an audience that does not include you. The effect of such a message can be to arouse laughter or anger instead of the change desired by the source. A billboard showing a bathing beauty in a bikini to advertise a new car, for example, may arouse contempt in a viewer who is sophisticated enough to recognize and resent the obvious suggestion that having the car will also get one the woman. Sometimes errors in audience analysis can make the message have an effect that is the opposite of the one intended. Recently this happened with some antismoking advertisements that were placed in late afternoon commercial television children's programs. Some of the advertisements were designed to be very ironic, showing a person enjoying a cigarette while a "voice over" talked about the dangers and tragedies of smoking, clearly pointing out to the listener that the person depicted would not live to enjoy the pleasures of a full lifetime. The visual picture had a powerful impact on children who could not detect the irony; they responded to the message by picking up sticks and imitating the smoker in the advertisement.

SUGGESTION: THE STILL, SMALL VOICE

Remember the television and radio advertisement that goes, "You can take Salem out of the country, but you can't take the country out of Salem?" The advertisement ends with the singing of just the first half of the phrase (up to word *but*) followed by the ding of a bell. It compels the listener to complete the phrase in his or her own mind and, thus, plants the name of the product in the listener's consciousness through a creative jingle, a catchy phrase, and a memorable tune. The listener is stimulated to remember the name of the product without ever having responded to the product in a critical way at all. He or she may even find that the tune will constantly recur and will be whistled or hummed in idle moments. This process, through which persons respond more or less uncritically to persuasive stimuli, is known as *suggestion*. The degree to which a persuader is aware of suggestion and controls it may determine his or her effectiveness.

Suggestion works in a variety of different ways. Like many of the other components of communication, each suggestion technique can be adapted to a specific situation. We will mention the use of ethos as it relates to suggestion. We will also note how the presence of other people contributes to suggestion. Creating an appropriate atmosphere can be important. Finally, we will mention a variety of other techniques that the persuader can use to suggest a change to the listener. Variety and flexibility should be considered in the use of any or all of the techniques mentioned.

Advertising gimmicks represent a significant portion of the persuasive stimuli that affect us in our daily lives. Advertisers, of course, spend millions of dollars to get the "right" saying or the "right" music for their product. With the tremendous amount of money expended on behalf of creating this kind of suggestion, it is little wonder that we are almost constantly bombarded! Most advertisers are satisfied if their product gains the attention of the listener because it is thought that this recognition alone will cause the listener to buy the product since he or she will have been subconsciously influenced to purchase it by the suggestion of the advertisement.

A technique which is commonly used by advertisers is *ethos,* persuasive power that operates through suggestion by association. Many writers refer to ethos as "prestige suggestion." Advertisers use this technique when they pay prestigious figures to endorse their products. You have undoubtedly believed something or done something simply because a source you considered important suggested it. Popular sports figures and film stars are often used in this manner—partly because they are accustomed to eliciting the attention of audiences. It is interesting to see Joe Namath, Mark Spitz, or Patricia Neal perform in an advertisement.

The influence of prestigious figures does not operate in advertising alone. One of the authors of this text, for example, once went out and bought an expensive long-playing record of the sounds of earthquakes, ionospheric swishes, whistlers, tweeks, and the dawn chorus just because a high-school science teacher spoke so highly of it. It was a once-in-a-lifetime opportunity to have these sounds on record—and the record was listened to once in the author's lifetime! This, too, was uncritical acceptance. Ethos is often at work when someone says, "I'd believe (or do) it, if I were you." Your action is then dependent on the prestige value of the source. Even if we rationalize the behavior with a phrase like, "Oh, I was going to do it anyway," the prestigious figure may have been the final stimulus that tipped the scales and caused you to act. This kind of suggestion is unlikely to do much more than simply tip the scales, but in many cases, this is all that is desired.

Another source of suggestion is a crowd of other people. Have you ever noticed how your behavior changes when you are with a large group? James A Winans, an early writer on communication, noted that men's minds are "overcome by mass suggestion" when in a "psychological crowd." We are less critical and discriminating—more emotional and responsive. "A crowd of men, usually polite," according to Winans, "will hoot at strangers, women, or authorities. Men usually reserved will slap each other on the back, shake hands with strangers, parade in lockstep, laugh, shout, sing with abandon."[1] An effective public speaker capitalizes on this tendency when he encourages his audience to sit close together down in front of where he or she is speaking. People who are seated close together are more susceptible to *social facilitation*—each person's responses will be increased by the mere presence of others. The speaker's jokes will be funnier, a sorrowful message will be more grievous, and inspirational sentiments will be more uplifting. In a sense, other people around us give us implicit suggestions on how to act. We may laugh at another's joke because those around us laugh, even if we then have to ask a friend to repeat the punchline. We may applaud a performance because those around us applaud, even if we dislike it. When we are with others we also feel less inhibited, and their reactions and responses are more readily communicated to us.

There are also certain sounds and body movements that tend to affect the audience psychologically when they are performed in rhythm by the group. The use of rhythm can help to create an atmosphere for uncritical acceptance. Rituals, chants, songs, hand-clapping, cheering, and the like heighten suggestibility by lowering your critical abilities in a particular setting and reducing your *will* to evaluate critically. Some church services rely heavily on these techniques in their worship. You may recall rhythmical performances occurring at political conventions, pep rallies, and rock concerts as well.

Suggestion also occurs when an appropriate atmosphere is created. Often, a great deal of time and effort are expended to produce a con-

---

[1] James A. Winans, *Public Speaking: Principles and Practice* (Ithaca, New York: The Sewell Publishing Company, 1915), p. 287.

ducive climate. When a public-speaker delivers his message in an assembly hall, tabernacle, or synagogue, the speech seems important and grand. A location can affect your suggestibility. When Presidential candidate Edmund Muskie declared his intention to run for office to the nation, he did so sitting in a room in rural Maine with all the blandishments of a Lincolnesque setting—suggesting the "honest Abe" image through the surroundings and decorations. When a person wants to suggest making love, the persuasive communication can be heightened by soft music, dim lights, and wine.

We tend to think of the analysis of crowd behavior as being a fairly recent study, dating perhaps from the mass rallies in Germany in the 1930s, but mass behavior had been studied in depth even before that time. H. L. Hollingworth, writing in *The Psychology of the Audience* in 1935, noted several ways through which suggestion can operate. Suggestion is more likely to have impact if the persuader will attempt to have the suggestion seem to originate with the listener. It is likely to be more effective if it is presented with force and vividness, if it is made positively rather than negatively (the persuader argues in favor of his own ideas rather than against an opposing view) and if it is presented more than once (that is, if it is repeated). The power of suggestion will be increased as well if the persuader increases his own prestige, aligns his suggestions with the dynamic motives and beliefs of the listener, and refrains from suggesting opposing or rival courses of action.[2]

Each of the following techniques also can increase the possibility that suggestion will occur: the persuader asks questions to which the listener can answer "yes"; creates an appropriate emotional tone or mood for the message; assumes that the listener will agree with him or her; achieves common ground with the listener by appealing to his or her beliefs, wants, needs, and desires; identifies himself or herself with the listener's causes; and phrases his or her ideas to utilize the energy of the listener's motives.

Suggestions and associations are generated in the minds of listeners with or without the specific intention of the source whenever communication occurs. The persuader who attempts to channel those suggestions to his or her own ideas, beliefs, or actions is simply capitalizing on a present and unavoidable force. The persuader who successfully controls the force is using suggestion positively—in his or her own behalf—rather

---

2 H. L. Hollingworth, *The Psychology of the Audience* (New York: The American Book Company, 1935), pp. 142–144.

than being controlled by it or allowing the suggestion to occur in random fashion.

Persuasion by suggestion is one of the most subtle forms of exerting control through communication. Becoming aware of the power of other's suggestions, whether they are intentional or unintentional, begins when you ask yourself why you do what you do and believe what you believe. Your behavior and your values come, in part, from the influence of others, and much of that influence is in the form of suggestion. It is one of the main communication techniques, for example, through which parents train their children to behave in ways that are acceptable to the parents and to society at large.

PROTEST: THE URGE TO SHOUT

At the other end of the persuasion continuum is the range of communications that have been labeled *protest*. Unlike suggestion, protest communication is very obvious; it works for change through confrontation between the source and receiver in which the source is very open about his or her intention to produce a change in the receiver.

When we speak of protest communication in America, we usually think of the turbulent decade of the sixties. However, protest goes back to the earliest periods of American history. The period preceeding the American Revolution was filled with revolutionary tracts whose modern equivalent would be the underground newspaper. Early demonstrations included such famous events as the Boston Tea Party and the Boston Massacre. Long before the Civil War, there were speeches, writing, and demonstrations for and against slavery. Even the current women's movement has a historical precedent—at the beginning of the twentieth century and until the end of World War I, women were involved in the suffragist movement, which was concerned with obtaining the right to vote. Protest was justified and encouraged by such influential early Americans as Thomas Jefferson who wrote "timid men . . . prefer the calm of despotism to the boisterous sea of liberty."[3]

Yet even with historical precedent and philosophical justification, the period of the sixties was a time of great shock and dismay to many Americans. Perhaps this shock was intensified because of the passivity of the fifties. Students of the fifties were described as the "silent gen-

3 Thomas Jefferson, Letter to Mazzei (1796).

eration" and the decade was largely one of apathy and "do-nothing." We will probably never be able to conclusively answer why one decade is quiet and another is turbulent. However, we do know that the conditions for protest exist a long time before the actual act of protesting occurs.

The Conditions for Protest

Kennth Boulding has written of the conditions that provoke protest:

> Protest arises when there is a strongly felt dissatisfaction with existing programs and policies of government or other organizations, on the part of those who feel themselves affected by these policies but who are unable to express their discontent through legitimate and regular channels, and who are unable to exercise the weight to which they think they are entitled in the decision-making process. When nobody is listening to us and we feel we have something to say, then comes the urge to shout.[4]

Perhaps the conditions for protest are best characterized by the feeling of frustration on the part of the protesters. The traditional democratic institution has broken down, and the protester feels powerless.

> When one person or a few people in a group or society possess all the guns, muscles or money, and the others are relatively weak and helpless, optimum conditions do not exist for discussion, mutual influence, and democracy. Discussion in such circumstances occurs only at the sufferance of the powerful; and generous as these people may sometimes be, they are not likely voluntarily to abdicate their power when vital interests are at stake. . . . The most solid and enduring basis for democracy exists when the participants possess relative equality of power. Discussion is assured only when those desiring discussion—usually those who are dissatisfied with the present state of affairs—have sufficient power to make those in control of the situation listen to them.[5]

The Dynamics of Protest Groups

All protest groups have a great deal of intrapersonal and interpersonal communication within the group that is not intended for outsiders. The purpose of this communication is to unite group members and to form group goals. This process is particularly important to long-term groups because it gives the movement continuity.

[4] Kenneth E. Boulding, "Towards a Theory of Protest" in *The Age of Protest*, Walt Anderson (ed.) (Pacific Palisades, Calif.: Goodyear Publishing Co., 1969), p. vi.

[5] Dean C. Barnlund and Franklyn S. Haiman, *The Dynamics of Discussion* (Boston: Houghton-Mifflin, 1960), p. 12.

The first intrapersonal function of a protest group is what women's groups have labeled "consciousness raising." As we have pointed out in the Self and Communication chapter, many of us have an idea of ourself which is based on who other people think we are. The purpose of consciousness raising is to reject society's definition of you and to define your own self. Self-definition is a profound concept which goes right to the central core of a human being. How does it work in practice?

For many years, blacks used skin lighteners and attempted to straighten their hair. This behavior has been seen as an attempt to imitate whites and to conform to white standards of beauty: a beautiful person has light skin and straight hair. By performing these two acts, blacks accepted the white definition of beauty and hence rejected the idea that dark skin and nappy hair could be attractive. When blacks began to define themselves, they stopped using skin lighteners, wore their hair in "naturals" or Afros, and said, "Black is beautiful." Similarly, in the women's movement, women began to admit that they were not finding fulfillment in being only wives and mothers, and they began to reject this narrow definition of themselves. Many homosexuals have rejected the widespread idea that homosexuality is a mental sickness, and they are now maintaining that it is an alternative life style that can be deliberately chosen by healthy persons.

In order to aid the identity process, the groups also create a group mythology by discovering and writing their history. Arthur Smith, who has written about the black protest movement, says, "Convinced that the white man had dominated other peoples of the world because his myths were stronger, the black rhetors [speakers and writers] saw an opportunity to re-direct and re-structure reality. . . . The intent of this rhetoric is to get on the offensive by defining one's world in relationship to one's self, as indeed, the black revolutionists insist the white man has done for five hundred years."[6]

This group awareness of history has had implications outside of the group. Many schools are offering courses in black studies and women's studies. Interested groups are working to counteract the image of Indians that has appeared in numerous cowboy-and-Indian films. Homosexuals celebrate Gay Pride Day with parades in major American cities.

The idea behind the creation of mythology and history is to give individuals a collective group identity. Group identity is also developed

[6] Arthur L. Smith, *Rhetoric of Black Revolution* (Boston: Allyn and Bacon, 1969), p. 19.

in other ways. All of these groups have ways of identifying themselves to other members or potential members. These range from pins they can wear to handshakes. The blacks and the homosexuals also have a group language that is not understood by people who are not members. This private language ties members of the groups more closely together. There is also ridicule of potential group members who pretend to be different from what they really are. All groups speak scornfully of the "sell-outs"—those who are on the side of conformity. Sometimes these nonmembers are specifically labeled with terms such as "oreo," "Uncle Tom," or "closet queen."

Communicating Protest

Recent protest has been either issue-oriented or group-oriented. Issue-oriented protest occurs when persons get together to protest a specific issue or social evil. Typical past examples have been the protest of the Vietnam War, the demonstrations staged at the 1968 Democratic National Convention, and various challenges to university and college administrations. Individuals involved in the protest may be very different from each other in their everyday life—their main purpose in grouping is to protest the issue and after the problem is solved (or the issue loses interest) the group disbands.

Generally issue-oriented protest has only short-term goals. Group protest, on the other hand, has long-range goals, and protest may continue for several years. Group protest occurs when individuals form a group to protest against discrimination of themselves as a group. Typical examples would be blacks, women, Indians, and Chicanos. Members of the group have a common identity—their blackness, their femaleness—and their protest is a long-term ongoing process.

Generally protest communication goes through various stages. In the first stage, it is not true protest for the intention of communication is to produce dialogue and discussion. The persons who have a complaint get together to discuss the problem with the authorities—those who have the power to bring about a change. A typical example might be a group of students discussing the college grading system with members of the administration. If those in power are responsive to the complaints and to solving the problem, then the complaining parties disband. If the authorities are not responsive, however, the communication changes: dialogue and discussion become protest. Even if the protesters expect no cooperation from the authorities, this attempt at dialogue-

discussion is essential because if those in power refuse to negotiate, then the parties concerned will feel that they have a legitimate reason for protest.

In the second stage, the protesters attempt to win support for their position. They may picket, erect posters, distribute leaflets, hold a mass meeting, or attempt to get media coverage. This particular step is largely informational and educational. It attempts to attract as many sympathetic followers as possible. In this stage an attempt is made to build group unity, to determine goals and strategy, and to eliminate those people who do not belong in the group. (We have elaborated on the ways this is done in the preceding section.)

The next stage of protest is nonviolent resistance. Nonviolence is aimed more at the policy than at those who invent or perpetuate the policy. Typical examples of nonviolent policy are sit-ins and boycotts. For instance, a group of civil-rights workers successfully used a sit-in in Jackson, Mississippi. They occupied the seats of the lunch counter at Woolworth's until the store changed its policy of not serving blacks. Boycotts have been used in the same way. Groups of people refuse to buy at a store until the store changes its policy of high prices or not serving certain groups of people.

Nonviolent demonstrations have the intent of bringing change peacefully. However, past nonviolent demonstrations have often provoked violence on the part of the authorities: times when they have refused to negotiate and have reacted violently against the demonstrators. This reaction causes some demonstrators to go into the new stage of confrontation that may involve using violence deliberately. In fact, in the late sixties, some persons became disillusioned with nonviolent demonstrations and bypassed the nonviolent resistance stage, moving immediately to confrontation.

Bowers and Ochs have discussed the confrontation stage in great detail in their book *Rhetoric of Agitation and Control*. They say that the purpose of the confrontation stage is to irritate the authorities so much that they react violently. When society at large sees those with power reacting violently, then society will demand that reform take place.[7]

A good example of this kind of reaction from society occurred after several students were shot by National Guardsmen during a protest in 1970 at Kent State University. Previous student protests often seemed remote to the American public and many Americans asked, in some con-

---

7 John Waite Bowers and Donovan J. Ochs, *The Rhetoric of Agitation and Control* (Addison-Wesley: Reading, Mass., 1971), pp. 35–37.

PROTEST: THE URGE TO SHOUT 197

fusion, why students could not appreciate their opportunities and priviledged place in society. The Kent State shootings changed the picture drastically. The victims were the sons and daughters of the middle-class; the neighborhood baby-sitter, the boy-next-door. Because Americans could identify with these victims, they were outraged; their outrage led them to demand explanation and "justice" from the authorities as well as reassurance that such actions would never happen again.

A few days after the Kent State shootings, several black students were wounded and two were killed by state and local policemen at Jackson State College. This incident did not provoke nearly so much outrage. Although it is possible that the American public could not bear any more grief and tragedy, there was also the factor that most people simply could not identify with black students. We do not maintain that Kent State and Jackson State students deliberately provoked violence; however, these examples seem to point out that if violence is going to be effective as a protest tactic, it will work only if there is potential identification between society and the protestors.

Many protestors use tactics to push the authorities into violence. They may spread rumors that large numbers of people are going to turn out for the demonstration and that there will be violence. This causes the police to appear in large numbers, which creates a greater potential for trouble. The protestors may use nonverbal signs to provoke their antagonists. These symbols include such nonverbal behavior as giving the peace sign, a black power sign, or making an obscene gesture. Language is also used to provoke. Insults and profanity are shouted to enrage the enemy. Desecration is another possible tactic. Those in authority are often upset when radicals or hippies wear the flag—they are even more upset when they burn it. Finally, if the protesters cannot provoke their antagonists into reacting violently, they may try some token violence. This may include throwing rocks, spitting on establishment members, or actual physical assault—acts all calculated to bring about violence.[8]

Even though the protesters have provoked the violence, the authorities may be seen by society as the villain for they are the ones with the guns while their opponents usually have only sticks, stones, and bottles to use as weapons.

The confrontation stage is the end of the protest process. If confrontation does not lead to negotiation, then the protesters must try additional confrontations or previously mentioned protest strategies. It is important to remember that even through the confrontation stage, the

8 Bowers and Ochs, pp. 35–37.

protest group still has the ultimate goal of integrating into the mainstream of society.

Some groups ultimately decide that they want no more to do with protest, and they go another step which is beyond protest—that of *separation* from society. Sometimes this separation is peaceful as in the case of students who dropped out of school to pursue alternative life styles in places such as communes. In other cases, separation leads to violence. The Weathermen, for example, have gone underground with the intention of forming a revolutionary group to overthrow the government.

No single group can be described as being in a specific stage of protest. For example, there are some blacks who are interested in discussion, some who are interested in protest, and others who are interested in separation. Individuals may also change. Bobby Seale, a Black Panther leader, has been in both the confrontation and separation stages; running for office put him into the dialogue-discussion stage. The period of time in history also seems to make a difference. The early sixties were characterized by nonviolent protest while the late sixties were a period of confrontation. It is almost impossible to predict what the future will bring.

Mass Media and Protest

One characteristic of the protest movement is a wide-scale use of the mass media. The media are used in two ways: within the group to reach their own members and outside the group to bring their cause to the attention of the general public.

The mass medium most often used within the protest group is the underground newspaper or some similar publication that appears periodically. Some of these publications have a long life such as *Muhammed Speaks,* the newspaper of the Black Muslim movement, while others come and go. The underground publication has two functions: it creates a sense of group unity, and it reports news that would probably not be reported by the general mass media. By reporting their own news, the group is assured of having the information presented as they want it to appear—without the press establishment's bias or slanting.

Beginning with the civil rights movement in the early sixties, all protest groups have made wide use of the media to present their cause to the rest of society. They have been particularly interested in network television coverage because this medium reaches the largest possible audience. The obsession with media coverage is so great that some critics have observed that many protests appear to be staged specifically for the mass media. *Newsweek* comments on this phenomenon on the occasion of the 1973 Indian occupation at Wounded Knee: "As in the 1969 occupation of Alcatraz Island and last fall's seizure of the Bureau of Indian Affairs in Washington, the militants had gained attention in what was essentially a media maneuver. . . . Like any media maneuver, it demanded a climax—and the danger was that neither side would feel able to back off."[9]

All protesters must learn to use the media; protesting, as an act in itself, carries no assurance of media coverage. Most protesters now realize that the media is not interested in reporting ideologies, debates, speeches, or news of lawsuits. Instead the media, and particularly television, want action and drama. Therefore the protesters deliberately stage events that they know will be newsworthy. The Indians did this at Wounded Knee. There was also a good deal of staging at the 1968 Democratic National Convention in Chicago. "In particular, the demonstrators understood the passion of TV for action shots. On the eve of the convention one group obligingly staged rehearsals—for the cameras—showing how they would break the police lines. No statement or prediction seemed too eccentric to get TV attention."[10] When protesters plan for media coverage and stage events for the mass media, they have completed a crucial step in their strategy.

Can Protest Communication Be Positive?

As we have looked at protest communication, we can see that it is filled with ritual, strategy, and even a sense of theatre. As a form of communication, it seems far away from the ideals of openness, honesty, identification, and reasoned discourse that we have discussed in other chapters. Yet protest communication deals with real grievances and involves people who have suffered great physical and psychological damage. Its accomplishments have been notable; American society is far away from the attitudes of complacency and apathy they held in the fifties. Many people are aware of injustices—in their lives and in the lives of others; this awareness has been brought about by protest.

Some people believe that the wave of protest is over and that the future will be a quieter period. Many people have become newly aware of discrimination against themselves, however, and it seems likely that

9 *Newsweek*, March 12, 1973, pp. 27–29.
10 James McCartney, "Must the Mass Media Be 'Used'?" in *Mass Media and Mass Man*, Alan Casty (ed.) (2d ed.; Holt, Rinehart and Winston: New York, 1973), p. 234.

they will fight to gain the rights of which they are newly aware. There seem to be three possibilities open for the next decade: the first is that it will be one of violent confrontation as was the decade of the sixties. The second possibility is that those in power have become receptive to new ideas and will accept formerly disenfranchised groups. This book is being written during the Watergate hearings, and while it is difficult to assess their final impact on American society, it seems impossible that Americans will retain their blind faith in the establishment—especially in the present one. Watergate and similar events may open American eyes to some of the alternatives. The third possibility, and the most dismal one, is that the authorities will become more unyielding and will be unwilling to assimilate any dissenting groups. Then the protesters have no alternative; if they are to continue, they must go underground and turn revolutionary. Protest, then, will give way to increasing acts of terrorism. Only time will tell the direction we are going to take.

USING PERSUASION TO CHANGE ATTITUDES

A person's attitudes, like his or her behavior and beliefs, are learned. Your attitudes are the result of your experiences, the influence of individuals and groups in our society, and your personal values. What a person is at any one time depends in part upon his or her past. Exposed to a stimulus to change—like a persuasive message—you may resist because the change represents an alteration of past behavior and involves some feeling of risk. This is true even if the stimulus to change comes from within yourself. Thus, change is likely to occur slowly and over a long period of time. The realistic persuader will limit his or her expectations and not be disappointed when changes take time to happen.

The rate and degree of change that is possible in any situation depends upon the attitudes of the source and the receiver toward that change. Changes in behavior begin with changes in attitudes. An *attitude* is a positive or negative feeling that we associate with an object, an event, another person, a situation, and so on. It is the mental position that we take for or against something. A shift in your attitude about something will often eventually result in a change in your behavior. If someone convinces you to dislike a course you are taking and attending regularly, you may begin to attend it less regularly—a behavioral response corresponding to your shift in attitude.

The speaker in a persuasive communication is likely to have a stable and predictable attitude toward the message. Since he or she is advocating the change, the speaker will have a favorable attitude toward the message, usually an attitude that is quite definite and compelling. The listener, on the other hand, may have almost any attitude toward the message. He or she could be favorably disposed—showing moderate interest or even great enthusiasm. The listener could be negatively disposed toward the message—showing strong antagonism or rejection. He or she might also have a neutral attitude—showing apathy, ambivalence, indifference, or ignorance about the topic.

In addition to the listener's attitude toward the particular message that the speaker wishes to have received, the persuader should note a general attitude toward change which many people exhibit. Generally, it is safe to assume that people believe what they want to believe. Most of us are ego-centered, strongly invested in our own interests. When presented with a persuasive message, people will select, organize, and interpret stimuli in line with their existing motives—that is, they will modify their behavior according to what is important to them or gratifying for them. Because most people act and think this way, you should do more than simply tell another person what you wish him or her to accept or believe. Although telling the listener clearly and distinctly is important, you also have to show how his or her acceptance of your message will be personally gratifying.

You have to be concerned with the needs which motivate individuals to action or belief. If you wish to change your listener, you must first influence his or her attitudes, and individual feelings are almost always tied up in some kind of self-interest. This is not necessarily ruthless or selfish since people associate their own self-interest with many positive values, both for themselves and for others. You might be able to change an attitude, for example, if you showed a person that your idea would satisfy his or her physical well-being—an appeal to the desire for good health, which we all agree is a worthwhile attitude. You could appeal to the need for pleasurable feelings—sex, adventure, or fun. You could appeal to the listener's interest in having money or material things, in gaining the good will or attention of others, in achieving personal success or social status or esteem, or in enjoying freedom or acquiring individual desires and ends. These are all desirable goals for which most people in our society strive.

We also have feelings of duty, and to those who are duty-conscious, you could appeal to their obligations to family, state, nation, business, religion, and so on. Most of us have positive attitudes toward telling the truth, keeping promises, and otherwise maintaining the mores and rules of our culture. An effective persuasive message might indicate that the change proposed will satisfy one of these needs. Finally, we could appeal to the listener's desires to engage in commendable behavior—maintaining one's self-image; being kind and fair; exhibiting courage, honesty, tolerance, persistence, or sincerity, for example. When a person feels that your idea will satisfy his or her needs, the listener will be disposed to change his or her attitude.

You are not likely to arouse an emotion simply by describing it or by telling the receiver he or she ought to feel it. The appeal should be vividly presented with illustrations that show real people in real situations so that the receiver can be lead to sympathize and emphathize. The receiver will become part of the persuasion process if the right mood is present and if the persuader has succeeded in getting on *common ground* with him or her—offering ideas with which the listener can identify and feel strongly.

As a persuader, you can create attitude change through three processes identified by Herbert C. Kelman, a writer on opinion change.[11] Kelman says that attitudes can be changed by compliance, identification, or internalization. If you provide the receiver with either rewards or punishments for adopting behaviors and attitudes, you are using *compliance*. The receiver is likely to alter his or her behavior and attitudes for the moment but not to change basic attitudes, his or her fundamental reasons for holding those attitudes or acting the way he or she does. The mother who rewards children with candy for behaving while she is grocery shopping may alter their mischievous behavior for the moment, but such behavior is likely to recur in another moment or as soon as the children are outside the supermarket.

A persuader who seeks to have receiver(s) be more like the persuader or some other person is using *identification*. The receiver may be encouraged to adopt attitudes similar to those of the source or of others. When a persuader uses himself or herself as the "model," he or she is using *ethos* to promote the cause. If others are used, they are established as "idols" for emulation. It might be possible, for instance, for you to encourage a son to be more like his father, a young woman to be more like her teacher, a parishioner to be more like his or her minister, or a citizen to be more like a politician he or she admires. Often, this change, too, is temporary for it is based on identification rather than intellectual agreement. If the new attitude or behavior is not reinforced by others or if the receiver and the "idol" are separated for a period of time, the atti-

---

11 Herbert C. Kelman, "Processes of Opinion Change," *Public Opinion Quarterly*, 25 (1961): 57–78.

tude or behavior is likely to change back to the way it was originally.

If the persuader can convince the receiver that the change in behavior or attitude is in agreement with the receiver's basic values, then the message is likely to be internalized and integrated with the receiver's existing values. This process—*internalization*—encourages the receiver to be influenced at a deep level and to adopt the recommended course of action because he or she is truly convinced of it intellectually. A salesman might use this technique to convince a person to buy a product because of the utilitarian value of the product—that is, the person could see himself or herself making a great deal of use of the product.

We cannot control other people's behavior all the time; thus, we try to persuade them to change their attitudes in an attempt to eventually alter their behavior. The effects or outcomes of our attempts will be different with different situations, different participants, and different messages, but in every case, lasting changes in behavior will result only if attitudes are changed.

WILL THE CHANGE LAST?

If you are able to cause another person to change his or her attitudes and, thus, his or her behavior, how enduring can you expect these changes to be? A receiver may experience an immediate change in attitude, but this is no guarantee that the change will be long-lasting. Time will decrease the effect of the stimulus to change. Regression of attitudes back to their previous position will also be effected by contrary information or by information that reaffirms the original feeling. The credibility of the source or the stimulus for change and how often a receiver is reminded of the fact of and reason for the change will also determine how long that change will be sustained.

The type of communication—interpersonal, public, or mass—from which one received the persuasive stimulus may also determine the effects that can be expected. In all cases, attitude change takes time, but the permanence of the change is likely to vary with the type of communication used. In the interpersonal arena, for example, changes often require the support of continued transactions, but interpersonal influence is vitally important in securing even small amounts of attitude change in a receiver. Although it is unlikely that one interpersonal encounter will alter your life, continuing encounters do affect both your attitudes and behavior.

Attitude and behavior change often result when we join groups as well because in groups we engage in numerous transactions with others. Some change in attitudes will occur just by sheer number of encounters alone. It is within interpersonal and small-group communication situations that the largest shifts of attitudes occur. To test this possibility, notice the group members' attitudes sometime when you are part of a new group and see if they become more alike as the group develops together. Notice what happened to your own attitudes when you went to college; the changes that occurred will be affected by further changes as you leave college and join different groups.

Interpersonal and small-group communication have a direct influence on communication received from both public speeches and the media because in our intimate or friendly conversation with others, we discuss what happens publicly. There are few, if any, research findings on the long-range effects of public speaking. Long-range effects are difficult to determine because important speeches are often criticized and evaluated immediately and, too, because of the role of interpersonal and small-group communication on the effects of the public speech has not been studied. Remember the last time you heard an important Presidential address—one that covered issues that touched your life and that of your friends? It probably became the topic of conversation the day after it was given. For most people, the conversations they have about the address are more important in changing or freezing attitudes than the address itself. This fact reaffirms the importance of interpersonal and small-group communication in changing our attitudes. Seldom do we make independent judgments based on a single public speech that are not influenced in this manner.

Even the media, surprisingly enough, play a small role in effecting attitude and behavior change. They influence how we generally view events, but this occurs over a period of time. Advertisers, who are perhaps the heaviest users of the media for persuasion, only have to persuade a small percentage of their audience to achieve success. The increase in sales that results from effective advertising is due to the size of the mass media audience rather than from the powerful effects of the media. Much of the successful persuasion that occurs in advertising affects relatively unimportant matters in our lives, like which brand of toothpaste we buy. In more vital matters, the media are more likely to reaffirm and stabilize our attitudes rather than to change them. It is likely that in the programs you watch, for example, your life style is reaffirmed—a college education is useful, parents are respected, athletics are admired, nice cars are esteemed, bright teeth are socially necessary. Seldom do the media challenge these habitual life-style behaviors and,

thus, the media play a major role in reinforcement rather than in creating new attitudes or changed behavior.

Another reason for the media's lack of influence on viewers' attitudes is simply the viewers' own awareness. Receivers are harder to persuade because just as the techniques of mass persuasion have become more sophisticated, so have the receivers. They know the intent of advertisers, of politicians, and of some editorial comments. Because of their sophistication, their resistance is increased.

RESISTING PERSUASION

As a persuader, you need to know methods of bringing about change; as a listener you need to know how to resist persuasive attempts. Knowing the possible techniques—the skills a persuader might seek to use—is one means of resisting or, at least, listening intelligently. When another person attempts to appeal to altruistic motives, to keep your mind filled with a desired action, to achieve identification, to create a favorable mood, to arouse an emotion, or to find a *key need*—something you desire greatly—you can respond with some knowledge of the intent.

The more committed the listener is to an attitude, the less likely it is that anyone will be able to change it. Often, attempts to change a listener so committed results in greater adhesion, not less, to the original attitude. A person whose approach to life results from his atheistic beliefs, for example, will not be very receptive to a person who promotes a fundamentalist religious viewpoint or a proreligious message of any type. Such a message will provide the atheist with more reasons for resistance and may even provoke him or her to anger. For this reason, members of some fundamentalist sects are instructed not to encourage friends or spouses to join, providing they are not already members, if their feelings or beliefs lie elsewhere. The likelihood of arousing an antagonistic response is too great.

Public commitment by a listener causes him or her to become resistant to persuasive communication. A man who calls himself a "nondrinker" may consume alcoholic beverages at home but prefer not to do so in front of others. If, however, at a social gathering, because of his mood or because of this feeling, he refuses a drink, saying, "I don't drink," he will probably feel that his future behavior must become consistent. The "nondrinker" may become even more resistant to alcohol than previously because of this public commitment. Had this public position not been taken, he might have been willing to accept an occasional drink "just to be social." When a commitment is announced publicly, however, people become inflexible—note, for example, a doctor and a diagnosis, a lawyer and an opinion, a teacher and a grade, a student and a paper, or a manager and a policy decision. In each of these situations, the person who has the power to make a decision—whether it is giving a grade or determining why a patient shows particular symptoms—will be much more resistant to making a change in that decision after he or she has become publicly committed to it.

Understanding the relationship between public commitment and resistance is useful for both persuaders and listeners. As a persuader, you should realize that trying to change someone else's public stand will be much more difficult than trying to alter a view which he or she has expressed privately to you. This is one of the reasons that negotiations between labor unions and management are held in private, often with total black-out of information to the public. Each side realizes that public announcement of a position makes it much more difficult to then negotiate and change that position.

If you are a listener, and especially if you wish to remain open to the possibility that you will change your attitude about something, it will help to avoid public commitment to a particular attitude until you have weighed all of the alternatives. Because a public statement of your attitudes tends to cause them to become frozen, the authors advocate a *suspension of judgment* until all of the evidence is in, when you wish to remain open to new ideas. On the other hand, when you are confident that you wish to hold on to your attitudes and to resist efforts to change them, you will find it helpful to announce your attitudes as publicly as possible. This will reinforce your conviction that the attitudes are not easily changed.

Another means of resisting persuasion is active *refutation*—proving that a proposed change is undesirable by arguing against it. We build defense systems against major influences on our basic values and needs, and most of us have been trained to resist by arguing. The receiver is not a passive sort, prone to sit by and see his or her values and needs —especially those that buttress the receiver's life pattern—dashed to the ground with no resistance. In most situations in which a listener tries to refute persuasion, the logic or sophistication of the listener's argument is not as important as the energy with which he tries to resist. Intense energy will lend support to the listener's resistance just as it will lend power to a persuader's effort to effect change. In a sense, the listener persuades himself that he wants to resist, perhaps in spite of a refutation that seems superficial, based on strong biases, or supported by weak evidence. Thus, the persuader has the job of breaking through the listener's energy as well as dealing with misunderstanding or lack of logic.

People are seldom converted overnight. Even the mass conversions that are exhibited at Billy Graham's rallies do not reflect an immediate change of belief or a change in one's way of life by those willing to make the public display. Many of those who go forward are already believers—they are reaffirming their current beliefs. Attitude change occurs slowly for most people because they know something about the persuasion process, because they are personally committed to their current views, because they have made a public commitment, or because they actively argue against change.

ETHICAL CONSIDERATIONS

Like anything else, persuasive communication can be critically evaluated and judged. When you say that a particular communication transaction is "good," you may mean literally hundreds of different things. Some judgments of communication have nothing to do with morality, with the rightness or wrongness of the message, or the motivation of the source. You may, for example, see a film that presents values that are completely different from yours; it is still possible for that film to be a "good" one in the sense that it uses skillful photography. Sometimes a "good" communication is simply one that turns out well for you; if you have a discussion with a friend in which you each express your affection for each other, you might come away feeling that it was a "good" conversation in the sense that it made you feel good.

Ethical judgments of communication are different from both of these examples. *Ethics* deals with rules or standards of right conduct. When we refer to the ethics of a communication, we usually apply words like *good* and *bad, right* and *wrong* in their moral sense. We express our judgment that the source or the message is praiseworthy or blameworthy; that is, we evaluate the communication in the light of our own personal value system.

If you say that a communication transaction is unethical, you may be referring to the source's purposes or goals, to the means or methods used in the communication, or to the accuracy of the information in the message. It is generally thought, for example, that it is wrong to communicate with the intention of harming someone. It is usually considered wrong to use communication techniques to manipulate a receiver without his or her knowledge, as is done in subliminal communication or in other techniques that affect the unconscious mind. It is also considered wrong for a source to present as true a message which he or she knows is not true.

There are no strict ethical guidelines that can be neatly applied to every persuasive situation; however, there are some broad criteria that you can apply as a source and as a receiver when you are trying to evaluate the ethics of persuasion. One of these is that the persuader should not place his or her own special ambitions above the welfare of the receiver(s). A car salesman who convinces you, for example, that this is *not* the time of year to buy a car, who tells you that you would be better off keeping your present car, or who says that you should consider what is best for you goes a long way toward convincing you that his intentions are "good" because he seems to value your welfare more than making a sale. If, on the other hand, you try to talk your roommate into cutting a class because you need a ride to town and your roommate is the only person around with a car, you probably need to reevaluate the ethics of that persuasion.

Often a persuasive source will recognize that it adds to his or her credibility to *appear* to be ethical, even though his or her real motives are unethical. Car salesmen have to continually fight the image of being untrustworthy, smooth operators who are out to make a fast, easy buck; thus, the admirable social values expressed in the salesman's comments about your keeping your present car would probably be weighed in relation to his later behavior. If the salesman follows his speech about how you should use your own judgment with an offer to take you for a test drive "just because you are here in the showroom," you are probably sensible to suspect his motivation and to question the ethics of his communication.

The central ethical principle in these examples involves satisfying oneself that the communication being tested does not show a source who is more concerned with his or her own welfare than with the welfare of others. This is not to say that it is unethical to be concerned about your own needs. It is to say that you may not ethically satisfy your needs at the expense of someone else.

Another broad guideline that is useful in judging the ethics of a persuasive communication is that the ends do not justify the means. It is clearly wrong, by this criteria, to lie to your roommate in order to convince him or her to cut a class to take you into town. If you say that you have urgent personal business when you actually just feel like going shopping, you have violated this ethical principle. Sometimes, of course, the situation is not that clear-cut. You may be convinced that it would be good for your best friend, who has been working hard on a term paper all week, to get out on Friday night. One way to persuade your friend to take a break would be to say that *you* need to get out and that you do not want to go alone. In this case, the end (getting your friend to take a break) involves another's welfare rather than your own, but the means (lying about your own motivation) is still considered wrong.

Public speakers, like communicators in any type of communication situation, should observe another ethical standard, the demand that information be made available to all. This standard of fairness is reflected in our constitutional protection of the freedoms of speech, press, and assembly. It places a burden on the communicator for often he or she has had some special opportunity to explore and analyze the idea or subject matter and, thus, holds an advantage over the receiver. Aware of this possible advantage, the ethical communicator will, in addition to expressing ideas clearly and frankly, show the receiver fully and fairly why he or she holds them. This implies, too, that the communicator needs to be informed—possessing enough information on an idea or topic so that he or she can respond intelligently to another person's question.

Deliberate suppression of information is considered unethical, as are distorting information and doctoring quoted materials and statistics. Reporting with accuracy should be the goal of every communicator. Through deliberation and good judgment, the rational activity known as persuasion can result in mutual understanding, but only if the communicator is careful to make all possible information available to the listener.

People who give advice to others, either in a professional capacity or in interpersonal relationships, also have special ethical obligations. All of us need the support of someone else's perspective occasionally as we try to make decisions about our own lives. We can get this support from family members, friends, and professional counselors such as social workers or psychologists. It is unethical, however, for the advice-giver to impose his or her values on the person whom he or she is helping. This means that a therapist, for example, must be careful not to simply tell the client what to do about problems. This kind of advice makes the client dependent on the therapist instead of more able to figure out his or her own difficulties. In interpersonal relationships you should be careful to respect your friend's right to make up his or her own mind. The temptation to persuade someone that you understand the problem and know what is best for him or her can be great, and people who are in trouble often ask for this kind of persuasive "support." In the long run, however, such advice is probably not helpful. Often the best support you can give a troubled friend is to listen and to respond to what you hear your friend saying about the problem. This kind of understanding response is better than trying to impose your solutions on other people's problems.

Propaganda

The term *propaganda* is generally associated with schemes devised to spread ideas that might not otherwise be heard—that is, it is the artificial and cultivated dissemination of particular ideas. It is the feeling of those who spread propaganda—whether it be nations, governments, organizations, or individuals—that others would not learn about these ideas without their intervention.

At the present time, the word *propaganda* has negative connotations. People believe that propaganda is a process that is sinister, involves lying, and is based on the deliberate attempt to manipulate by concealed and underhanded means. These feelings date from the First World War when propaganda was employed in an attempt to influence the final result of the war. More recently, Watergate and the attempts by the government to regulate public attitude toward it by selectively controlling information to favor their particular viewpoint and by doctoring information to create a particular impression enhance the general negative feeling associated with the word.

Propaganda, as it is used today, relates to persuasion because it has become associated with the practice of influencing the emotional attitudes of others. It relates to suggestion because suggestion is the "fundamental mechanism employed by all forms of propaganda."[12] It relates to protest because protest movements use it to advance their ideas. Through propaganda they catch the audience's attention and attempt to propagate their unfamiliar doctrine. Often it requires a considerable period of time to build a receptive frame of mind in others.

A chapter on persuasion is incomplete without some mention of propaganda for it *is* possible to take persuasion too far. Whatever the specific means employed—whether they be the use of stereotypes, selecting only those facts that are suitable, repetition, assertion, appeals to authority, or downright lying[13]—to be forewarned is to be forearmed. We should not underestimate the power of the determined propagandist. When one media presentation may reach millions of people; when we

---

12 J. A. C. Brown, *Techniques of Persuasion: From Propaganda to Brainwashing* (Baltimore, Maryland: Penguin Books, 1963), p. 25.
13 *Ibid.*, pp. 26–28.

know that man can be an irrational animal; when we know that political and religious propagandists, as well as advertisers, spend a great deal of effort, time, and money to appeal to our emotions—we begin to realize the possible impact of propaganda.

In some instances—as in political discourse—we can accept half-truths because we also know that politicians are not philosopher-kings. "Culture," however, "cannot long withstand perversions of truth. When culture becomes politics, revolutionary politics in particular, there can be no criterion for truth and its inseparable companion, rationality. . . ."[14] It is our responsibility as citizens to recognize propaganda for what it is and to beware of its effects. Not enough can be said about the essential importance of truth-telling in maintaining both personal and national sanity.

SUMMARY

Persuasive discourse has as its purpose the change of existing attitudes or behavior in another person. Changing another's attitudes is difficult because attitudes are imbedded deeply in one's patterns of behavior and belief. A communicator does not really persuade a listener to change an attitude or a behavior; the listener persuades himself or herself.

Persuasion, to be successful, must wear away attitudes as water wears away stone. No matter what means are used—whether it be logos, pathos, or ethos—extreme patience and skill are required before change can be expected. The effect of persuasion is likely to be short range unless continuous reinforcement is provided. The less a listener has to "give," the more likely he or she will be to change an attitude or a behavior.

Suggestion is the most subtle form of persuasion. Common techniques in suggestion include persuasion by association, by encouraging social facilitation in a crowd, and by creating an appropriate atmosphere. The communicator who uses suggestion will be most effective if he or she attempts to make the suggestion seem to originate with the listener and presents the persuasive message with vividness, force, and a positive approach.

Protest communication is an attempt to produce change through confrontation. It occurs when people cannot get satisfaction through le-

---

14 "Six Big Lies About America," *New York Times Magazine,* June 6, 1971, pp. 32–33.

gitimate channels and when dialogue and discussion break down. Protest communication may go through several stages—stopping at the stage where satisfaction is obtained. The stages of protest include dialogue-discussion, attempts to win support, nonviolent resistance, and confrontation. Protest stops when satisfaction is reached, when members get disillusioned with the protest process, or when members decide to withdraw from society and go underground.

Although it is difficult to change attitudes, there are several methods which the persuader can use: he or she can associate the desired change with the self-interest of the listener, present the message in such a vivid manner that the listener's emotions are engaged, use punishment or reward to encourage the change, attempt to identify the changed behavior with a model or an idol, or convince the listener that the change is congruent with his or her basic values. The most lasting changes in behavior require a previous change in fundamental attitudes.

The permanence of a change in attitude or behavior depends upon the type of communication used to effect the change. Interpersonal and small-group situations are the most effective settings for effecting permanent change because they permit the communicator to engage in many persuasive transactions with the listener. The persuasive effect of a public speech depends upon the degree to which that speech is discussed in interpersonal and small-group situations. Messages that we receive through the mass media are more likely to confirm our existing attitudes than they are to change them.

To understand persuasion is to understand how to resist persuasion ourselves and to understand why others resist. Resistance is the natural posture. Our fundamental pattern of beliefs, or of living for that matter, guides us, and when we are in doubt, we stick to it or fall back on it rather than change. On most issues, we just do not care, but on those that affect us, our minds are already made up. That is what makes persuasion difficult, and that is what makes understanding of it important.

Ethical judgments about persuasion refer to the communicator's moral responsibility. One may question the ethics of a source's purposes, goals, means, or methods, as well as the accuracy of his or her message. It is generally considered unethical to manipulate the listener, to communicate with the intention of harming someone, or to distort the truth in a communication. Another ethical requirement is that the persuader should not place his or her own welfare above the welfare of the listener. Those who give advice to others should be careful to avoid imposing their values on the listener. It is possible to take persuasion too far, and we need to be aware of the influence of propagandists.

Persuasion is a powerful communication intention that can be used effectively and ethically to alter the attitudes and behavior of the listener. Understanding persuasion is important for both the source and the receiver; the source can develop effective persuasive messages through this understanding; the listener can comprehend the intention of the persuasive source and, if appropriate, resist these messages.

FURTHER READING

Saul D. Alinsky, *Rules for Radicals: A Pragmatic Primer for Realistic Radicals.* New York: Vintage Books, 1971.
This book outlines the techniques of political organization for those who want to fight the establishment. The author emphasizes communication both within the reform group and with the enemy. Full of examples, this vivid and exciting paperback is written with both passion and compassion as a kind of revolutionary's handbook for gaining social and political justice.

J. A. C. Brown, *Techniques of Persuasion: From Propaganda to Brainwashing.* Baltimore: Penguin Books, 1963.
This is a very interesting book which questions the notion that man is a rational animal. The author demonstrates, through the use of numerous examples, how man falls easy prey to advertisers and political propagandists. In this paperback book, he discusses everything from propaganda in advertising and the media to attitude formation, religious conversion, indoctrination, and brainwashing.

Jerry Bruno and Jeff Greenfeld, *The Advance Man.* New York: William Morrow, 1971.
This book tells what goes on behind the scene in the planning of a political campaign. It is invaluable for anyone interested in politics or in understanding the political process.

Richard L. Johannesen, *Ethics and Persuasion: Selected Readings.* New York: Random House, 1967.
This is an excellent collection of articles on the relationships between ethics and persuasion by some outstanding writers. It provides a broad perspective covering the democratic premise, some philosophical perspectives, and mass persuasion. The articles in this paperback book provide stimulating and challenging reading which require no background, prior introduction, or special vocabulary for understanding.

Irving J. Rein, *Rudy's Red Wagon: Communication Strategies in Contemporary Society.* Glenview, Ill.: Scott, Foresman, 1972.
This is a book about manipulators. The author uses cartoons, ads, newspaper columns, and menus to illustrate his points. His chapter on the rhetoric of the used-car salesman is particularly interesting and useful.

Carl P. Wrighter, *I Can Sell You Anything.* New York: Ballantine Books, 1972.
Here is a paperback book about the persuasion of advertising. It is a straightforward look at how advertising works told by a Madison Avenue adman who minces no words, hits you between the eyes by naming products and practices, and enjoys letting you in on the details. The excitement reflected in the writing—like a good ad—makes you part of the product. The author tells you how admen do it, how they get away with it, and how *you* can see through it.

7

Small-Group Communication

Contemporary American culture has been referred to as a "tribal society" because of our dependence on groups. We are born into a group; we go to school in groups; we worship in groups; we play in groups; we are laid to rest in a ritual group meeting. Our society itself is a large group composed of many small ones. It would probably be impossible to survive without participating in group activities.

As a college student, you may spend several hours in a single day communicating in small groups of various kinds as you take part in a seminar discussion, argue for change in a student government committee, and chat with friends who meet for coffee after class.

People join a group to complete a task; for personal growth (as in sensitivity or encounter groups); in connection with their work with the PTA, the League of Women Voters, their business, religion, or local government. An individual may be part of the research and development section of a corporation, a long-range planning committee of a university, an ad hoc committee to study pollution problems, a standing committee of a social club, or an on-the-job group where he or she earns a living. We are all part of a family, which is another group. There are, then, task-oriented small groups, therapeutic groups, short-range and long-range work groups, social groups, and discussion groups. The concepts and characteristics in this chapter relate to groups such as these—groups of a variety of different types.

Groups function to increase understanding, to render judgments, to heighten sensitivity, to facilitate social give-and-take, and to solve problems. Many times, one group will serve several of these functions at the same time. The executive committee of a social group, for example, needs to keep members informed, render evaluations about the progress and health of the organization, and solve the problems of the group—all in addition to providing the social give-and-take which is the organization's primary reason for being and the function that makes all the work seem both worthwhile and enjoyable.

A *small group,* in the way we are using the term, has several characteristics which distinguish it from other communication settings. These characteristics are determined by the relationships and the interaction among the listeners and speakers who are members of the small group. 1) There should be some similarity and interdependence among members —as Kurt Lewin, an early researcher on groups, pointed out.[1] Similarity, according to Lewin, refers to an awareness by all members of the existence of every other member as an essential part of the total group. Interdependence means that members influence each other; one member's behavior is modified by the action and behavior of all other members of the group. 2) Another prerequisite is that there be interaction and communication among members. Interaction means reciprocity—the mutual action of members on each other. Communication in a small group involves the mutual interchange of thoughts, opinions, and information both orally and nonverbally. 3) Members of a small group share common needs or goals. The desire to complete a task or work out a problem in a joint and united way is an example. Finally, 4) there is a set of norms—or expectations—for the group as a whole or for specific members. A *norm* is simply a standard. A group may set standards that regulate behavior, participation, interaction, or almost anything else. Norms that refer to specific members are called roles. A *role* is the part that a member plays or the function he or she performs in the group.

Every small group is a social event because every person involved in a group's process plays the role of inquirer—wondering how he or she will relate to the other people of the group as human beings. When people share ideas, an important social dimension is present that should

---

[1] Kurt Lewin, "Field Theory and Experiment in Social Psychology: Concepts and Methods," *American Journal of Sociology,* 46 (1939): 868–896.

not be overlooked in analyzing small-group behavior—no matter what task the group is pursuing. To achieve full participation and full productivity, a congenial atmosphere of trust and understanding is needed. For this reason, attention must be given to certain group norms that treat the human side of small groups. Encouraging behavior that makes members feel liked, admired, and respected and producing a climate that allows each member to enjoy the company of others and to consider the ideas of all important and worthwhile are essential. The establishment and maintenance of this norm should override all other considerations because the closer all groups come to this ideal, the more successful they are likely to be.

The communication model presented in the introduction describes a *bilateral* situation in which messages are sent and received from one person to one other person. Small-group communication is *multilateral* —that is, it takes place from one person to several others, and any one of those several others is free to respond. Thus, feedback occurs between a number of individuals, each person responding to all of the others as potential sources of communication. All members speak and listen with equal responsibility because the primary source of communication is constantly changing. Individuals switch from speaker to listener and back to speaker again, instantaneously. This multilateral communication gives small-group members a shared purpose and stimulates the development of a structure of roles and norms.

In this chapter we will investigate five major aspects of small-group communication. We will first examine some of the variables that affect the success of small groups. Secondly, we will examine the kinds of communication that occur in small groups. In the third section we will examine small-group leadership and the components of effective leadership. We will then consider several methods of evaluating small groups. Finally, we will discuss the problem-solving group as a case study of the small-group process.

WHAT MAKES A SMALL GROUP WORK?

The factors that affect small group success include size, spatial arrangements, roles, norms, and cohesiveness. These essential variables will affect the amount and quality of the communication that is likely to occur as well as the ability of a group to complete its task successfully and the likelihood that leadership will be effective. These factors form the foundation for good group functioning and will help determine the outcome of group work. No matter what type of group it is—social, business, educational, legal, scientific, literary, or religious—and no matter what its task may be—making arrangements for a party, discussing a company's sales, learning about biochemistry, deciding on an interpretation of a law, talking over a new discovery, arguing about an author's approach, or conversing about church doctrine—the factors discussed below will affect that group's success.

Group Size

The amount and the quality of the communication that occurs between members of a small group is affected by the size of the group. Group size will also affect the way that members relate to each other since relationships are developed by communicating.

Think about how you would react in a group of three individuals discussing your experiences in looking for a job. In a group of three, you would likely be fairly open and communicative, revealing those times when you had to search the classified ads for weeks or when you were interviewed by a tough personnel manager. Now, add two members to the hypothetical group and imagine the changes that might occur. You have fewer responsibilities for holding up your end of the conversation because you now have four other members to do it instead of two. You are not looked at as often; your ideas are not sought as much. You retreat slightly—but you still feel very much a part of the group, showing your willingness to contribute if you want to. If you double the number of members in your hypothetical group—making it ten instead of five—the likelihood of your participating in the group's activities diminishes even more. "Why should I contribute when there are nine other people?" might be your feeling. Your responsibility is decreased, and perhaps you begin to feel that your experiences do not mean so much to the group—they might even sound ridiculous if presented. You "clam up"!

This description reflects the behavior of many people when group size is increased. Larger groups do not give you as much time to speak. When more people are involved, you cannot maintain social relationships with all the members. Anxiety, fear, and inhibition become more likely because members find it harder to express their true feelings—particularly disagreements—and feel the threat of other group member's attitudes and feelings on their own. Passivity results, and the communication becomes a bilateral experience rather than a multilateral group sharing as two or three of the more forceful individuals carry the burden of the communication. The other group members begin to behave like an audience, and the situation resembles public speaking more that the small group. As an audience member, an individual becomes anonymous—losing himself in the group. Willingness to communicate, thus, is replaced by eagerness to conceal and retreat as groups get larger.

To maintain quality communication in a small group, the group's size has to be controlled. The ideal size will vary within certain limits according to the task of the group and the personalities of the members. A task which involves far-ranging and extensive gathering of information —like a town government's task-force committee to investigate the effects of a proposed bypass—might, of necessity, require more members simply to accomplish the task than, perhaps, a policy-making subgroup of a larger organization—such as a constitution-revision committee set up by the student-government association.

There are other factors that will influence decisions about group size. Robert Freed Bales, a researcher of small-group interaction, suggests that members of small groups should be able to meet face-to-face.[2] He also points out that members should be able to receive a distinct impression of every other member of the group—an impression that can be recalled. Face-to-face interaction could, conceivably, involve from three people to upwards of fifty people—depending on the size and flexibility of the room. A circle of fifty people might be called a small group by this standard. The second factor is more limiting, however, since it is unlikely that anyone except a person with a photographic memory could recall a vivid impression of many more than fifteen or twenty individuals. Recalling *that* many would be possible only with concentration on the task of remembering and only after meeting together over a period of time.

Acquiring a vivid impression of others depends on extensive interaction and communication with them. This occurs most successfully in groups of three or more and nine or less. Members of groups with less than five complain that their group is too small; when the size is greater than thirteen, the tendency is to form smaller groups—to splinter. Groups composed of an odd number function better than groups totaling an even number since a majority decision can be attained in an odd-numbered group; thus, groups of five or groups of seven are generally more efficient than groups of four, six, or eight. Research indicates that five is an ideal number for most small groups. Larger groups often end up with a core group of five or so among whom talk becomes centralized

---

2 Robert Freed Bales, *Interaction Process Analysis: A Method for the Study of Small Groups* (Reading: Addison-Wesley, 1950), p. 33.

anyway. Bales recommends committees composed of more than three but less than seven. Our class experience demonstrates that students prefer collecting, exchanging, coordinating, analyzing, and evaluating information in groups of five—as opposed to groups of three, four, six, or seven.

Spatial Arrangements

One of the influential factors in determining the flow of communication during a small-group meeting is eye contact, the extent to which group members communicate eye-to-eye with other members. Just sitting and talking around a table in the local hang-out with a bunch of friends may reveal some of the effects of eye contact. Even in this small group you will probably interact more with those whom you can observe directly and readily, and you will likely direct most of your comments to those seated opposite from you. Also, in this same situation, the closer the chairs are arranged to each other, the more likely that communication will be facilitated rather than inhibited. Note the intention of inhibiting communication revealed by the arrangement of chairs in a library— chairs are often removed from the heads of tables, and some distance is often put between the chairs around a table. Erving Goffman, Edward T. Hall, and Ray Birdwhistell—all writers and researchers on nonverbal communication—agree that direct visual contact can be uncomfortable and disconcerting under ordinary conditions, and even produce feelings of anxiety. It is sometimes difficult for people to "break through" their customary reactions to sustained visual contact.[3] For some, it takes concentration, but the effort is worth the value gained in small-group situations, where dependence on the quality and the quantity of communication is at a premium.

The expected psychological relationship among members of a group may also affect choices about the spatial distance. In an encounter group, for example, physical closeness is preferred because it is the intimacy of the group relationships that aids in increasing individual understanding of group process and personal potential. In a conference where members represent different points of view, on the other hand, distance is often preferred.

Small-group communication is also affected by the task. Members

---

3 See Erving Goffman, *Behavior in Public Places* (Glencoe: Free Press, 1963), Edward T. Hall, "Silent Assumptions in Social Communication," in *Disorders of Communication,* 42 (1964): 41–55, and Ray Birdwhistell, "Field Methods and Techniques," *Human Organization,* 11 (Spring, 1952): 37–38.

who engage in a task which requires a high degree of cooperation generally select spatial arrangements that facilitate interaction—adjacent, side-by-side, corner, or face-to-face arrangements. Distant seating is preferred when no cooperation is required, when members are working on different tasks, or when members are competing.

Member Roles

The function of role-playing in the communication of self and in interpersonal relationships has been discussed in Chapters 1 and 2. Role-playing is also commonly found in small-group situations. Most of us play a role of some kind much, if not all, of the time, no matter what context we are in. These roles are a kind of public self and reflect our cultural training, our expectations of our self, our reactions to the expectations of others, and so on. In small groups, as in other communication settings, playing a role can be positive or negative.

One of the positive functions of roles in small groups is to allow division of labor among the members according to their capabilities and specialized knowledge. As groups begin to operate—whatever their function—certain people begin to specialize. When a member and the group discover that this is occurring, the member establishes a role in that group. Such roles are not necessarily consistent from one group to another. Roles change from group to group just as personalities do. For example, a person could be the leader of his religious-study group but show no leadership tendency in his classes. Your role will be determined by the situation, by the people around you, and by the task at hand, as well as by your own personality. It will be negotiated by you and the group.

Some people are more skilled or talented than others in certain areas or when it comes to special fields of interest. A group faced with a task that involves math, for example, will likely have at least one member with some skill in mathematics. A group faced with a creative task will probably have at least one member with creative talents. In circumstances requiring their special skills, such members will play the role of group expert; in other circumstances they may fade into the background. Inherent capabilities cannot always be estimated or anticipated, and groups need to stress their need for specialized knowledge and to encourage this kind of positive role-playing by talented group members.

Roles also are related to specific group responsibilities; for certain groups to operate efficiently, necessary tasks must be performed by someone. One such role is the coordinator of group activities. Sometimes the coordinator will be the president, the chairman, or the program director. Sometimes, it will just be one member to whom the others look for leadership. There is also likely to be an energizer, who gets the group moving and pushes them toward greater activity. There is often a recorder, who keeps track of group progress and notes accomplishments and defeats or agreements and disagreements. There might also be an evaluator-critic, who examines the productivity, the decisions, or the reflections of the group and seeks to render some judgment of their worth. These roles or functions are likely to overlap, and several may be fulfilled by the same person. They vary with the group and with the task.

In a group that meets briefly for coffee between classes, such task-oriented roles are inappropriate, but even in groups whose chief function is social, individual roles do come into play. Think about the last time you shared coffee with a group of friends. Did you find that someone was more aggressive than the others? Did someone seek recognition? Did someone play the role of self-confessor? Playboy? Dominator? Help-seeker? Special-interest pleader? In such a group, these roles are not necessarily irrelevant to the group's behavior. They can make the group experience interesting and exciting as they stimulate conversation, provide a sounding board for ideas, and generate new ideas for consideration.

Individual role-playing may have a negative effect on the group, however, because the roles which some people assume get in the way of the group's progress. Whether the group meets simply for the social purpose of getting to know each other better or there is a specific task that the group is trying to accomplish, certain individual roles can short-circuit the group's functioning.

We have catalogued a number of roles that are commonly found in human relationships. When these roles are played in small groups, they can significantly hinder the group's process.[4] We have listed those that we have observed being played most often; it is not a complete list, nor are they necessarily listed according to frequency or importance—simply, those we have noticed occurring most often are near the begining of the list. Many times, a person will play several roles or a combination of roles. Think about yourself and those with whom you associate, and note the effects that such roles have had in groups in which you have participated.

4 Kenneth D. Benne and Paul Sheats, "Functional Roles of Group Members," *Journal of Social Issues*, IV, No. 2: 41–49, reported in Robert S. Cathcart and Larry A. Samovar, *Small Group Communication: A Reader* (Dubuque, Iowa: Wm. C. Brown, 1970), pp. 137–138.

There are the people who are *anxious*. These individuals often make others in the group feel tense because of their own uneasiness. Sometimes, these people are disturbed just by being in a group bcause they are feeling apprehensive about working with others. Such group members may also be concerned about making personal feelings known, or the topic or task may cause the worry. A relaxed, informal atmosphere in which feelings are readily shared does the most to relieve unnecessary anxiety. If such people are encouraged to participate and are made to feel part of the group, anxiety soon disappears.

Authoritarian members want to control all of the other group members and everything that happens in the group. Not surprisingly, they often generate quite a bit of group hostility since the rest of the group is likely to see them as selfish and thoughtless. An authoritarian can create an atmosphere in which other group members suppress their feelings and reduce their communication. An informal group may show the authoritarian that such behavior is not welcome, especially if the group establishes a norm of cooperation. In more formal task-oriented groups, thorough preparation by all may create equality among members. Indicating the need for ideas from all members may serve to tone down the influence of the dominator.

People who are *silent* also affect small-group communication. Because of certain fears, many people are reluctant to open to others; they prevent communication by saying very little. Left alone, the silent people will retreat farther and farther until they become hostile and bitter and either leave the group or become antagonistic and unhappy. Individuals who are silent suffer from the need to be supported by the group so that they can feel safe in expressing their true ideas and feelings.

Some *intellectuals* avoid full emotional relations because they are uncomfortable with feelings. These people are likely to stress rational procedures in group process and to discount affection, anger, and other personal feelings as irrelevant. Effective small-group communication requires human beings who can express emotion as well as ideas. To help make intellectuals comfortable, the emotional can be played down if the group is involved in a problem-solving task. Some intellectuals work best independently; thus, they can be given a task or responsibility that can be accomplished alone. Since many group members value emotional expression as part of the group process and since all groups need opportunities to develop member relationships through emotional exchange, often the emotional issue must be faced squarely. Failure to permit expressions of feeling may cause hostility or anxiety. Also, dealing with intellectual issues separated from emotional issues causes sterility in group deliberations; that is, the deliberations become dull, dry, and boring, lacking both depth and feeling.

The *know-it-alls* are individuals who care more about winning the arguments than about evidence, listening, or learning from others. The know-it-alls can be quite uncomfortable in groups that have problem-solving as a major function because such groups require cooperation and willingness to suspend judgment until all the evidence is in. Clarifying group goals, stressing cooperation, and delegating specific responsibilities to the know-it-alls may encourage such members to become more responsive to the needs and wishes of others.

Verbose members fill every void in communication by saying so much that nobody can possibly sort out all the words and figure out anything about these members' ideas or feelings. More than anything, verbose members need the support of the group. Feeling accepted and wanted, they will express their true ideas and feelings.

Conformists need the acceptance of others more than individual expression. Since conformists are unwilling to disagree, most small groups have little interest in what they say. Conformists need to be encouraged to offer personal viewpoints. Reinforcement of their ideas will often call forth more ideas and more positive behavior.

Indecisive people avoid making decisions as long as possible for fear that the decision will turn out wrong. Remaining indecisive is safe—a means of self-protection—but serves little useful purpose in a small group, especially a group in which decision-making, policy-formation, or problem-solving is the standard operating procedure. Uncertain members become roadblocks to effective small-group operation when there is a need by the group for the ideas, efforts, and contributions of everyone. Delegating individual responsibilities by giving task assignments and stressing the importance of deadlines and "due dates" may help the indecisive people. Respecting their contributions may also be helpful.

Rivals in a small group make every situation a contest and every other member a competitor. They become hostile to anyone else who strives for superiority. Discussions become debates because in debates someone wins and someone loses. Setting a tone of cooperation at the outset may help to "steal the thunder" of members bent on competition. Aligning these members' goals with those of the group—the desire of the group to excel and succeed—may also help integrate their efforts with those of other group members.

Cynics distrust everybody else in the group. Often these people have been disillusioned by some profound disappointment, and they are dissatisfied with life. Cynics have trouble being neutral about any idea or proposal. They are likely to belittle, to argue for the sake of arguing, and to dismiss any constructive suggestion as naive. Cynics are difficult members for a small group to contend with, and they often affect the whole atmosphere in which the group works. Showing a sincere interest in cynics and their information and demonstrating that people really do care may help to make those people more receptive to the group members and to the group's ideas.

Group members who play the role of the *comedian* are seeking visibility; they want to be seen by the group. If, in this role, these people would provide comic relief, the role could supply a badly needed characteristic that many groups lack. Unfortunately, comedians often take nothing seriously and hinder the work of the small group by constant laughing, joking, and playing the role of fools for others. Pointing to the importance of the group's task, the seriousness of the matter at hand, or the need for full group attention to the problem may help gain these members' help.

There are other roles, but the important thing here is to recognize that such roles can be destructive in small groups. Often we act out roles unconsciously, but once we are aware that we are doing it, we can look for ways to change our role or the role structure of the situation or of the group so that the total resources of the group can be used. We can stop and talk about problems that occur because individuals in the group are playing roles that are causing problems. Becoming aware of the roles that we and others play and being able to discuss these roles in relation to the group's process will go a long way toward helping all of the group members to reevaluate and change their role-playing behavior.

In the social circles in which you move, you can probably think of friends of yours who always seem to fulfill certain roles when your group gets together. Some of these roles are positive and some are negative, but when this group of people gets together, the roles are generally predictable. The more groups in which you participate, the more likely you are to observe a variety of different roles in others and to play a wide range of roles yourself.

Group Norms

Sometimes roles are determined by norms—standard, accepted ways of behaving, of participating, or of thinking that govern membership relationships and modes of operating. Pressures in the group cause members to conform. Norms are acceptable when they result from the collective wisdom of the group. In some cases, when a person chooses to enter a group, he or she also agrees to accept the norms of that group. In other cases, tension is created between individuals and the group because of disagreements over norms. Deviation from a group's norms will result in the norm being changed or overlooked, or in the deviate member leaving the group by pressure or by choice.

Cohesiveness

The extent to which members assume positive roles, the degree to which negative roles are minimized, and the extent to which members willingly subscribe to the norms of a group will often determine the group's cohesiveness. *Cohesiveness* is simply the group's ability to stick together, to work together as a group, and to help each other as group members. Group size is related to cohesiveness since the larger the group, the less likely that it will be cohesive and the more likely factionalization, the opposite of cohesiveness, will occur. A group that has "pulled itself together" spatially is also more likely to create cohesiveness because physical closeness generates close feeling.

Cohesive groups generally display high motivation and morale, positive group performance, and greater possibility for success. When group members are united behind a common cause or need—even if that need is simply conversation or the pleasure of each other's company—members are more cheerful, confident, and eager to expend more energy on behalf of the group. With more enthusiasm, positive group performance naturally follows. Members of a cohesive group willingly interact conversationally, which provides pleasure, a measure of positive performance in any group.

Positive performance may also be related to a task. Because cohesiveness often results in increased pressure for all members to agree, task completion is facilitated by strong cohesiveness. This can be negative when pressures to conform prevent, hinder, or otherwise obstruct tendencies to disagree. All sides of an issue are often best presented through disagreements, as evidence and ideas are challenged and questioned by nonconforming members. This strength should not be sacrificed—even if it means some loss of cohesiveness.

High motivation and good group morale may also be valued by some group members. If individuals derive pleasure from such feelings, it is likely that cohesiveness will increase in a cyclical manner—building on itself. Better decisions, freer participation, and even higher motivation to carry out and support group decisions are likely to result.

Cohesiveness does not mean total uniformity nor total agreement. As a matter of fact, those groups that demonstrate high cohesiveness are often noisy, full of good-natured teasing, disagreement, even argument—all characteristics of strong interaction and a healthy group atmosphere. Individuals in such groups enjoy being together, sometimes disregard time limits, discuss even after the meeting is over, and raise important questions, which they discuss thoroughly. There is cooperation, consideration for others, some defined group goals, some discipline, and some differentiation among roles as well.

A group *personality*—the aggregate of the individual personalities combined together at a particular time and for a specific purpose—depends upon the size of the group, the way the group arranges itself, the roles the members play, the norms of the group, and the degree of cohesiveness achieved. Together these factors can create a group that is greater than the sum of its parts. In successful small groups, the personalities of the individuals in the group combine with, intensify, and complement each other as the members interact in the group setting. No group experience can duplicate another; every meeting of the same group is different just as every group is different because the personality of the group develops and changes as the group works together.

PATTERNS FOR COMMUNICATING IN SMALL GROUPS

Much of the communication that takes place in a group results from an individual's needs to learn what the others believe, to modify his or her own opinions, to try to change the beliefs of the others, and, thus, to bring his or her view of reality into line with that of other members of the group. *Group process*—the carrying out of the group's functions—depends upon this communication. Unity within the group is created as group functions are negotiated, appraised, and agreed upon. Decisions regarding size, spatial arrangements, individual roles, and group norms are reached through communication just as cohesiveness is achieved through communication.

Ineffective communication can result if the size of the group is too large, if the spatial arrangements do not allow for close face-to-face interaction, if the members' roles do not support the group effort, or if the norms are broken or disregarded. Successful group process also depends upon establishing constructive patterns of communication among group members and utilizing good communication skills.

The patterns of communication between individuals in a group are produced by the flow and direction of message exchange. Effective communication involves everyone; messages flow among all members rather than resting statically with one or being exchanged by only a few. Communication is dynamic—continually circulating and proceeding smoothly among members in a spontaneous manner—unprogrammed and unstilted.

The direction of the message flow is often affected by the roles of members or by their status in a group. If one member's role is considered important for the situation or for the task, the others in the group are likely to direct comments to that member and to acknowledge his or her contributions more than those of others. A group of friends deciding to go to the movies may, for example, recognize the suggestions of one member who is a film major in school or is known to keep up with movie reviews. In this group, this member plays the role of a knowledgeable source. The direction of communication in such a group is represented in the pattern in Figure 7.1.

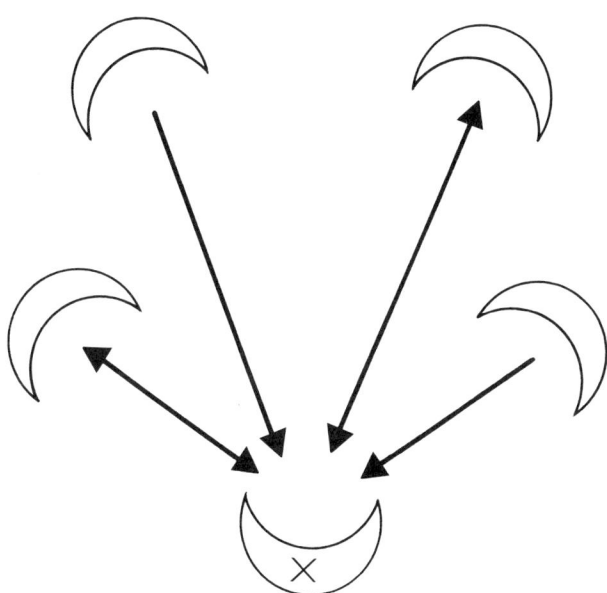

FIGURE 7.1

The direction of the communication may also be influenced by member status. If a manager calls together a group of employees to discuss changes in company policy, their communication would probably be directed according to the pattern in Figure 7.1. If, instead, the manager is not present, and the employees decide to get together as a group to prepare a slate of grievances, the communication patterns would be more like Figure 7.2.

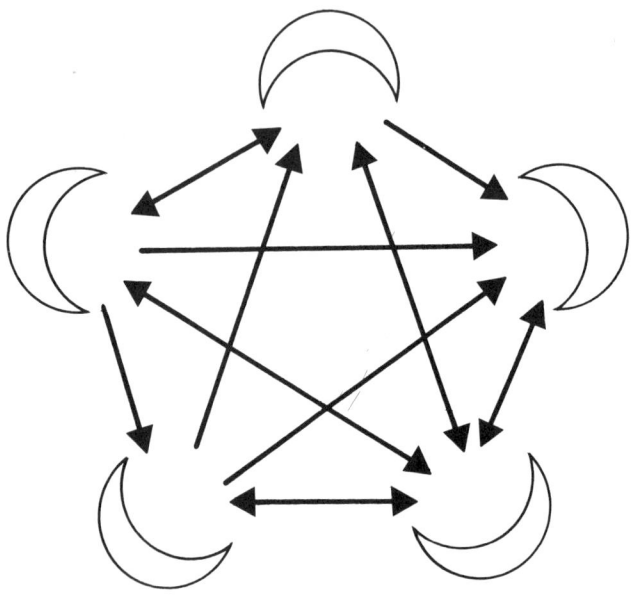

FIGURE 7.2

This second pattern for the direction of communication is more likely to encourage a free exchange of ideas and to result in members feeling that they have had a chance to express themselves because participation is fairly equal, with communication directed to all members of the group.

Patterns of communication in small groups should not be static. Direction and the extent or degree of flow in any single discussion are likely to change as the group functions. The group of friends who are selecting a movie, for example, will use the pattern in Figure 7.1 while they get suggestions from their knowledgeable source; they will use the pattern in Figure 7.2 when they decide which showing of the film is the most convenient time for most members.

The best communication patterns are those which encourage widespread participation in fulfilling the group's task. Thus, the manager-directed meeting is really not a small group at all. It is a public-speaking situation because the manager is not interested in receiving messages from the group of employees in order to change his views; he is simply interested in sending a prepared message. When employees meet to exchange grievances, on the other hand, the pattern of their communication involves all of the group members in the transaction; this is a true small-group situation.

Effective small-group communication depends upon the same speaker and listener skills that produce effective interpersonal or public communication. Each speaker should be audible, use variety, be clear and fluent, and coordinate the verbal and nonverbal channels of communication so that they support each other. Each listener should give attention to all channels of the message and should provide clear feedback so that the speaker will know his or her message is being received. These skills are crucial in small-group situations because the whole group process depends upon a continual flow of clear messages among the group members.

It is important for both listeners and speakers in small groups to be flexible in their use of communication. Sometimes it is best for the listener to interrupt—to say that he or she does not understand the message, for example. At other times, it is more helpful to allow the speaker to complete his or her message before imposing another message on top of it. Sometimes the best way to communicate in a small group is to say nothing, to send an I-am-waiting-to-see-what-the-others-say message nonverbally, and to wait. Small-group communication sometimes requires such restraint. Each member should be sensitive to what is happening with all of the others as well as to the effect of such nonverbal factors as room size and extraneous noise on the quality of the communication.

Good communication is an important factor in cohesiveness; the cohesive group will likely demonstrate effective use of communication skills because all members make every effort to cooperate with each other—which means sending and receiving messages in a way that does not obstruct or build barriers to the exchange of meaning. They will interrupt others and willingly be interrupted by others to help generate the spontaneity good discussion requires. Cohesiveness encourages good communication, too, because as members begin to care about the group, they will speak up, ask questions, and seek more information.

LEADERSHIP

Some people see all leaders as coercive, inflexible, dogmatic tyrants. To others, leaders are impotent, "wishy-washy," ineffectual opportunists who got where they are by accident. The effective small-group leader resides somewhere in between, revealing characteristics of both extremes when the context calls for it. He or she is a leader, perhaps, because of special training or ability, because of the purposes of the group, because of pressures put on the group from outside, or because of the way the people in the group relate to one another. People do become leaders by accident; they are also appointed, chosen, and voted into office. Often, too, they rise to the occasion in a group because of some specialized knowledge or ability that is appropriate at the time.

A *leader* performs actions that direct the group toward achieving a desired outcome. A group may, thus, have one leader or many—as many leaders as there are members—depending upon the situation, the participants, and the task. Any member who influences a group is, in a sense, leading it. For a group to have a leader, then, someone need not be designated to perform the leadership task; it is rather a question of the degree to which members of the group are willing to lead. We are all leaders since even a member's silence may influence the group. However, some people will, very likely, lead more than others.

Understanding leadership and how it operates in small groups helps in two ways: it makes us more aware of what leaders in general do, and it helps us to know what is expected when we play a leadership role in a small group. To provide this understanding, we will examine the emergence of leadership, the function of leaders, and the styles of leadership.

The Emergence of Leaders

There are, basically, two ways that leaders become leaders. They appear in a group because they are imposed on it—like the employee who is asked by an employer to "head up" a study group to determine how the company can educate employees in ways of using their leisure time. They may, on the other hand, emerge from the group during its deliberations. A group of tenants, for example, may meet to discuss what kind of a reaction they should make toward their landlord's raising everyone's rent. Each of the members has his or her own alternative which is considered, in turn, by the group. As each tenant suggests and defends a particular alternative, he or she is leading the group. A group that operates without an imposed leader is likely to experience *functional*

leadership, in which the role of leader is distributed among the group members in this way. If the group selects one of its members as a leader, the group is imposing a leader on itself.

Just because a group has an imposed leader, does not mean, however, that functional leadership cannot also occur. When an individual senses at a particular time that he or she can best mirror the group's needs and influence their behavior, that person may take a leadership role even if another person has been designated group leader. An effective imposed leader will create a permissive atmosphere by supporting free discussion and, thus, provide an environment hospitable to, and encouraging of, functional leadership.

Leadership is a role which is given by the group; it is not a property of an individual. A leader cannot function in that role without the group's permission, in spite of the fact that groups often do not realize this nor do leaders often acknowledge it. Leadership is conferred upon various individuals by the group during the process of interaction. How this occurs is not always clear since the process varies with the task, and the role of leader may move very quickly from individual to individual, but leadership is likely to remain with an individual who is most influential at a particular time until he or she no longer meets the group's needs.

The Functions of Leaders

There are essentially, four major leadership functions that need to be filled in a small group. These functions can be fulfilled at the appropriate time by anyone in the group. A group with a strong imposed leader may look to him or her to satisfy most of these needs whereas a group with no imposed leader will, very likely, find that these needs are satisfied by a variety of individuals. The four major functions of a leader are establishing procedures, raising questions, focusing on answers, and encouraging social-emotional growth.

Establishing Procedures A small-group meeting is conducted according to a plan which structures the group's work; establishing and maintaining this structure are procedural functions. If an effective procedural framework is established, the task of the group will be easier and more efficiently fulfilled. Procedural functions include beginning the communication, selecting and ordering the topics, encouraging participation, achieving progress, and calling for self-assessment. The need for procedures such as these varies with the task of the group, but the leadership of any group includes providing a structure within which the group can best function.

A strong start sets the precedent for effective group process. Just as first impressions count in interpersonal relationships, they also influence group procedures. The group leader who begins with a brief introduction, makes his or her remarks clear and interesting, and shows the group through manner and responsibility that the task is worth considering and capable of solution will stimulate the group to productive activity. Any member who helps to get the group off to a good start is fulfilling this leadership function.

When no order is agreed upon by the group, chaos may prevent the group from making any progress with its task. Some sequential ordering is necessary for most discussions just as road maps are for traveling long distance. The pattern should result from group deliberations and, generally, should not be imposed on a group. The leader's role here is simply to point out the need for order and to encourage the group to discuss the structuring of their work. Order should be flexible—able to change as a result of the actual discussion—and the leader may also warn the group about imposing too rigid a structure on itself at the beginning.

The leader who makes all group members feel that they have adequate opportunity to speak will also create a positive group atmosphere. Participation cannot be completely equal, of course, and the silent member often feels satisfied with the group. However, contributions from as many members as possible will be solicited by an alert and conscientious leader.

The best way contributions can be clarified is by using the mirroring response in which a person simply seeks to find out from a communicator whether or not he or she understood what the communicator said. A leader who is skilled in paraphrasing the contributions of others will keep all group members informed on the comments of other members and keep the discussion on the topic. Through paraphrasing, the digressions and extraneous material can be weeded out. When misunderstanding occurs, it should be cleared up at once. Full participation is generated when all members realize that they are being heard by the rest of the group.

Groups cannot move ahead when members spend excessive amounts of time dealing with trivial matters or dealing with only a certain phase of a problem. An effective small-group leader will move the group toward another phase of the problem when the leader feels that a sufficient amount of information has been presented, when information is being repeated, when a point being discussed is trivial, or when members engage in purposeless conversation and small talk. Often, achieving progress requires some aggressiveness on the part of the leader. The leader must be willing to interject himself or herself and the group's agenda upon the group. This requires some discretion and diplomacy because group members do not like to be bossed; it also requires the ability to recognize useful digressions which can promote harmony, encourage humor, or permit the expression of new ideas within the group.

It is often necessary for a group to take time out to find themselves. Misunderstandings occur, material is omitted, direction is misfocused, and digressions take place. Many such problems can be solved if the group feels free to take time out from the task to discuss how they are progressing. An effective leader will call for this self-assessment when it is needed.

Summarizing is one good way to provide self-assessment. It serves to alert the group to where it has been, what it has accomplished, where it is now, and where it is going. Conciseness and brevity require that only basic ideas are stated in a summary—not complete details. It is essential that the leader who summarizes be accurate; if a leader reports what he wishes the group had said instead of what they actually said, conflict will result from the summary, and time will be lost instead of gained. Summaries do not need to be given by an imposed leader alone; they should be provided as needed by anyone in the group who feels that clarity, efficiency, and understanding will be promoted by summarizing the group's progress.

Raising Questions Questions are asked by the leader during small-group deliberations for specific purposes: to identify goals, to gain information, to evaluate information, to find solutions, to evaluate solutions, to resolve differences, or to ask for a plan of action. Leaders who are effective in getting answers to such questions are able to ask them in such a way that the leader does not place group members on the defensive or make a member feel that the question is designed to "catch" him or her off guard or to challenge his or her integrity.

Group members who are not clear about the nature of specific group goals are likely to direct their efforts toward different objectives. Goal-seeking questions provide a common focus. Changes that occur during a group's deliberations often require modifications in the goals or changes in previous commitments on goals. A leader who asks group members about limiting the discussion to the goal at hand, who inquires about making clear aspects that have not been previously discussed, and who comments that the group appears to be off the track is focusing on group goals. This leadership intervention may help individual focal points to become group focal points.

Seeking information is an integral part of many kinds of groups. If the task of the group is to solve a problem, the group should be encouraged to delay a consideration of solutions until all the facts are in and have been analyzed. When there is insufficient information, profitable discussion is impossible since a pooling of ignorance is ignorance. In encounter groups, the most important information has to do with what members are feeling or how they are reacting to something that another member has said. Once the information is discovered, it should then be shared to the fullest extent possible.

Often a group receives information which must be evaluated. Effective leadership can be exercised if a member asks questions such as these about information: How recent is the information? Who is the source of the information? Is he or she biased? Is he or she an expert? Under what circumstances was the information collected? Does the information mean what it appears to mean? Is there contradictory information? These questions are as appropriate for information about personal feelings and judgments as they are for information about objective knowledge. Facts and opinions should be scrutinized carefully for possible errors or misinterpretation.

When the group is seeking solutions, leadership can be exercised to encourage members of the group to be flexible in their thinking. People often become prisoners of their own thinking because they suffer from "hardening of the categories." Questions can be designed which will free these prisoners from their stereotyped, typical, or common-knowledge responses. Roadblocks to discovery can be overcome when a leader is prepared to offer alternative courses of action which will motivate group members to achieve a higher level of critical thinking. This is equally vital whether the group is discussing a political topic or a personal one.

Solutions should be evaluated with consideration for their advantages and disadvantages. Some solutions rejected earlier in the discussion can be offered again as new insights are gained and new combinations seen. A useful leadership role is played by members who ask questions such as these: What are the consequences that are likely to occur? What are the costs that are likely to accrue? What barriers have to be overcome and how serious are they?

Good leadership includes allowing for disagreements to occur and encouraging their expression by all members of the group. If the group establishes a norm of permitting differences to be expressed, questions about various positions and statements of opposition will not appear offensive. The energy that is generated by conflict in a group can be a strong and positive force for pushing toward the fulfillment of the group's task, but conflict is difficult for many people to handle. Careful leadership is required if disagreement is to be used constructively by the group. The leader can mediate controversies by phrasing questions about opposing views in a neutral manner which focuses on the points of difference; this is clarifying behavior. Leadership is also exercised by the member who distinguishes between the controversial idea and the person who expresses it; members should avoid attaching a controversial position to a particular speaker when this is possible.

Complete unanimity is seldom possible in small-group process when minds are actively operating in a mature and intelligent way. The success of the group depends on satisfaction with the process—not whether everybody agrees all the time. If the atmosphere is warm and friendly, conflict can be tolerated by the group and members are less likely to become angry or embarrassed over the statement of controversial ideas.

In some groups the task includes formulating a plan of action, a group commitment to do something to solve the problem with which the group has been struggling. If you decide in a group that the only course of action is to demonstrate against the administration for its unfair practices, your group will be faced with making plans for that demonstration. How are you to publicize your grievances, get recruits, and carry out the protest so that it will effect the changes your group wants? Effective leadership includes helping the group to plan carefully for the action that it has decided to take. It is important to remind the group that a superior plan for action that is ineffectively implemented is of less value than a mediocre plan that is well executed.

Focusing on Answers To accomplish its task, a group needs answers. If the function of the group is to solve a problem, members need to keep their attention on solutions. One of the most frustrating discussion-group experiences is to be a member of a group which just talks and talks without seeming to come any closer to clarification of the issue under discussion. In groups in which social-emotional growth is the main task, members need to feel that they are finding some answers to the personal difficulties which brought them into the group. Effective group leadership in each of these situations involves focusing the group's attention on the need for answers and supporting members who work toward answers without imposing the leader's answers on the group or any individual in the group.

In a group composed of definite factions, where intragroup conflict is strong, or in which the potential for controversy is great, the leader should exercise restraint—assuming a position of neutrality and playing the role of receptive listener. His or her answers should be scrutinized to the same extent as the answers of other members. It is very important in such a group that all positions are heard and that summaries and interpretations be given fairly.

When conflict is not as great, the leader can make more frequent substantive contributions. He or she should place greatest emphasis on the substantive contributions of others, however, assuming primary concern for the procedural aspects of leadership. The leader should not excel in providing answers at the expense of others but should provide facts, evaluations, and solutions whenever these would be helpful to the group.

Encouraging Social-Emotional Growth Personal growth is one of the by-products of any effective small group. This growth is achieved when people are recognized and accepted by others, when they feel secure, and when they are valued. The main task of encounter groups is to encourage personal growth through accentuating humanistic values which emphasize the dignity and worth of the individual. The group engages in supportive behavior which builds a person's sense of worth and importance. But the need for these feelings is not confined to encounter groups; any group to which a person belongs needs to provide that person with the same reinforcement. The more friendliness, mutual trust, respect, and warmth exhibited, the more likely that the member will find pleasure in the group and, too, the more likely he or she will work hard toward the accomplishment of the group's goals.

The development of an informal group atmosphere will aid in the reduction or elimination of anxiety, discomfort, embarrassment, and strain. Status differences can be minimized by the arrangement of chairs. The leader can encourage the use of "we," "us," and "our" to show group spirit, and he or she can use the first names of all persons.

The effective leader will strive to reinforce desirable traits, worthy contributions, and helpful additions to group deliberations. Reinforcement simply means strengthening. When behavior is rewarded, we can expect more evidences of the same desirable behavior in the future. The leader who understands others, provides conclusive proof of his understanding—through paraphrasing, for example—agrees with others, and helps others, goes a long way in promoting higher levels of participant satisfaction.

Styles of Leadership

In a successful small group, members know that others in the group are behaving in accordance with the demands of the situation for a certain style of leadership. In some situations, complete freedom for full participation by all members is desired. There are other situations, however, in which forceful, unchallenged leadership is expected. These are the oposite ends of a continuum. There are, essentially, three kinds of leadership styles: authoritarian, democratic, and laissez-faire. In addition, some groups function best with no leader at all.

Authoritarian Leadership Using the authoritarian style, the leader determines all policies, dictates the particular work task, and, generally, remains aloof from active group participation. One would expect this style in the military establishment. At times, too, one sees signs of it in elected political officials or in business bureaucrats. They appear to possess virtue, realize that justice resides with the strong, share leadership with no one, insist on deference and respect from others, and treat others as means to an end.

Although one would think that a person who demonstrated such characteristics would be easy to identify, these characteristics are probably not all demonstrated by one person in a small group. Sometimes two or three members in a group exhibit authoritarian leadership styles; if they are strong enough or remain unopposed by other members with different styles, these individuals establish the leadership style for the group. Often such persons play the role of dominators. The authoritarian may well be a skillful manipulator who engineers consent in a subtle and unforceful manner. Cleverness is often a trait of the leader who seeks to control by authoritarian means.

Democratic Leadership Using the democratic style, the leader encourages and assists the group in the determination of policies. The group is also responsible for determining the general steps required to meet the group goal. The leader maintains objectivity by giving the group choices, suggesting alternative procedures, being fact-minded in praise and criticism, and in trying to be a regular group member rather than dictating procedure or courses of action, praising or criticizing members themselves instead of their information, and maintaining aloofness.

Democratic leadership lies between the extremes of authoritarian and laissez-faire leadership. The democratic leader draws characteristics from both these extremes. Some control and guidance from the leader is necessary to obtain order, efficiency, and forward progression and some permissiveness is also beneficial—with the minimum amount of restraint—to encourage full participation and the widest possible range of input of alternatives—ideas, suggestions, feelings, courses of action, or whatever.

Democratic leadership is also beneficial for the group members. Members like to share in the process—in the way things are accom-

plished. Members reveal greater degrees of friendliness, more willingness to work as a team, and more satisfaction with the group as a whole because of democratic leadership. When they have been an integral part of the process, they not only speak positively of other members and of the way things were done, but they are also more willing to support conclusions, decisions, or other group results and products.

Laissez-faire Leadership Using the laissez-faire style of leadership, the leader will participate in the group very little, allowing complete freedom for group or for individual decisions. The laissez-faire leader is still a leader because he or she will provide information when asked. He or she takes no part in the discussion, however, and this leader's usual behavior could be described as almost complete nonparticipation. There is, thus, no attempt to appraise, regulate, question, or direct except for occasional spontaneous remarks on member activities—unless otherwise requested by the members.

The Leaderless Group In contrast to these styles of leadership is the leaderless group. There appears to be a trend toward such groups because of the reactions people have toward leaders in general and because of some of the negative models presented for us by those in high administrative places. Much communication and discussion occurs in groups without the presence of a chairman or other high-status person to take over the leadership role. When a group of students meet casually to plan a program, a petition, a platform, or a presentation, no single member may be recognized as the leader.

Robert Freed Bales found that in leaderless groups there are usually two complementary types of individuals who appear, one who tends to specialize as a task-oriented person and one who becomes a social-emotional specialist. He also found, in asking group members to rate one another, that the "best liked" individual was the one who most actively initiated social-emotional interactions.[5]

Discussion may occur in which no one emerges as a leader. All of the functions are diffused among all the members but with no division of labor or specialization. Feelings of equality, of freedom, of informality, and of activity are sometimes experienced in such groups; however, one may soon discover, depending upon the situation, the participants, or the topic or task, that procedure breaks down. Minority views may be slighted, perhaps, even unknowingly; progress toward a specific goal may be absent; efficiency may deteriorate. When minority views, goal-orientation, and efficiency are unimportant or irrelevant—as they may be when a group of students who have had some training in group methods meet to discuss politics, religion, or sex—then a leaderless situation may work well. It may work, too, with a group that meets casually with no particular purpose except sociability or compatibility.

Styles of leadership often result from the style of the group. Often a group composed of members with strong personalities needs to be democratic—the preferred leadership style for most groups. Members will either press for or provide an atmosphere for their leader to operate democratically. Leadership is often contextual as well as personal; it is

---

[5] Robert Freed Bales, "Task Roles and Social Roles in Problem-Solving Groups," in *Readings in Social Psychology,* Eleanor Maccoby, *et. al.,* eds. (New York: Holt, Rinehart and Winston, 1958), p. 441.

what it is because of the context of the group and not just because of the individual personality of the leader, although it is likely that both affect each other. A group leader will probably not be able to operate democratically if the members are unwilling to receive his coercion, help, protection, or restrictions in the benevolent manner in which they are proffered. Benevolence—the desire to do good for others—distinguishes the democratic leader from the undemocratic leader in his or her use of power.

There are other characteristic ways in which groups behave which have a tendency to inhibit the operation of democratic leadership. Members, for example, would not be recipients of democratic leadership if they became excessively task- or productivity-oriented rather than concerned with the degree of representation of group members. If the pressures toward conformity—inducing members to go along with an idea because everyone else is—become too great, democratic group functioning may cause the loss of democratic leadership. Efficiency, too—being overly concerned with the time element—may cause a group to dispense with democracy in favor of more efficient procedures. Thus, one can see that the needs of the group will determine the appropriate leadership style for that group.

EVALUATION IN SMALL-GROUP PROCESS

Evaluation sometimes occurs spontaneously after an interpersonal communication when you find yourself thinking, "Oh, I wish I had thought to say that." After you have given a speech, you often find yourself delivering the speech you wish you had given in your head. In the same way, you are likely to evaluate the small-group situations in which you participate; you may think about how you behaved as a group member, and you will probably have an overall reaction to the group, labeling it "good," "bad," "a waste of time," "productive," or "fun." Criticism and evaluation are bound to happen; thus, it is worth briefly considering useful techniques for judging small-group communication. For groups that continue to meet over a period of time, evaluation can improve the process and product of the group. For groups meeting only once, evaluation will facilitate better understanding of what happened in the group and why it happened. In addition, members may discover information that might enable them to become better participants or leaders in other groups.

There are, essentially, two aspects of the small-group as a group that can be evaluated. The first is the process—the things that occurred while the group was carrying out its task. Analysis of the process includes criticism of the development of relationships in the group, the degree to which members got along with each other and formed a group, as well as cohesiveness and attitudes; problem-solving patterns; the quality, quantity, and spread of communication; and the leadership. In evaluating leadership, you could ask: Who was leader? How did he or she perform? What style was exhibited? What effect did it have on the group? What functions were fulfilled by the leader?

The second focal point for evaluation is the product—the end result of the group's work together. You might examine the quality of the product; how satisfied group members were with it; the feasibility of the solution, if one was reached; the amount of information obtained by group members; possible changes in attitudes; the quantity of the product; or the extent to which the group achieved its goal.

Individual group members may also be evaluated separately in an analysis of their effectiveness as participants in this particular group. We can look at the participants and the way they handle information, reason, structure their contributions, use language, relate to others, and communicate. We can also look at the leader and the group to determine how the various parts combined to make the whole.

Evaluation can be accomplished by the group members themselves —although members may not be as objective as they might be if they were not focusing on themselves. Self-evaluation is a useful exercise for each individual, especially when performed along with other kinds of evaluation. Evaluation by other group members is also useful; however, a great deal of variation often occurs between ratings, and averages are often useful to achieve a balanced criticism. Trained observers sitting on the sidelines are often more objective than we can be ourselves or than other group members can be about us. A final type of appraisal may be made by people who have had nothing to do with the discussion and who see it on film or videotape, or hear it on tape recording.

Evaluation during the group process allows members to see problems when they occur, to halt the discussion while in process, and to act before a serious difficulty gets in the way of the group's functioning. The group can, thus, alter its process or change its course to a more fruitful line of action.

Perhaps the most useful time to evaluate is immediately after the discussion or meeting when the whole picture is vivid and while the process is still clear in the minds of participants. To delay the evaluation is to blur the images somewhat, which may spoil the sharp contrast of the picture even though delayed evaluation may allow time for reflective thought and for testing the decisions reached by the group.

There are several methods of evaluation. One useful method is simply to discuss, orally, what occurred. Another method is to use rating forms that might include such items as knowledge of the subject, analysis of the subject, reasoning ability, familiarity with the process, communication skills, and awareness and concern for others. Another type of form is the open-ended one, which allows the evaluator complete freedom in response. In some groups, one can test the feasibility or workability of the group's decision as a method of evaluating it. Simply raise the flag to see if it flies! Finally, one can judge the holding power of a group by finding out who comes back. If members keep coming back, there is no question that they feel they are engaged in a worthwhile activity, an enjoyable experience.

THE PROBLEM-SOLVING GROUP: A CASE STUDY

Much of the communication that occurs in small groups is directed toward solving problems. All groups must determine procedures, set norms, and negotiate individual member roles, for example, and each of these decisions may be seen as a problem which the group needs to resolve if it is to function well. In addition, some groups are created specifically to find the solution to a particular, predetermined question. A work group such as a committee that is formed to investigate an issue and bring back recommendations to its authorizing body is an example. Since problem-solving is such a common group task, we will consider in some detail the functions of a successful problem-solving group.

The main form of communication in problem-solving groups is discussion. The group meets to exchange information and ideas in an effort to gain better understanding of particular issues or situations. *Discussion,* in this sense, is restricted to situations characterized by free interaction among members in which specific objectives are outlined by the group, relevant information is offered to substantiate ideas, consideration of the ideas is thorough, and group responsibility is directed toward moving from conception of the idea to its disposal or solution. It is, thus, different from that communication that normally occurs in bull sessions, coffee klatsches, encounter groups, and sensitivity sessions.

In 1910, John Dewey wrote a book entitled *How We Think,* which provides a guide to reflective thinking—a scientific pattern of thought which requires a high degree of rationality, a deep respect for evidence, and a careful consideration of possible answers or solutions to problems.[6] Dewey's reflective pattern includes five steps in a sequence that leads from the determination of the problem to the determination of the solution: 1) recognition of the problem, 2) description of the problem, 3) suggestion of possible solutions, 4) evaluation of solutions by reasoning and the discovery of the best solution, and 5) development of the plan of action. The reflective pattern provides a useful structure which can be put into practice—in part or *in toto*—in small problem-solving groups. The entire pattern, which is presented here, is probably best suited to formal, task-oriented groups. The structure may be adapted, however, for use in less formal group situations in which problem-solving is part of the group's process.

Recognizing the Problem

One of the most difficult tasks for students involved in practicing discussion techniques is the selection of a topic. In real-life situations, topics arise naturally out of the situation: school boards are faced with formulating a policy about the "open classroom"; company administrative committees must make a decision about the four-day work week; or a group of town selectmen try to determine how to handle the problem of sewage disposal. Students planning for in-class situations may find fruitful topics in the areas of business or education, in the social or political arena, or in considerations of personal opinion about local issues. Such topics include business monopolies, educational grading policies, the social problem of crime, political scandal, and a person's right to privacy.

After the topic has been selected, it should be formed as a proposition. *Propositions* are simply formal presentations of anything selected for discussion; they may be in statement or question form. There are three types of propositions: fact, value, or policy. Propositions of fact allege the existence of something—an object, an event, or a relationship. They are found to be either true or false, based on the evidence that is accumulated to affirm or deny them. Propositions of fact are most appropriate for groups whose primary purpose is the accumulation of information or evidence—fact-finding groups. For example, seeking to encourage shopping in a downtown area, a group of businessmen may get together to resolve a proposition that might be phrased "Business in the downtown area can be expanded." The businessmen might wish to

---

6 John Dewey, *How We Think* (Boston: D. C. Heath, 1910), p. 72.

present information on this topic such as the *likelihood* that it can be expanded, current sales this year versus last year at the same time, parking availability, and so on before deciding that something should be done. They may find that business is operating at near peak capacity considering the parking spaces available, or they may find that most businessmen are not at all dissatisfied with the present level of business. Either of these findings would make their proposition false.

Propositions of value express evaluative judgments concerning the goodness or badness of some person, institution, or idea. This kind of proposition involves making a judgment only; it is not concerned with recommending a policy or action. "Business in the downtown area is good," is one example. Another might be "Is the present system of electing the President detrimental?" Commissions selected to determine the possible harm of a current trend or of a proposed change treat value propositions: "Is pornography harmful to society?" "Pollution is damaging our environment." "Will the proposed bypass be harmful to downtown business?" "Will the pass-fail grading system be detrimental for future employment?" Questions regarding judgments of value are often resolved before a group takes action on a policy.

Propositions of policy are those types of questions most often discussed in small-group problem-solving discussions. Such propositions propose a new policy, a change of policy, or some other specific action. A proposition of policy asks, should this be done? "Should business in the downtown area be advanced?" "Should our system of electing the President be changed?" "Should pornography be legalized?" "Should pollution be controlled?" Almost any topic can be phrased as a proposition of policy. Policy questions can often be detected by the presence of the word *should,* or one of its synonyms: *ought, has to,* or *must.*

Knowing whether you have a proposition of fact, value, or policy is only part of recognizing the problem. The actual phrasing of the problem is just as important, for a poorly worded proposition can affect every other stage of the pattern. The proposition can be phrased as a question or as a statement, but a question often attracts more attention and provides more impetus for active discussion since it challenges rather than just declares. The proposition should be clear. Ambiguous wording will cause discussion time to be wasted in figuring out what the words of the proposition mean. The topic should be narrowed to just the part of a broad topic that can be reasonably handled in the time allotted for the discussion. Trying to treat "Should stricter measures be employed to reduce crime?" in an hour discussion is certain to be frustrating because the necessary information cannot possibly be covered in that amount of time. Discussing a single subtopic such as recidivism, rape, or shoplifting in an hour is a bit more feasible.

Good discussion can be encouraged, too, if the proposition invites many-sided responses rather than simply a yes or no. It is better to begin with "To what extent should . . ." or "What should be the role . . ." than simply to begin with "Should. . . ." Finally, the proposition should not reflect the biases of the formulators. You should try to avoid using words in a policy proposition like *irresponsible, unnecessary, irrelevant,* or *unreasonable.* Let these judgments be discovered in the discussion of the topic and supported with evidence.

Early consideration of these problems in finding and phrasing topics encourages productive discussion. A group that finds an exciting and stimulating topic and phrases it precisely and clearly is well on its way toward generating effective communication and strong group cohesiveness. If everyone agrees with the topic choice and its phrasing, a healthy group spirit and atmosphere will probably accompany all group deliberations. A well-phrased proposition also provides the foundation for the remaining steps in the Dewey reflective-thinking procedure.

Describing the Problem

One way to describe a problem is to look at its effects. To study the proposition "Should television violence on children's shows be reduced?" you would need to find out the immediate effects of violence on the children who watch it. Do children who are exposed to televised violence commit more aggressive acts than children who are not exposed? What is the relationship between juvenile crime and televised violence? Your group might also look into long-range effects such as the extent to which violence in children's shows has affected adults who are in prison for committing violent crimes.

Often it is difficult to determine cause-effect relationships of this kind. If the group is unable to link a particular effect with televised violence, the group has still uncovered useful information since it may conclude that no such relationship exists. Thus, no information is sometimes as helpful as positive information in the description of the problem.

Another way to describe a problem is to examine its underlying causes. Some consideration of the history of the problem is often helpful. How long have children's shows depicted violence? Has there been an increase in juvenile crime or in aggressive acts by children since television has become widespread? These sorts of questions will help to place the problem in historical perspective.

Finally, in describing the problem, specific information about the immediate causes should be sought by the group. Who writes television shows depicting violence? Why is it depicted? Why do advertisers support shows with violence in them? To what extent is violence ignored by parents? Learning about the immediate causes of the problem will help the group to clarify exactly what the problem is; it will also prepare the group to consider solutions.

Finding Solutions

Following a thorough and complete description of the problem, discussion should turn to the discovery of solutions. Information gained from the description phase will help the group to determine the conditions to be met by an acceptable solution. A solution to the television-violence problem, for example, would have to be agreeable to writers, advertisers, and audience members. In another example, a solution to our transportation problems would have to satisfy the needs of automobile users, be reasonably inexpensive, and be efficient.

With conditions outlined, possible solutions—including a variety of alternatives—can be determined. A high degree of creativity is desirable in this step. New solutions, or unusual approaches, often result from the combination of individual contributions. Group members who try to integrate and synthesize are often the ones who see the big breakthroughs, the uncommon, the unpredictable, and the new. Such combinations, however, result from a base created through careful study and preparation, the accumulation of knowledge and methodical planning as well as imaginary wandering, hunches, intuitions, and the ability to juggle many different responses.

Realistic discussion of solutions includes consideration of the kinds of attitudes that exist regarding the problem. If the topic is abortion, it is important for group-discussion members to understand the Roman Catholic position on abortion. The degree to which a negative attitude is held toward a topic—and the number of people who hold such an attitude—could determine the workability of a particular solution as well as the plan of action to be used to institute it.

Evaluating Solutions

Once a number of solutions have been discussed, they can be evaluated and the best one accepted by the group for action. The best solutions come out of group discussions in which evaluation of the various possibilities is delayed until all solution alternatives have been discussed. Sometimes a solution that would have been rejected by premature evaluation becomes part of the accepted solution because the group did not judge it too soon.

In evaluating solutions, members should discuss their merits and weaknesses, keeping in mind that each solution may offer a partial answer. It is essential that disagreement as well as agreement be expressed so that the group can come up with the best possible response to the problem. Often a multiple solution—one that has different parts, phrases, or steps, and combines several responses—is the best answer. The final judgment of a solution will be determined by whether it has the potential for changing present undesirable effects, whether it creates new undesirable effects, whether it corrects the causes of the problem, and whether it satisfies the other conditions to be met by an acceptable solution that have been agreed upon during the discovery of solutions step. Some initial testing might be necessary.

The Plan of Action

The final step involves the plan of action—the determination of how the accepted solution will be put into operation. What group or what individuals will have to carry out the solution endorsed by the group? How will they do it? What barriers need to be overcome? How will they be contacted? How will they be supervised and evaluated? To consider the solution in light of how it can be put into action is to look at it in light of reality—what really might happen when it is publicized and promoted.

It is easy for a group to be idealistic, especially a group of students sitting in the classroom, generating creative and interesting ideas that look good and sound good. There is, no doubt, merit in the consideration of such paper policies—but often the test of a group's success is whether they come up with ideas and courses of action that can be practiced, utilized, or implemented. To consider the plan of action is to keep an eye on the real world.

Using Dewey's pattern of reflective thinking encourages active, persistent, and careful consideration of ideas. It also promotes the investigation of the evidence which supports ideas and the conclusions which lead from them. Discussion that is characterized by the use of this structural format reflects definite purpose; systematic and logical procedure; effective oral communication; consideration of all available ideas, facts, and opinions that bear on the topic; group cooperation; and leadership in one form or another. This is what successful problem-solving small-group communication is all about.

SUMMARY

We depend upon various kinds of small groups in much of our living. These groups have different kinds of goals, from the solution of a specific problem to the pleasure of social interchange, but all of them have certain characteristics in common: the members are similar and interdependent; there is interaction and communication among them; and they share common needs or goals.

Small-group communication is multilateral in that members play the role of speaker and of listener interchangeably. Successful small groups have between three and nine members in most cases to permit maximum interchange among the members. The arrangement of space for small-group communication depends upon the expected psychological relationships of the members and also upon the group's task. Members of small groups play roles that may be either helpful or destructive of the group's purposes. Each group also develops a set of norms for the group's behavior. The degree of cohesiveness in a group depends upon the group's size, its spatial arrangements, the roles that members assume, and the extent to which the group develops and adheres to group norms.

Constructive patterns of communication in small groups permit the greatest flow of messages among all of the group members. The direction of the message flow in a group is affected by the roles of the members and by the relative status of various group members. Among the most important communication skills in groups are the ability to listen, the ability to give good feedback, and the ability to be flexible.

A leader directs the group in performing its task. Any member who influences the group may be said to be leading it. Leaders may be imposed on a group, or they may emerge from the group in response to a need felt either by the leader or by others in the group. Among the functions of a leader are to establish procedures, to raise questions, to focus on answers, and to encourage social-emotional growth. Of the three leadership styles—authoritarian, democratic, and laissez-faire—the democratic style works best for most groups. Some groups also function successfully without leaders.

Evaluation need not always occur in small-group communication; however, if one intends to improve group behavior, evaluation should be part of the group's operations. Evaluation may center on the group's process or on the end result of the group's work. It may be carried out by the group members, collectively or individually, or by trained outside observers. Good timing is important: it may be useful to stop during the group's work to evaluate; evaluation is also effective right after the group has met or later, when the results of the group's decisions are known.

Communication in small groups is often directed toward problem-solving. Following Dewey's pattern for reflective thinking, a problem-solving group can move from recognition of the problem to description of the problem to discovery of solutions to evaluation of solutions and, finally, to a plan of action.

Many of the skills discussed in the chapters on interpersonal and public communication also apply to small-group communication. A person who is effective in any one setting is likely to find success in other situations as well; however, each format has special characteristics and makes special demands on the communicator functioning within that format. In small groups, perhaps the single most important characteristic of a good communicator is his or her ability to interact constructively and clearly with all of the others in the group. Since small groups are a large part of our everyday existence, some knowledge of how to perform better in them will make our lives more satisfying and rewarding.

FURTHER READING

Eric Berne, *The Structure and Dynamics of Organizations and Groups.* New York: Ballantine Books, 1963.
   This paperback book discusses group process from a psychological perspective; one section treats group relationships from the transactional point of view. Although the book is intended for professionals or laymen, it uses a fairly complex vocabulary for the beginning student. The glossary which is included is very useful. Written in an informative and interesting manner, this original work is required reading for those interested in the psychological aspects of group behavior.

Erving Goffman, *Relations in Public: Microstudies of the Public Order.* New York: Basic Books, 1971.
   This is a collection of six articles in which the author details the social understandings necessary for the orderly conduct of the larger group—society. His thesis is that there are delicate connec-

tions between social relationships and public life. It will be clear from reading this book that almost all activity in which we engage is group regulated.

Jane Howard, *Please Touch: A Guided Tour of the Human Potential Movement.* New York: A Delta Book, 1970.
One of the few books available that reveals what encounter groups, sensitivity groups, and T-groups are all about in plain terms. Vivid and witty, Howard's paperback is also honest, personal, and objective. She doesn't just tell you about the movement, she lets you know what participating in the movement feels like by immersing you in it!

William C. Schutz, *Joy: Expanding Human Awareness.* New York: Grove Press, 1967.
The purpose of the author's work is to provide theories and methods that people can use to achieve their full potential—joy. This paperback book makes use of much of the philosophy of the human-potential movement. To develop openness and honesty, you must proceed through various levels—body-structure, personal functioning, interpersonal relations, and, finally, organizational relations. Having achieved the final level, the "fully-realized" person will be more capable of having satisfying relations with others and with society.

Clovis R. Shepherd, *Small Groups: Some Sociological Perspectives.* San Francisco: Chandler, 1964.
Here is an introduction to sociological and social-psychological theory and research dealing with the small group. Designed for the serious student with little or no background in sociology or social psychology, this paperback includes a thorough bibliography and provides a stimulating starting point.

8

The Mass Media

The mass media are a major force in American society. In 1972 there were over 11,000 newspapers, 9,000 periodicals, and 25,000 new books available to the American public. The broadcast industry includes over 900 television and 7,100 radio stations; in the average American home the television set is on seven hours a day. Women are exposed to 305 commercials every day and men to 285. More than 200 new films were produced in 1973. John M. Culkin estimates that by the time a typical American student graduates from high school, he or she has seen more than 500 films and has watched 15,000 hours of television. (The same student has spent a total of 10,800 hours in school during the same period).[1] Whether you are aware of it or not, you are probably exposed to more mass communication than any other type of communication.

THE MASS-COMMUNICATION PROCESS

Basically, *mass communication* can be defined as a communicacations system in which an identical message is originated by an insti-

1 John M Culkin, S.J., *Film Study in the High School*, in *The Electric Humanities*, Don Allen (Dayton, Ohio: Geo. A. Pflaum, 1971), p. 164.

tutional organization and sent to a large number of receivers through public channels. The institutional organizations include radio and television networks and stations, newspaper and magazine publishers, and film companies. The receivers consist of a large, diversified audience. The messages are identical because all of the receivers are sent the same message; they are public in the sense that they are available to anyone who wants to watch, listen to, or read them. The *mass media* are the communication channels through which these messages are sent —radio and television, print (newspapers, magazines, and books), and film.

Mass communication has the same components of source, message, receiver, and feedback as do other forms of communication. However, these components have some unique characteristics in the mass communication setting.

Sources in Mass Communications

There are almost always several different sources in mass communications. For example, a newspaper reporter may call in a story by telephone. Another reporter in the newsroom writes the story, and someone else edits it. In television, the writer prepares the script; the producer puts together the various production elements of actors, set, and lighting; and the director decides how to shoot the story. In both cases the final message may be changed considerably from the message sent by the first source. The story called in by the reporter or conceived by the writer will be altered by each successive source. In a small communication enterprise, such as an underground newspaper, there may be a single source who does all of the writing and editing, but this is unusual.

Of all of the sources in communications, the mass-communication source has the least specific knowledge about the receiver. The larger the individual medium, the more this is true. The potential audience for a television special may number in the millions, for example, so the source can only have a very general idea of the receivers' likes and dislikes. Some of the media aim at a smaller and more specialized audience; their ideas of receivers may be more specific. A radio station with black-oriented programming may assume that most of their audience is black; *The New Yorker* magazine may assume that their readership is predominately urban and sophisticated. Yet even the more specialized media cannot be sure of very much more than that their audience is interested in the special area of messages which that medium transmits.

In interpersonal relationships, the message is very much influenced by the receiver, more so as the relationship grows and the source learns more about the receiver. In many public-speaking situations, the speaker can shape his or her content and delivery on the basis of what the speaker knows about the particular audience who will hear the speech. People who prepare messages for the mass media almost never have this kind of specific information about the audience.

Another characteristic that makes the mass communication source different from other sources is that there is very little the source can do to control its audience. In small-group situations, leaders help to direct the communication behavior of the group members. Public-speaking audiences are more or less captive; if they come to hear you at all, they will usually hear you out, and you have some chance of affecting them with your message. Controlling the mass-media audience is much more difficult; a disk jockey cannot keep people from turning off their radios, and a newspaper publisher cannot stop people from wrapping the garbage in their newspaper as soon as they have read the sports page.

Messages in Mass Communication

Because mass communication sources have less knowledge about and control over their audiences than other sources do, their messages are different. One basic principle of mass communications is the larger the audience, the more general the message. For example, in the thirties and the forties, films had very large audiences; they were made to reach the general American public. When television came along in the fifties, it captured the former film audience; films became more specialized as a result. In the late sixties and early seventies, films were made about surfboarding and motorcycles, for example, in an attempt to capture specialized audiences. The same thing is generally true of newspapers and magazines. Big city newspapers aim for a broad and diverse audience while magazines aim for a specialized audience. The age of the mass magazine seems to be over. *Colliers, Look,* and *Life* all died within a single decade, but small specialized magazines have flourished, and one can find magazines devoted solely to cats, super-8 filmmaking, and poultry breeding.

When the medium's audience is very large, as it is in television, messages are also more simplified and repetitious. Since the source knows little about the audience, an attempt is made to reach everyone. Messages are designed to be understandable to people who have little education as well as to nuclear physicists. The best example of simplified, repetitive messages are those used in advertising; these messages are understood even by very young children.

Mass communication messages are also carefully timed and spaced. Broadcast messages are timed to the second, and print messages are measured to the column inch. All television programs for example, commonly fall into thirty minute or sixty minute segments although occasional programs might be either longer or shorter. If a program series decides to tackle a particular social problem, it must do it in an exact number of minutes. Even though there might be a light news day, the television or radio news program must fill a certain amount of time and so additional stories, which would not be covered on a heavy news day, will be added as fillers. Newspaper stories are traditionally written with the most critical information at the beginning of the story so that the article can be cut to fit into the allotted space. Inevitably, the lack of flexibility in timing and spacing leads to distortion of the messages for mass communications.

Mass-Media Audiences

Certain generalizations can be made about the audiences for the mass media. Some media, including most newspapers and radio stations, tend to have local audiences that are limited to a particular geographical area whereas other media, including magazines, movies, books, and network television, are directed toward national audiences. Herbert Blumer has described four characteristics which distinguish national mass-media audiences. He says that the members of the audience come from all groups of society, the audiences are composed of individuals who do not know each other, they are separated from each other in that they cannot interact with one another or exchange experience, and there is no definite leadership for the audience because they are loosely organized—if they are organized at all.[2] Local audiences may differ from national audiences in that they are more likely to know and interact with each other.

A study by Paul F. Lazarsfeld and Patricia Kendall showed that people who are exposed to one medium are likely to be exposed to others so that a radio listener is also likely to be a moviegoer and a person who reads one magazine is just as likely to read three or four.[3] People may

---

2 Herbert Blumer, "Collective Behavior," in *New Outline of the Principles of Sociology*, A. M. Lee (ed.) (New York: Barnes and Noble, 1946), pp. 167–222.

3 William L. Rivers, Theodore Peter, and Jay W. Jensen, *The Mass Media and Modern Society* (2d ed.; San Francisco: Rinehart Press, 1971), p. 282.

THE MASS-COMMUNICATION PROCESS 261

have a greater attraction to one medium than to another, however. College-educated persons, for example, do more reading while high-school-educated persons depend more on the electronic media. Age may also be a factor. As Americans grow older, they are more inclined to use media for information than for entertainment. Media use also has a tendency to drop off in later years.

Research has indicated that individuals have a tendency to select whatever medium is most readily available. Television drama is usually more readily available than live theatre because the television play is as close as the "on" button while the live play requires a trip across town. Given this choice, most people will select the television play. He also found that people make media choices according to what fits in best with their leisure time. For example, a person who spends time on a commuter train may read his or her newspaper very thoroughly. Finally, researchers discovered, people choose the medium that will offer the greatest reward. For instance, a housewife might find a television soap opera a very satisfying means of escape.[4]

Specific media also have certain kinds of audiences. Schramm and White found that the young use newspapers chiefly for entertainment and read the human-interest stories, comic strips, and crossword puzzles while older persons use them more for news. The reading of public affairs and news increases with more education and a higher economic status.[5] Book readers have above-average education, and young adults and urban dwellers are the heaviest readers. Book readers also make use of the serious content of other media, for example, news and public affairs articles in magazines.

Film audiences are very specialized. The Opinion Research Corporation discovered that the majority of moviegoers are under thirty—in fact more than half are under twenty and a third are under fifteen. Persons over fifty seldom attend the movies at all. Of all of the mass media, movie going provides the most social activity and is commonly used by the young for dating. Four fifths of all film admissions are for groups of two or more.[6]

Radio also aims at a specialized audience. A station's programming may range from top-40 to country-and-western, and the programming

4 *Ibid.*, pp. 287–288.
5 Wilbur Schram and David Manning White, "Age, Education, and Economic Status as Factors in Newspaper Reading: Conclusions," in *The Process and Effects of Mass Communication,* Wilbur Schramm (ed.) (Urbana: University of Illinois Press, 1954), pp. 71–73.
6 Rivers, p. 281.

commonly determines the audience. Americans listen to radio on the average of two hours a day; this listening may be broken into several short periods. There is also a good deal of out-of-home listening on car and portable radios.

Television audiences best fit the Blumer description of national audiences given above. Audiences for national television are the largest mass-media audiences, and they also cover the widest age, economic, and educational range. Television audiences can, of course, become more specialized because of program content. News and educational programs, for example, attract more definable audiences. It is generally very difficult to describe a typical television audience for an evening entertainment program because the audience is so heterogeneous.

Feedback in Mass Communication

Perhaps the most outstanding characterstic of mass communication is the lack of feedback. When a message is sent by mass media, the communication is one-way because the receivers do not respond immediately to the source. If feedback exists at all, it is delayed and occurs in such forms as letters to the editor or producer, and increased sales for an advertised product. In the broadcast media, feedback is often determined by a third party, one that is not involved in sending or receiving the message at all. This third party is the audience-rating service, which is hired by broadcasters to discover how many people were watching or listening to a particular message. There is no attempt to find out whether or not the receivers liked or approved of the message—it is sufficient that they listened.

Although feedback may be delayed for days or even weeks, it is still important to mass communication. If large numbers of people watch a program, attend a film, or buy a newspaper, the institution or organization will continue to produce similar messages. When people do not listen, watch, or read, the organization changes or drops the message. Thus, feedback in mass communication is considered to be positive when the message has been received by a large audience. The fact that the message holds the attention of many people is more important than the quality of the message.

Because feedback in mass communication is largely a matter of measuring the size of the receiving audience, the best messages are considered to be those which are most popular. This type of feedback results in the repetition and imitation of similar messages. The success of *All in the Family* caused the television networks to attempt several imitations. Even though the *Whole Earth Catalog* decided to go out of business, its basic format has been copied, and there are several similar catalogs in bookstores. There are always a few people who are willing to experiment with new forms and messages, but most mass-communication messages are determined by what has sold in the past. Creators of mass communication strongly believe that nothing succeeds like success, and many critics of the mass media complain that mass communication messages are of poor quality for exactly this reason: they are geared to please the largest possible audience.

THE ECONOMICS OF THE MASS MEDIA

There are three types of financial support for the American mass media: they are bought directly by the receiver (books, tickets to films); they are subsidized by organizations (educational radio and television stations); or they are supported by advertisers (radio, television, and newspapers). In some cases there may be two forms of support for a medium; a magazine, for example, may be supported both by advertising and by readers who buy copies.

The economic structure of the mass media exerts a strong influence on message content. With the exception of the few media that are subsidized, the American media exist to make a profit, and profit is made by attracting audiences. Most of the broadcast media, the publishers, and the film studios would cease operation if they did not make money.

This desire and need to make money means that the American media offer mostly entertainment because entertainment attracts the largest audience. Even though they also provide information such as news, documentaries, and public-service material, the information function is secondary. In fact, an effort is made to make news and other information entertaining, too. The major television networks have created news teams in which the reporters are personalities with images like those of other media stars. These images have as much to do with a reporter's ability to entertain as they do with his or her ability to give information. Similarly, a murder in Chicago affects only a very few people, but people like to read about murders so newspapers carry homicide stories in disproportionate numbers to their real importance.

Finally, the mass media compete with each other for audiences. The newspapers compete with rival newspapers as well as with radio and television; a radio station may compete with several other stations as well as with television and newspapers. Success in competing is always determined by audience size so that the newspaper or the radio or television station which has the largest audience is successful because it is able to sell the most copies or attract the most advertising revenue.

Advertising and the Mass Media

Advertising is so critical to the American mass media that it must be considered as an independent economic force; one cannot discuss newspapers, radio, or television without discussing advertising because none of these media would survive without it. Media advertising is also crucial to the modern American economy. After mass-production techniques were developed, there was a profusion of goods on the market that had to be bought if the economy were to flourish. As mass production developed, people were also beginning to live in concentrated urban areas, and it became possible to reach consumers in large groups. Advertising developed to bridge the gap between the supplier and the buyer, and the most efficient way to advertise is through the mass media since they can reach vast numbers of people. Mass-media advertising is essential to the American economy because there is no other way to stimulate widespread demand for objects consumers have never heard of or try to persuade the consumer to buy one product over another one.

As well as providing a vehicle for making the public aware of goods, advertising provides the money that the media need for their operation. For example, advertising pays 60 percent of the cost of producing mass magazines and 70 percent of the cost of producing metropolitan newspapers. Someone once estimated that if the *New York Times* did not have advertising support, the daily edition would cost the reader $1.50 and the Sunday edition would cost $6.00. Radio and television are also very expensive media, and receivers would have to pay for programs directly in some way if there were no advertising support. Thus, advertising works to the benefit of both the producer of goods and the institutions that operate the media. In essence, the advertiser borrows the audiences of the mass media to show their products, and the media benefit by having programs or newspapers partially paid for.

This reliance on advertising, however, has many disadvantages; in many ways advertising is a two-edged sword. Although our media would not be able to exist in their present form without it, advertising has influenced the very nature of the media.

Advertisers represent the view of the big-business community. Among the 500 largest industries in America are companies whose advertising has made their names household words: General Motors, R.C.A.,

Eastman Kodak, Borden, Xerox, Coca-Cola, Johnson and Johnson. These industries are the heart of the American economy, and their advertising exerts a great deal of influence on Americans' ideas of what the good life is. Most of the people who can afford to buy the products that these companies make are white and middle class, and big-business advertising is directed toward them and toward confirming their values and life styles. It says to them, in effect, you are America. Because the advertiser directs his message to the majority—the largest audience—the many minorities in America are left out. Those whose race, creed, political outlook, or level of income or education is different from the largest audience are told that they are not America, that they do not matter.

The influence of big business in the media is much more far-reaching than simply determining advertising content, however. Big business in America is also dominated by white middle-class men who are most comfortable with a mass media that reflects their own values and attitudes. Since their advertising supports the media, these people have the economic power to force the media to portray the values of the white middle class—in their programming as well as in the advertising they carry.

There are numerous examples of similar advertising interference with program and editorial content. During the civil rights movement in the sixties, several advertisers stopped placing ads in newspapers that carried liberally oriented stories. If this is done on a wide enough scale, a newspaper can no longer survive. The newspaper has only two alternatives: to find new advertisers or to please the existing ones. In the broadcast media, networks deliberately choose programs that will get sponsorship. The programs most likely to be sponsored are those that do not offend anyone—thus listeners and viewers are given a steady diet of bland programs. Advertisers are also interested in large audiences and depend on rating companies to periodically supply figures on audience size for most radio and television programs. In television, even a program with a small but devoted audience and sponsorship is likely to be dropped by the network because they are afraid that it may affect the audience ratings of the program that follows. This control of programs by advertisers means that most successful television writers avoid controversy, unpleasantness, and innovation.

The final problem with advertising is that television and radio commercials are a constant interruption and take up program time. Newspapers and magazines are not faced with such problems. The reader can always skip the advertisements, and if many persons want to advertise, the newspaper simply adds more pages. The broadcast industry cannot do this. There are only so many hours in a day, and the time for advertisements must be taken from program time. Advertising interruptions also destroy some of the power of the message to establish mood and to build tension and suspense. Hitler may never have become so powerful if his radio speeches had been interrupted with commercials because he would not have been able to build the tension which was so crucial to his particular type of speaking.

Although all communications sources are influenced by outside forces, only the mass media, and particularly the broadcast industry, have such constant interference. In many cases the outside influence of the advertiser is as important in determining the message as the source is. This characteristic is unique to mass communication.

THE POWER OF THE MASS MEDIA

There is no question that the mass media have tremendous potential power, although this power is often misunderstood and unnecessarily feared. When you see a three-year-old browbeating his mother into buying a particular brand of cereal because the child has seen it on his morning cartoon program, you may conclude that television is the ultimate thought-control instrument. It is clear that the mass media influence many of our decisions; however, most receivers are not as easily manipulated as a three-year-old.

The effect of a mass communication message is determined by the results that the message produces in the receivers. If an evening newspaper advertises a sale in a local department store and the store is flooded with customers the next morning, the advertising message has the effect of producing customers.

Throughout its history, mass communication has produced both short-term and long-term effects. The invention of the printing press changed the entire structure of Western society. Before 1440, the date traditionally given for the invention of mass-production printing equipment by Johann Gutenberg, written materials were rare and costly to produce. With the printing press came volume production so that books and other printed materials became widely available. A rise in literacy followed; information that had been available only to scholars and the rich became accessible to many more people. Think for a minute about what you would be able to find out about your world if you had no printed material and your only sources were personal observation and word of mouth. This was the situation of most people before the invention of the printing press.

The electronic media (film, radio, and television) have had an equally important effect on contemporary society. Marshall McLuhan maintains that the media have created a "global village," a world that is instantly aware of events in all other parts of the world. Entertainment as well as political events are beamed to many areas of the globe—you can see *Gunsmoke* in Africa and *Ironside* in Japan. The mass media are most prevalent in the United States, however, where they influence everything from how we use our leisure time to how we elect our political candidates.

Early observers of the mass media were alarmed by the possible effects of mass communication. These observers saw receivers as helpless victims who could be controlled and intimidated by the media. However, these early fears were greatly exaggerated; subsequent research has brought the realization that media audiences are by no means passive. Zimmerman and Bauer have coined the phrase "the obstinate audience"—an audience that does not passively absorb and act on messages but selects and remembers what is useful to them.[7] Wilbur Schramm writes ". . . the trend in communications research over the past several decades has been away from concern with what communications do to people and toward the study of what people do with communications . . . what people bring to the media *interacts* with what the media bring to the people."[8] Thus, media receivers are active rather than passive—they participate and are involved in what they hear, see, and read.

The Effects of Mass Communication

Since mass communications is similar to interpersonal, small-group, and public-speaking communication, it also shares many of their effects. The following generalizations, as Donald F. Roberts points out, are common to all communication: 1) We tend to be more open to messages that reinforce our attitudes, beliefs, and values; we tend to ignore or avoid communication that goes against these beliefs. If you are a ded-

[7] Claire Zimmerman and R. A. Bauer, "The Effect of an Audience Upon What Is Remembered," *Public Opinion Quarterly,* 20 (1956): 238–248.

[8] Wilbur Schramm, "Approaches to the Study of Mass Communication Effects: Attitudes and Information," in *The Process and Effects of Mass Communication,* Wilbur Schramm and Donald F. Roberts (eds.) (rev. ed.; Urbana: University of Illinois Press, 1971), pp. 391–392.

icated Democrat, probably no amount of messages will turn you into a Republican. 2) We are more inclined to change our mind about certain aspects of our attitudes and beliefs than we are likely to change our entire value structure. We might discover that the Catholic Mass is very moving, but we won't change our religion from Jewish to Catholic. 3) We are more open to messages that are useful and that will help us reach our goals. If your house is full of roaches, you will pay special attention to advertisements about roach poisons. 4) We process information that will help us to structure our social and physical environment. If there has been a serious fire in your city. you will seek out information about it from the existing media or from people who have seen the fire. 5) Various aspects of the total communication situation may affect our interpretation of the message. You will be more likely to believe your state senator than the gasoline company in an explanation of why gasoline prices are higher.[9]

The range of research about the specific effects of the mass media is so vast that it could only be covered in several books; we will only mention some of the broader and more general theories. Paul F. Lazarsfeld and Robert K. Merton developed some mass media theories in 1948 which are still regarded as important today.[10] Their first observation about mass media was that it conferred status. Persons, organizations, social movements, and political issues become important because they are recognized and reported by the mass media. (To get an idea of what this really means, imagine yourself on the cover of *Time* magazine!) The second effect of the media they discussed was that it enforced social norms by showing what was acceptable and what was not. The media coverage of Watergate is a good illustration of this point. News of Watergate exposed deviations from the norm to public view. The third media effect they labeled as "narcotizing dysfunction." Basically this means that the viewer is narcotized (or numbed) by all she or he sees. The ultimate effect of narcotization is an informed and interested citizen who does nothing. The period at the end of the Vietnam war is a good example of this point. Many people were well-informed about the war, and the general American sentiment was against the war; however, in the latter days of the war it was almost impossible to mobilize people to protest against it. Lazarsfeld and Merton also say that the media has

9 Donald F. Roberts, "Nature of Communication Effects," in *The Process and Effects of Mass Communications*, pp. 369–371.
10 Paul F. Lazarsfeld and Robert K. Merton, "Mass Communication, Popular Taste, and Organized Social Action," in *The Process and Effects of Mass Communication*, pp. 554–578.

produced an overwhelming flood of conformist material and is responsible for a decline in popular taste and culture—an opinion held by many critics of the media.

Joseph Klapper, another important media researcher, has dealt with the influence of the mass media in changing beliefs, values, and attitudes. As we have already mentioned, most communication is unlikely to change basic value structures; this is particularly true of the mass media. Klapper says that most people select, perceive, and retain that which is compatible with what they already believe. Once they have received a media message, they subject it to considerable additional scrutiny. This may range from talking it over with their friends to evaluating it in terms of their group memberships.[11]

One of the most interesting examples of this process of evaluating messages can be found in the popular television series *All in the Family*. When the program first began, many people praised it as a great attack on bigotry and prejudice. Then it was discovered that it was as popular with conservatives as it was with liberals. Liberals saw Archie Bunker as a brilliant and cutting satire of a bigot, and conservatives saw him as a good guy with the right ideas. Regardless of who Archie Bunker is, he is a perfect example of how people see exactly what they want to see.

Roberts points out some additional media effects. He says that the media is effective in showing us parts of the world which we would have little opportunity to see first-hand. However, this media virtue can easily turn into a vice. If the media presents a distorted, stereotyped, or biased picture, the receiver has no way of checking on the accurary of that picture and therefore has a similarly biased view. For example, generations of Americans formed pictures of Africa based on *Tarzan* films. Roberts also says the media can make events, people, and organizations insignificant by *not* reporting them.[12]

Black Americans have particularly suffered from this lack of coverage. Prior to the sixties, one seldom saw blacks at all in any of the media. Although they have received coverage in the sixties and seventies, the coverage was more likely to concern urban disturbance and militancy than to show a well-rounded portrayal of black life in America. Quite often the most valid way to study propaganda is to study what is not covered rather than what is.

---

11 Joseph T. Klapper, *The Effects of Mass Communication* (Glencoe, Ill.: The Free Press, 1960), pp. 15–49.
12 Roberts, "Nature of Communication Effects," pp. 375–387.

Since children are great media users, many people have been particularly concerned about the effects of media violence on children. Roberts and Schramm have summarized some of the probable effects. They say that a disturbed child is more likely to be influenced by the media than a healthy child. They also say that a child may learn aggressive behavior from the media and may imitate what he or she has learned if faced with a similar life situation. Another possibility is that children may become desensitized to violence. These conclusions are tentative, and there will probably be a great deal of forthcoming research on the subject of children and media violence.[13]

Research of mass media effects is vigorous and far-reaching. Studies are carried out by the various media industries and by students of communication in academic settings. Additional research is being done by the federal government as well as by scholars in the fields of education, political science, sociology, and economics. The mass media are a concern of many people, and this concern is likely to increase in the time to come.

THE REGULATION OF MEDIA

Because the mass media are public, people have always been apprehensive about the potential impact they may have on readers, viewers, and listeners. There has always been controversy about how far the media can go in presenting controversial issues or ideas that may go against prevailing social norms. In spite of this concern, there are actually few set rules that limit all of the media, and, in practice, these limitations are very much determined by the mood of the time.

There are some general principles that both free and restrain all communication, however. The First Amendment of the Constitution guarantees that there will be freedom of speech which means that neither an institution nor another individual may keep you from saying what you will, so long as you are not jeopardizing the safety or security of the nation or of another person. There are libel laws that prohibit one from holding an individual or a small group up to ridicule, hatred, or contempt, and there are other laws which protect individual privacy. Copyright laws protect the work of authors and musicians from being used without per-

---

13 Donald F. Roberts and Wilbur Schramm, "Children's Learning from the Mass Media," in *The Process and Effects of Mass Communications*, pp. 596–611.

mission. There are also obscenity laws—some on the federal level which limit what can be sent through the mail and others which determine what can be seen, heard, or read on the local level.

All of the mass media are also subject to certain limitations which specifically affect them. The first type is self-regulation. Newspapers and the broadcast and film industries all have a code which governs their conduct within the industry. The newspaper code, or the Canons of Journalism, is a broad and idealistic code which emphasizes the necessity of truthfulness, sincerity, impartiality, and a respect for individual privacy. The broadcast and movie codes are more practical and specific. They stress standards of acceptability and good taste and often state what should *not* be shown rather than what is acceptable. There is no law which says the media must follow these codes; it is a matter of individual media responsibility.

The only media subject to rather stringent government control are radio and television. Broadcasting is bound by the regulations of the Federal Communications Commission (F.C.C.). The F.C.C.'s power to regulate is based on the assumption that the airways belong to the public because they are a limited commodity in that there is only enough room on the broadcast band for a few people to own radio and television stations. The main powers of the F.C.C. are to grant and renew radio and television licenses, to decide the frequency the station should use, and to determine whether or not the broadcaster is operating in the public interest. Although the F.C.C. has the power to prohibit obscenity and profanity, it does not have the power of censorship over program content.

The regulation and control of the media is an everchanging process. With a liberal government or Supreme Court there may be very little control; with a conservative government and Court, the control tightens. The mass media will always be subject to more control than any other communication because of their public nature.

PLANNING A POLITICAL CAMPAIGN: A CASE STUDY

So far we have discussed mass communications theoretically. Now we would like to look at it from a more practical point of view, and in light of how candidates running for office might use the existing media. Let us assume that there are two candidates named Ann Jones and Walter Brown who are going to run for the office of mayor in the hypothetical town of Farmington, Ohio.

Farmington has a population of 25,000 people. The town has one medium-sized university with 12,000 students and one small college with 3,500 students. The students are not included in the population figures, and they are not eligible to vote. They are important to the community, however, since many of the townspeople are employed by the educational institutions or work in or own retail businesses which serve the students. The university and college also influence the educational and income level of the residents of the town. The average yearly family income is $10,000. Sixty percent of the town's residents have completed high school while an additional 25 percent have completed college. Those persons who are not employed in education or retail businesses are employed in local industry or town services—police, electric company, library. The town is also a recreational center. There are several lakes and forests in the area, and tourists come from all over the state for recreation. There are two political factions in the town: those who favor attracting industry and those who oppose industry because they feel it is a danger to the natural environment.

One of our candidates, Ms. Jones, is an environmental biologist on the faculty at the local college. She has decided to run on a conservationist platform and is firmly opposed to any more large-scale industry coming to Farmington. Our other candidate, Walter Brown, is a local businessman who owns an appliance store in the town. He believes that more industry is essential to the economic well-being of the town and so he decides to run on a platform that encourages such industry. Both candidates have modest campaign budgets and must decide how to best use these budgets in media advertising.

Farmington offers several media possibilities—a daily newspaper, four commercial radio stations, and one local television station. The radio stations all aim at different audiences. When the candidates look at audience surveys and other station data, they discover the following facts: Station A is the oldest, the best established, and the most powerful station in town. Its programming appeals to a middle-class and upper-middle-class audience, and it provides popular, easy-listening music as well as an excellent local news coverage. Station B is a top-40 station which appeals to a younger audience. It has a high listenership on car radios and is especially popular during the morning and evening hours when people are driving to work. Station C plays contemporary rock, jazz, and folk albums and has an audience composed almost entirely of college students and young adults. Station D is a religious station and carries only religious programming. Since there is only one local television station, most Farmington residents subscribe to the cable and receive stations which come from other cities. The Farmington station is the only television station which carries local news.

Both candidates can, of course, depend on a certain amount of free coverage from all of the local media. Since they are candidates for the town's most important political office, the media will automatically cover them in interviews and news stories. Their main problem is to decide how to spend their modest budgets on political advertising.

Both candidates will be able to buy as much newspaper space as they want or can afford. Since they know that the newspaper is widely read and is influential with those with high incomes and educational levels, they both decide to allot the largest share of their budgets to newspaper advertising. Ms. Jones decides to spend 30 percent of her budget on the newspaper and Mr. Brown decides on 40 percent. Brown's share is larger because he is especially interested in reaching the business community—all of whom are likely to read the paper and to support him.

Their next decision is how to spend their money on broadcast time. For purposes of discussion, we will assume that they will be able to purchase any time they need. In practice, however, commercial time during the most popular broadcast hours may not be available since the station has only so many minutes they can sell and they usually give priority to advertisers who are best-established and who spend the most money on the station.

Both candidates again decide to advertise heavily on Station A—the established station. Brown uses 30 percent of his budget for this station because he feels that it is probably the only radio station the business community is likely to listen to. He also requests that his commercials be around the morning newscasts. Jones spends 20 percent of her budget on this station and also requests time around the newscasts as well as some time in the middle of the morning when housewives are likely to be listening.

At this point, you will note that Brown has already spent 70 percent of his budget on the newspaper and on Station A. Since he is mainly interested in reaching the business community, he has put most of his money into the media they are most likely to use. He uses 15 percent of his budget for the three remaining radio stations. He believes that there are only a few potential voters who will support him in these audiences because they are predominately youthful or religious. However, he does not want to give the idea that he is not interested in some of his potential voters so he spends some time in advertising on these stations.

Jones, on the other hand, spends 30 percent of her budget on the three remaining radio stations: 20 percent on Station B—the top-40 station—and 5 percent each on the other two. On Station B she buys time during the commuter hours to reach people going to and from work. She also buys time immediately following school since eighteen-year-olds are allowed to vote in Farmington. She divides 10 percent of her budget for advertising on Stations C and D. She also believes that the audience for Station C will not be very useful since they are ineligible to vote, and she advertises lightly on Station D because she doesn't want to be identified as a religious candidate.

Both candidates spend 10 percent of their budget on television commercials which occur during the local news show. The local news is likely to be viewed by an audience interested in local issues, and thus, in local candidates.

After the candidates have spent the bulk of their media budgets in these ways, Jones is left with 10 percent of her budget and Brown with 5 percent. Again, in an attempt to reach businessmen, Brown spends his remaining money on billboards along the town's major roads. Jones is opposed to billboards because she believes they violate the beauty of the natural environment and so she uses the remaining 10 percent of her budget for direct mailing. She obtains mailing lists of all persons and groups interested in conservation and writes to them directly—urging that they support her.

Both candidates vary their messages for the different media. Jones' newspaper advertisements and radio spots that might reach businessmen are built around the idea that recreational sites bring money into the community. With housewives she makes an appeal for a safe and healthy environment for children, and to the teen-agers she focuses on the pleasures recreational sites can bring.

Brown's appeals to the businessmen stress that increased industry brings more money into the business community. On his limited appeals to housewives and the young, he emphasizes a better standard of living, a larger variety of stores and goods, and more job opportunities for teen-agers.

The success of both political candidates' campaigns will depend on how much they meet the needs of the community. The elements of running a media campaign are similar to all other communication situations —in order to be effective you must find ways to analyze the needs of the audience. In a media campaign such as we have described, the audience is the entire community of Farmington. If the candidates were campaigning in New York City or in Albuquerque, New Mexico, they would need different tactics. All cities have newspapers, radio and television stations,

but if they are to be used effectively, messages must be responsive to community needs. The New York *Times* is different from the Kalamazoo *Gazette* because the people's needs and the issues are different in New York than in Kalamazoo. When the media recognize and respond to these needs, then they are successful.

SUMMARY

Mass communication is a communications system in which an identical message is originated by an institutional organization and sent to a large number of receivers through public channels. The media for mass communications are radio, television, print, and film.

As with other forms of communication, mass communication shares the components of source, message, receiver and feedback. In the mass communication setting, however, the source may be many people, the receivers largely unknown, and the opportunities for feedback limited. Messages become more simplified and repetitive when the audience is large.

Audiences for mass communication vary greatly. Generally radio, print, and film audiences are specialized while television audiences are general and diverse. An audience for a particular medium is usually determined by the variables of age, education, and income. When these variables change, a person is likely to change his or her pattern of media use.

Economic considerations are a major influence in American mass communication. The American media exist to make a profit, and messages are considered successful when large numbers of people read, listen to, or view the mass media product. Most producers of mass communication emphasize entertainment to attract larger audiences. In several of the media, advertisers play an important role—they provide economic support to a medium and also influence message content.

The mass media are powerful in that they have made information and entertainment available to the entire world. However, the media are not particularly powerful in controlling people; research indicates that mass communication works more to reinforce existing beliefs than as an instrument of persuasion. Media receivers are not passive—they interact with the media by combining their own knowledge and experience with the information they receive from the media.

Of all of the communication we have studied, mass communication is the most highly regulated. Depending on the medium, it may be regulated by federal, state, or local government. Of all of the media, broadcasting is the most regulated.

The need for and the uses of mass communication vary from community to community. Mass communication is effective to the extent that it adapts itself to the needs and desires of the audiences it is trying to reach.

FURTHER READING

Erik Barnouw, *A Tower in Babel* (1966); *The Golden Web* (1968); *The Image Empire* (1970). New York: Oxford University Press.

These three volumes contain a history of broadcasting in the United States. You will be fascinated after reading one or two pages. This series may be one of the most readable histories of *anything* ever written.

Les Brown, *Television*. New York: Harcourt Brace Jovanovich, 1971.

This book is an account of television from the business point of view. The author writes about rating services, program decisions, and a variety of other business problems with which network executives must deal.

Alan Casty, ed., *Mass Media and Mass Man*. 2d. ed.; New York: Holt, Rinehart and Winston, 1973.

A collection of essays of various writers about the entire field of the mass media and its impact on society and culture. The book includes a section on mass media and information.

Jack Dillon, *The Advertising Man*. New York: Harper's Magazine Press, 1972.

This novel by an advertising man about an advertising man gives some insight into those who dedicate their lives to ads and commercials.

Edward Jay Epstein, *News From Nowhere*. New York: Random House, 1973.

This book is the best in-depth account of how television network news operations work. The author shows how and why the news is different from what occurs in the real world.

William Fadiman, *Hollywood Now*. New York: Liveright, 1972.

This writer has worked for several major Hollywood studios so this book is an insider's view of Hollywood. As well as describing the present set-up of the industry, he speculates on the future of the American film industry.

Nicholas Johnson, *How to Talk Back to Your Television Set*. Boston: Little, Brown, 1967.

This is an essential book for individuals and groups who object to television station's programming and procedures. This book tells you how to control television rather than letting it control you.

Joe McGinnis, *The Selling of the President 1968*. New York: Pocket Books, 1970.

Appropriately, the last book we mention brings together many of the communication components we have discussed. McGinniss' paperback presents a media case-study of the power of persuasion as well as the force of both interpersonal and small-group communication. It treats the concept of ethos—image development—and touches the areas of role-playing and ethics. It is a frank exposé of our life and times.

Index

Action language, 86
Advertising, 264–266
Alcoholics Anonymous, 27–29
Alexander, Hubert G., 124
Analysis of communication. See Realistic message analysis
Analyzing messages. See Realistic message analysis
Anaxagoras, 34
Anxiety, 143–146; common among performers, 144; physical symptoms of, 144; in public speaking, 143–146; reduction of, 144–146; situational, 144
Anxious role (in small-group communication), 226
Appropriateness, 129, 131
Aristotle, 139
Articulation, 175. See also Delivery of public speech
Attention, 88–89, 165–167; building suspense, 166; delivery, 167; humor, 166–167; the important and familiar, 165–166; the novel and unusual, 166; responsibility of speaker, 165
Attitudes, 39, 44–50; audience, 183–186; changing, 202–203; definition of, 200; empathy and, 45; exploration of, 44; favorable, 185; hostile, 185; and needs, 201; neutral, 185; selective perception and, 45; sociocultural influences and, 46–48; source and receiver, 44; suspended judgment and, 44; using persuasion to change, 200–202
Audience analysis, 121, 142, 146–152; attitudes and beliefs, 148; dogmatism, 149; examples of, 150–152; prior commitment, 149–150; and self-esteem, 148–149; sociocultural background, 147; strategies for dealing with, 149; variables in, 147–150

Audiences, identification with, 146; of mass media, 260–262; and nonverbal communication, 78–79, 84–85
Authoritarian leadership, 242
Authoritarian role, 226
Avoidance, 26–27; awareness of, 27; characteristics of, 26; definition of, 26

Bales, Robert Freed, 221–222, 244
Bartlett's Familiar Quotations, 155
Bauer, R. A., 267
Beavin, Janet, 50
Bernhardt, Sarah, 113
Bibliography. See Organization of public speech
Bilateral communication, 219
Birdwhistell, Ray L., 87, 91, 222
Black audience, 168–169
Blackberry Winter, 12
Black Muslim movement, 198
Black protest, 16, 191–200
Blumer, Herbert, 260–262
Body movement, 86–98
Body of speech. See Organization of public speech
Book of Facts, 155
Books. See Mass media
Boulding, Kenneth, 192
Bowers, John Waite, 195–197
Brown, Claude, 123
Bunker, Archie, 269

Canons of Journalism, 271
Carmichael, Stokely, 16, 143, 167–169
Change, 200–206; in attitudes, 200–206; lasting, 203–206; and the type of communication, 203–206
Channels, 6, 34–36; definition of, 6; and the effectiveness of your communication, 36; increasing those used, 36

281

Civil rights movements, 195–197
Clarity, 128
Cohesiveness, 229–230
Colliers, 259
Comedians (in small-group communication), 228
Common ground, 202
Communication, the changing emphasis of 2; as dialogue, 4; increased mobility and, 3; model, *Figure 1,* 5; the need for, 1; process of, 5; protest groups and, 3–4
Compliance, 202
Complimentary relationships, 49–50
Conclusion. See Organization of public speech
Conformists (in small-group communication), 227
Connotative meaning, 126
Constitution, United States, First Amendment of, 270
Content meaning, 125–126
Conversational delivery, 61
Credibility, 60–61
Culkin, John M., 257
Culture, 105–109; and eye contact, 107; and gesture, 108; and space, 106; and subcultures, 105–106; and time, 106–107; and touch, 107–108; and voice, 108–109
Current Biography, 155
Cynics (in small-group communication), 227–228

Davis, Bette, 144
Defensive communication, 25; characteristics of, 25; definition of, 25
Delivery, 163–176; and articulation, 175–176; and inflection, 172; and keeping attention, 165–167; and language choices, 167–170; and loudness, 172–174; by memorizing, 163; and rate, 174; research about, 171–172; and pausing, 175; and pitch, 172; of public speech, 163–176; using a manuscript, 163–164; using notes, 163–165
Democratic leadership, 242–243
Democratic National Convention, 1968, 199
Denotative meaning, 126
Describing the problem in discussion, 250–251
Dewey, John, 247–248
Dialect, 116–117

Dialogue, need for, 1
Dictionary of National Biography, 155
Disarming communication, 25–27; definition of, 25. See also Defensive communication; Hostile and aggressive communication; Manipulative communication; Avoidance
Disclosure, 19–24; areas of choice in, *Figure 1.2,* 20; definition of, 19; as flexible and changing, 21; and reciprocity, 22, 24; risks of, 22; steps toward, 24; and trust, 24
Discussion, 247. See also Small group; Small-group communication
Dogmatism, 149
Dynamism. See Ethos

Emotional messages, 54–55, 63–65; analysis of, 63–65; improving, 54–55
Emotions, 35; inappropriateness in expression of, 64–65; in messages, 54–55
Empathy, 61–63
Emperor's New Clothes, The, 14
Energy, 129
Ethical considerations, 208–211; availability of information in, 210; concern for others in, 209; definition of ethics, 208; ends do not justify means in, 209; no strict guidelines for, 209
Ethnocentrism, 48
Ethos, 142–143, 184–186; after the speech, 143; definition of, 142; and dynamism, 142; and expertness, 142; on-going, 143; in "prestige suggestion," 187–188; prior, 142–143; and trustworthiness, 142
Evaluating solutions, 251–252
Evaluation in small-group process, 245–247; accomplishing, 246; methods of, 247; of process, 245–246; of product, 246; timing of, 246–247
Evaluative judgments, 26; characteristics of, 26; risks of, 26
Evaluative responses, 51
Example, the hypothetical, 56
Expertness. See Ethos
Exploration, 44. See also Attitudes
Eye contact, 87–90; attention and inclusion in, 88–89; and culture, 107; feedback in, 90; intensity in, 89–90

Face-to-face interaction, 221. See also Interpersonal communication

INDEX 283

Facial expression, 90–91
Facts, 56–57
Familiar Quotations, 155
Favorable audiences. *See* Attitudes, favorable
Federal Communications Commission, 271
Feedback, 6, 10, 34–37, 90, 140–141, 167, 169–170; and body movements, 37; definition of, 6; in public speaking, 140–141, 167, 169–170; and the self, 10; and transactions, 37; and verbal responses, 37; and vocal responses, 37
Feminist movement, 17, 193–194
Fidelity, 7, 38, 40, 53, 128
Finding solutions in discussion, 251
Formality and informality, 74–77; in interpersonal communication, *Figure 3.1,* 75, *Figure 3.2,* 76; spatial distance and, 76; time and, 81
Forms of support, 56–58; examples, 56; facts, 56; illustrations, 57; opinions, 57; statistics, 56
Fuller, R. Buckminster, 2

Gathering information, 154–156; academic sources and, 155; community resources in, 154; library resources and, 155; personal experience in, 154
Gay liberation, 193–194
Gesture, 92–94; and culture, 108
Goffman, Erving, 222
Gossip, 64
Graham, Billy, 143, 152, 208
Group personality, 230
Group process, 217–255. *See also* Small-group
Group size, 220–222
Growth, personal, 12–14; in relation to psychological safety, *Figure 1.1,* 12
Gutenberg, Johann, 266

Hall, Edward T., 72, 222
Hidden Dimension, The, 72
Hill, Phill, 144
Hitler, Adolf, 266
Hollingworth, H. L., 190
Hostile and aggressive communication, 25–26; characteristics of, 26; definition of, **25–26**
Hostile audiences. *See* Attitudes, hostile
How We Think, 247

Human needs, 10–14. *See also* Growth; Safety, psychological

Identification, 146, 202–203. *See also* Audience
Illustrations, 57
Improving interpersonal transactions, 59–65
Improving verbal style, 133–135
Indecisive role (in small-group communication), 227
Indian protest, 198–199
Inflection, 99, 172. *See also* Delivery of public speech
Information Please, 155
Informative Speech, 156; characteristics of, 156; organization of, 156–163
Intellectual role (in small-group communication), 226–227
Intensity, 99. *See also* Loudness
Intentional meaning, 125
Internalization, 203
Interpersonal communication, 4, 33–67; affected by, 34; definition of, 33–34; essential elements in, 35–38; listener responsibilities in, 61–63; process of, 35–38; related to communication model, 35; skills involved, 34–35; speaker responsibilities in, 59–61; taken for granted, 33–34; uniqueness of, 34
Interpreted Meaning, 127–128
Introduction. *See* Organization of public speech

Jackson, Don, 50
Jackson State College, 197
Jefferson, Thomas, 191
Jourard, Sidney, 11, 16, 17, 21, 22

Kelman, Herbert C., 202–203
Kendall, Patricia, 260
Kennedy, John F., 117
Kent State University, 195–197
Keys, Weldon, 86
Kinesics, 87
King, Martin Luther, 84–85
Klapper, Joseph, 269
Know-it-alls (in small-group communication), 227

Laing, R. D., 10
Laissez-faire leadership, 243–244

Language, 113–136, 167–170; adaptation in, 134–135; appropriateness in, 129, 131; casual or formal, 169; choices, 128; clarity in, 128; energy in, 129; identifying with audience through, 167–170; restatement in using, 169–170; as power, 117; profanity in, 170; for public speaking, 167–170; slang in, 170; specialized, 170; vividness in, 131–133
Lazarsfeld, Paul F., 260, 268
Leaderless group, 244
Leadership, 234–245; emergence of, 234–236; functions of, 236–241; styles of, 241–245
Lehmann, Lotte, 144
Level of meaning, 124–128; content, 125–126; intentional, 125; interpreted, 127–128; significative, 126–127
Lewin, Kurt, 218
Life, 259
Listener roles, 38–40; and attitudes, 39–40; and predictions, 39–40
Location, the, 79–80; and space, 79–80; and time, 85–86
Logos, 184–186
Look, 259
Loudness, 99, 172, 174. See also Delivery of public speech

Magazines. See Mass media
Manchild in The Promised Land, 123
Manipulative Communication, 26–27; awareness of, 27; characteristics of, 26; definition of, 26
Manuscript speaking. See Delivery of a public speech
Maslow, Abraham, 12, 43; relationship between personal growth and psychological safety, *Figure 1.1,* 12
Massachusetts Quarterly, 168
Mass communication, 257–278; audience in, 257, 260–262; definition of, 257–258; effects of, 267–270; feedback in, 262–263; messages in, 259–260; related to communication model, 258; sources in, 258–259
Mass media, 5, 198–199, 257–278; and advertising, 264–266; audiences of, 257, 260–262; economics of, 263–264; extent of in United States, 257; power of, 266–267; and protest, 198–199; regulation of, 270–271; using to plan a political campaign, 271–276

McCroskey, James C., 81
McLuhan, Marshall, 267
Mead, Margaret, 12–13
Meaning, 121, 123–128; connotative, 126; denotative, 126; is in people, 123
Meaning in Language, 124
Mehrabian, Albert, 69, 95, 98
Memorization. See Delivery of public speech
Merton, Robert K., 268
Message, 6, 35, 69, 114, 140–141, 183, 219, 258; definition of, 6; impact of, 69; and interpersonal communication, 35; in mass communication, 258; and nonverbal communication, 69–71; and persuasion, 183; and public speaking, 140–141; and the small group, 219; and verbal communication, 114
Message structure, 58–59
Misunderstanding, how and where it occurs, 125–128
Mixed messages, 104–105
Model of communication process. See Communication, model
Muhammed Speaks, 198
Multilateral communiciation, 219

Needs, motivation and individual's 201. See also Human needs; Growth; Safety, psychological
Neutral audiences. See Attitudes, neutral
Newspapers. See Mass media
New York Times Review of Books, 168
New Yorker, 258
Noise, 6–7, 34, 37–38; and feedback, 38; physical, 6–7, 37; psychological, 6–7, 37; reducing, 38; and redundancy, 38; and the speed of communicating, 38
Nondisclosure, 19–24
Nonverbal communication, 4, 35, 64–65, 69–111; and action language, 86; body movement in, 86–98; control over, 70; cues in, 70; and culture, 101–104, 105–108; diffuseness of, 70–71; elements of, 69–71; and eye contact, 87–90; facial expression in, 90–91; and formality and informality, 74–77; and gesture, 92–94, 108; impact of, 69; and intimacy, 74; and mixed messages, 104–105; and object language, 86–87, 101–104; posture and emotion in, 94–98; related

to communication model, 71; and relationship and status, 77–78; space in, 71–80, 106; time in, 80–86, 106–107; and touch, 93, 107–108; and voice, 98–100, 108–109; warmth and coldness in, 72–74
Norms, 218, 228–229; definition of, 218; group, 228–229
Notes for a speech. See Delivery of public speech

Object language, 86–87, 101–104
Occasion, the, 79; and space, 79; and time, 85
Ochs, Donovan J., 195–197
One-to-few communication. See Interpersonal communication; Small-group communication
One-to-one communication. See Interpersonal communication
Onomatopoeia, 132
Opinion Research Corporation, 261
Opinions, 57
Oral communication, 122; adaptation in, 134–135
Organization of public speech, 156–163; bibliography, 160; body of speech, 157; conclusion, 160; informative speeches, 156; introduction, 157; outline of, 159–163; persuasive speeches, 156–163; sample outline, 160–163; statement of purpose, 156–157; supporting materials, 56–58, 159; transitions, 159–160
Outline of public speech. See Organization of public speech
Oxford Dictionary of Quotations, 155

Pacifying response, 52
Paraphrasing, 53
Pathos, 184–186
Patterns for communicating in small groups, 230–233
Pausing, 175
Perception, 40–50; and attitudes, 44–45; and complimentary and symmetrical relationships, 49; and projection, 41; and role playing, 42–44; of self by others and others by self, 40–50; and self-fulfilling prophecies, 41; and selectivity, 45–46; and sociocultural influences, 46–49
Persuasion, 181–215; to change attitudes, 200–203; effectiveness of, 203–206; and ethics, 208–212; ethos, 184–186; logos, 184–186; means of, 183–186; pathos, 184–186; and propaganda, 211–212; and protest, 191–200; and public commitment, 206–207; refutation, 207–208; resisting, 206–208; and suggestion, 186–191; and suspending judgment, 207
Persuasive speech, 156–163; characteristics of, 156; organizaton of, 156–163
Physical noise, 37–38
Pitch, 172
Plan of action, the, 252–253
Posture and motion, 94–98
Powell, S. J., John, 65
Power, 181–215; of communication, 181–182; ethics of, 208–211; of persuasion, 182–186; 200–203; and propaganda, 211–212; through protest, 191–200; resistance to, 206–208; through suggestion, 186–191
Practice, 135
Pragmatics of Human Communication, 50
Prior commitment, 149
Problem-solving group, the, 247–253; a case study, 247–253
Process of communicaton, 5–7
Projection, 41
Proof, 117
Propaganda, 211–212; and suggestion, 211
Propositions, 248–250; fact, 248–249; phrasing of, 248–250; policy, 249; value, 249
Protest, 5, 191–200; characteristics of, 193–194; communication of, 194–198; conditions for, 192; future of, 199–200; groups, 192–194; and the mass media, 198–199; and separation from society, 198; stages of, 194–198
Proxemics, 72
Psychologiical noise, 37–38
Psychology of the Audience, The, 190
Public commitment, 51
Public speaking, 139–178; as art, 139; and changes in form, 140; and democratic decision-making, 139; influences of mass media, 140; an ongoing process, 141; as a planned event, 140–142; as science, 139

Radio. See Mass media
Rate, 98–99, 174–175

Rational messages, 54–59; examples in, 56; facts in, 56–57; forms of support in, 56–58; illustrations in, 57; improving, 55–59; message structure in, 58–59; opinions in, 57; statistics in, 56–57
Reader's Guide to Periodical Literature, The, 156
Realistic message analysis, 63–65
Receiver, 6, 35, 141
Recognizing the problem in discussion, 248–250
Redundancy, 38
Reflective pattern, the, 247–253; describing the problem, 250–251; evaluating solutions, 251–252; finding solutions, 251; the plan of action, 252–253; recognizing the problem, 248–250
Relationships in communication, 49–50; complimentary, 49–50; and status, 77–78; symmetrical, 49–50
Responding, 50–53; evaluative response, 51; pacifying response, 52; by paraphrasing, 53–54; by probing, 52; supportive response, 52; through understanding, 53–54
Restatement, 169–170
Rhetoric, 139
Rhetoric of Agitation and Control, The, 195
Rivals (in small-group communication), 227
Roberts, Donald F., 268
Rogers, Carl, 16–17, 26–27, 29
Role playing, 42–44, 224–228; adaptability in, 43; awareness of, 43; effectveness in, 42–43; honesty in, 43–44; in the small group, 224–228
Roles, 11, 14–19, 27, 226–228; changing, difficulty of, 17, 19; congruence with self-image, 16–17; damage to individuals and society, 16; definition of, 14, 218; expectations of, 14–15; group memberships and, 15; in the small group, 218, 226–228; sociocultural, 15; violation and abandonment of, 15–16
Role-taking, 63
Ruesch, Jurgen, 86
Rumor, 64

Safety, psychological, 11–14, 21–27; related to personal growth, *Figure* 1.1, 12

Schramm, Wilbur, 261, 267, 270
Seale, Bobby, 198
Selective perception, 45–46, 124
Self and communication, 4, 9–31; self-concept, 10; self-fulfillment, 10; self-knowledge, 10
Self-esteem, 148–149; high, 149; low, 149. *See also* Audience analysis
Self-fulfilling prophecies, 41
Self identity, 10–16; sense of, 15. *See also* Roles
Selfishness and unselfishness, 81–82
Sharing, 60
Silent Language, The, 72
Sign language, 86
Significative meaning, 126–127
Silent role (in small-group communication), 226
Slurring, 175–176
Small group, 4, 217–255; cohesiveness in a, 229–230; communication patterns, 230–233; definition of, 218; evaluation of a, 245–247; leadership in a, 234–245; making one work, 219; member roles in a, 224–228; norms in a, 228–229; the problem-solving, 247–253; size, 220–222; spatial arrangements, 222, 224
Small-group communication, 217–255; evaluation in, 245–247; patterns for, 230–233
Smith, Arthur L., 193
Social facilitation, 188
Sociocultural influences, 46–48; and ethnocentrism, 48; and shared experience, 47
Socrates, 10
Source, 6, 35; definition of, 6; in mass communication, 258–259; in public speaking, 141
Space, 71–80; the audience and, 78–79; body, 72; choices about, for speakers, 78–80; and culture, 106; formality and informality and, 74–77; the location and, 79–80; the occasion and, 79; relationship and status and, 77–78; in the small group, 22, 224; the topic and, 78; warmth and coldness and, 72–74
Speaker roles, 38–40; and attitudes, 39–40; and predictions, 39–40
Speaking is not writing, 121–122
Speech evaluation, 176–177
Statement of purpose. *See* Organization of public speech

Statistical Abstract of the United States, 155
Statistics as forms of support, 56-57
Style, 113-136; appropriateness in 129, 131; and attention, 118; clarity in, 128; definition of, 115; and dialect, 116-117; differences in oral and written, 121-122; energy in, 129; improving verbal, 133-135; inadequate, 115; personality and, 116; as proof, 117; vividness in, 131-133
Suggestion, 186-191; and atmosphere, 189, 190; channeling, 190-191; rhythm in, 188; prestige in, 187; social facilitation in, 188
Supporting materials. *See* Organization of public speech
Suspended judgment, 44, 207
Symbol, 118
Symmetrical relationships, 49-50

Television. *See* Mass media
Thesis statement. *See* Organization of public speech
Time (Chronemics), 80-86; the audience and, 84-85; choices about, for speakers, 84-86; and culture, 106-107; formality and informality in using, 82; the location and, 85-86; the occasion and, 85; selfishness and unselfishness in using, 81-82; tasks and, 83; the topic and, 84
Time, 268
Times, New York, 264
Tone, 99-100
Topic, the, 78; and space, 78; and time, 84
Topics for speeches, 152-154; and the audience, 153-154; experiences with, 152-153; knowledge of, 152-153
Touch, 93; and culture, 107-108
Toward a Psychology of Being, 43
Transactions, 7, 38; improving interpersonal, 59-65; listener responsibilities in, 61-63; speaker responsibilities in, 59-61
Transitions. *See* Organzation of public speech
Transparent Self, The, 11
Trustworthiness. *See* Ethos
Two-way communication, 35, 37, 46. *See also* Interpersonal communication, Small-group communication

Understanding, 123; the core of meaning, 123
Understanding responses, 53-54; appropriateness of, 53; through paraphrasing, 53-54
Unselfishness, 81-82

Verbal communication, 4, 113-136; appropriateness in, 129, 131; clarity in, 128; and dialect, 116; energy in, 129; as proof, 117; related to communication model, 114; and style, 115-116; and your verbal image, 115-116; vividness in, 131-133
Verbose role (in small-group communication), 227
Visual materials, 170-171; attention and, 170-171; choice of, 171; display of, 171; retention and, 170; value of, 170-171
Vividness, 131-133
Vocabulary, 133; increasing, 133-134
Voice, 98-100; and culture, 108-109; and inflection, 99; and loudness, 99; and rate, 98-99; and tone, 99-100

Warmth and coldness, 72-74
Watergate Committee, 200, 211
Watzlawick, Paul, 50
Weathermen, the, 198
Weight Watchers, 27-29
Whtie, David Manning, 261
Whole Earth Catalog, 263
Who's Who in America, 155
Winans, James A., 188
Women's liberation. *See* Feminist movement
Words, 113-136; and audience analysis, 121; distortion and misunderstandings in using, 120; how they work, 118-121; and the listener, 121; as symbols, 118
World Almanac, The, 155
Wounded Knee protest. *See* Indian protest
Written language, 121-122

Yates, Brock, 144

Zimmerman, Claire, 267

Picture Credits

Page xiv
Photo by Steve Rose/Nancy Palmer Photo Agency

Page 18
David A. Krathwohl

Page 23
Sue Goldbaum

Page 32
Photo by Steve Rose/Nancy Palmer Photo Agency

Page 39
Photo by Renee

Page 55
Gib Fullerton

Page 62
Photo by Renee

Page 68
Joyce Kosofsky

Page 73
David A. Krathwohl

Page 92
Steve Schmidt

Page 97
David A. Krathwohl

Page 104
Bill Beggs

Page 130
Steve Smith

Page 138
Pete Manera

Page 147
Steve Quigley

Page 180
Photos by Renee

Page 195
Photo by Howard Petrick/Nancy Palmer Photo Agency

Page 216
Karasu

Page 223
Kevin Mack

Page 256
Alan Chapman

Page 275
Mark Majeski